Spirit of Love

Spirit of Love
A Trinitarian Theology of Grace

AMOS YONG

BAYLOR UNIVERSITY PRESS

© 2012 by Baylor University Press
Waco, Texas 76798-7363

All Rights Reserved. No part of this publication may be reproduced, stored in a retrieval system, or transmitted, in any form or by any means, electronic, mechanical, photocopying, recording or otherwise, without the prior permission in writing of Baylor University Press.

Cover Design by Dean Bornstein
Cover Art: "Love; Agape," by Rob Lawlor, www.lawlorgallery.com. Used with permission of the artist.

Library of Congress Cataloging-in-Publication Data
Young, Amos.
  Spirit of love : a Trinitarian theology of grace / Amos Yong.
  246 p. cm.
  Includes bibliographical references (p. 211) and index.
  ISBN 978-1-60258-326-9 (pbk. : alk. paper)
  1. Love--Religious aspects--Pentecostal churches. I. Title.
  BV4639.Y58 2012
  231'.6--dc23
                    2011051770

BAYLOR®
UNIVERSITY

Printed in the United States of America on acid-free paper with a minimum of 30% pcw recycled content.

To Alma, the love of my life

with gratitude for the 25 years we have shared together,

and with eager anticipation of all that will come next . . .

...

Contents

• • •

Preface

I must begin this book with a confession. Up until a few years ago, I never would have thought I would have written a book on theology and love. That is, not until I was invited, in 2007, to be an advisory board member of the core research group for a John Templeton Foundation funded project: "The Flame of Love: Scientific Research on the Experience and Expression of Godly Love in the Pentecostal Tradition." For this interdisciplinary research project intended to bring social scientists and theologians together, I was supposed to provide theological perspective. The first core group meeting of advisors and others in the spring of 2008 launched us all into vigorous discussions about the possibility and feasibility of combining interdisciplinary and theological perspectives on researching love as well as about the nature of Pentecostalism.[1] More importantly, it opened up extended consideration of the nature of godly love, why love language was not prominently featured in the pentecostal tradition, and what that might mean for the fortunes of this research endeavor.[2]

I will return in the third chapter to further discuss the Godly Love project. At the moment, however, I recall being quite skeptical that the project itself was based on a mistaken categorical association. Pentecostals were known for talking about divine power—the power of the Holy Spirit, to be exact—not about love; at least that was my initial reaction to the whole idea. And if I was right, we were going to be looking in vain for enough references to love in general (never mind "godly love") within the pentecostal tradition, and our failure to uncover this would end up undermining the project. Or even if we were to find love in the pentecostal tradition, its secondary status would call into question our project assumptions, objectives, and even methods. Whatever it was we were supposed to be studying, at that time I thought the project itself was quite wrongheaded in its approach.

I have come quite a long way in the last three years. Much of it has had to do with the patience of the project directors and other core group members with me. Along the way, I have come to realize two things, which are at the heart of this book. First, while references to love are not as prominent in the pentecostal tradition as are references to power, they are there, both in the contemporary landscape and, more important, at junctures early in the history of modern Pentecostalism. Second, there are untapped resources in pentecostal spirituality and theology for understanding a theology of love that can contribute to the wider discussion about godly love, its effects, and its redemptive and transformative power. The combination of these two intuitions that formed early on through our vigorous debate has led me on the path toward researching for and thinking about this book. What has emerged is a pleasant, but I should also say not totally unexpected, surprise: that there is a link between divine power and godly love in the person and work of the Holy Spirit, who is at the core of pentecostal spirituality and piety. In short—and here is my thesis for this volume—pentecostal understandings of the Spirit of God can shed new light on God as love and loving, and on what it means for creation as a whole and for human beings in particular to receive the love of God who gives graciously. I am optimistic that such pentecostal perspectives can be helpful for those in other Christian traditions as well as ecumenical theological discussions more generally.

I need to register three important caveats before proceeding. First, this volume makes no pretentions to presenting any exhaustive theology of love. We will indeed be covering a good deal of historical, scientific, and theological ground, but our coverage will be selective in each case, designed to engage with and undergird the overarching thesis of this volume, that regarding what might be called a pneumatological theology of love. Of course, such an endeavor is itself fraught with ambiguities and complexities since now we are hoping to unravel not just one mystery but two: that related to the Holy Spirit and that to divine love! But I make no apologies. The biblical witness unambiguously declares both that "God is spirit" (John 4:24) and "God is love" (1 John 4:8, 16). The Christian tradition has spent the last two millennia attempting to elucidate the obscurity surrounding each revelatory claim. This book is motivated by the intuition that our understanding of each one can illuminate the other.

Yet before proceeding to our second caveat, it is imperative that I say just a bit more about what I mean by "spirit" and by "love"—the two central notions of this book. Of course, it is impossible to define "spirit" exhaustively and I will not even try that here. Suffice to say that in this book, I assume that the biblical claim that "God is spirit" can be understood at least in part by what Christians refer to as the experience of the Holy Spirit. This is not to collapse God as spirit into God the Holy Spirit—I am surely aware that there has been a longstanding historical debate about the relationship between these two notions—but it is to say that the Christian encounter with the Holy Spirit provides at least one window into our understanding of the spiritual nature of God. More precisely, for my purposes, writing as I am from the perspective of pentecostal–charismatic experience, God as spirit is understood at least partly in terms of the Spirit poured out on all flesh on the Day of Pentecost (Acts 2). The rest of this volume will fill out this rudimentary claim.

If it is impossible to delineate "spirit" concisely, it is just as difficult to do so for "love." In order to provide some orientation for the discussion to come, however, let me suggest the following working definition: love is the affective disposition toward and intentional activity that benefits others.[3] It is the last clause that allows for translation of the preceding into a theological key. The benefit of others understood theologically is suggestive of what the biblical witness calls health, wholeness, and salvation, and this is finally comprehensible in terms of what Jesus called the kingdom or reign of God. For our purposes, Jesus came to announce and inaugurate the reign of God in the power of the Spirit. Hence, our approach will be specifically pneumatological, with the goal of seeing if some aspects of this topic can be opened up through considerations specifically related to the Holy Spirit.

Caveat number two clarifies how this volume answers to some of my critics, in particular those who have been concerned in my work about what they feel to be a division between the economies of the Son and the

Spirit, an overly optimistic view of the Spirit's work in the world, and an eliding of the differences between the Spirit of creation and the Spirit of redemption. All of these are important matters in the classical theological tradition that get us into the thickets of the trinitarian mystery of salvation and of grace. While I have already provided some preliminary responses to these questions,[4] the following pages unfold a more expansive answer, portrayed as a pneumatological soteriology of love and trinitarian theology of grace. Part of the challenge is that my work proceeds with one foot squarely in the evangelical tradition of theology, broadly defined, and with the other foot resolutely in the pentecostal movement, as complex and unwieldy as it is. For some, these two traditions overlap to a large extent, while for others, there are major differences that at present prohibit any substantive dialogue. Yet my theological career from the beginning has been to make a contribution from a pentecostal perspective to the wider theological conversation, both evangelical and ecumenical. Those to my right probably do not think this can be done (they think I should move further right), while those to my left probably wonder how I can maintain my evangelical sympathies. I have thought all along that it is precisely my pentecostal intuitions and sensibilities that might help us carve a via media between an inflexible conservatism and an unbridled progressivism in the contemporary theological landscape.

Such a conviction certainly drives what might be called the soteriology of love in this book. What follows is not only a pentecostal and pneumatological theology of love but also a pentecostal and pneumatological soteriology intended to provide a "big picture" about where pentecostal theology might be going. In brief, the Spirit of love is also the Spirit of the Father and the Son who is graciously given to the world so that she might sanctify and redeem the world for the glory of God.[5] This is my pentecostal version of the pneumatological and trinitarian theology of grace beautifully envisioned by Catholic theologian David Coffey, especially in his early work which depicted the Spirit's gracious outpouring of the Son as bringing about not only the incarnation but also, through Jesus' Spirit of sonship, the gracing of many sons and daughters.[6] It is also my pentecostal and pneumatological version of the trinitarian theology of grace brilliantly articulated by evangelical theologian Stephen Webb, for whom God is Giver, Given, and Gifting, and for whom the Gifting Spirit makes present and active the saving grace of God for the world.[7] What is minimally emphasized in both Coffey and Webb is that the gracious God and the Gifting Spirit of God is also the God who is love, who loves unconditionally, and whose Spirit of love never ceases to work for the salvation of the world.

In other words, this book in one sense brings together the various threads of speculative theology woven in my previous work but reenvisions them around the themes of God as spirit and God as love. As before, I proceed convinced that the pentecostal "gift" to the church ecumenical is continuous with that of the broader Christian tradition, but with a difference, one revolving around our encounter with the Spirit of God in Christ. As opposed to so-called trinitarian theologies which seem inevitably to collapse into binitarian notions or even christocentric or christomonistic formulations (because of a marginalized, neglected, or even forgotten pneumatology), starting with the Spirit contributes to a more fully and robustly trinitarian theology which also adjusts our doctrines of creation and redemption in an eschatological direction. Further, the point is not about either a pessimistic (few shall be saved) or optimistic (oh, no, too many shall be saved) soteriology but one that captures the gospel—the good news—of the Father's loving, unconditional, and gracious Gift of the Son through the Spirit for the salvation of a world otherwise awash in sin. In effect then, to think deeply from out of the pentecostal experience is to start with a charismatic God whose charisms (gracious gifts) are less supernormal capacities than they are the God of love himself, given in an unqualified way in the Son through the Spirit, and what difference such gifts might make for those of us who have been caught up in them. The following unfolds this trinitarian theology of grace, with a pentecostal accent. It presumes the work I have done before, but brings this forward in the hopes that such a pentecostal and pneumatological theology of love makes a resounding difference at the heart of the dogmatic and theological tradition, in particular its soteriology, trinitarian theology, and theology of grace.

Now my final caveat builds on the preceding more explicitly theological concerns toward a full, more personal confession and self-disclosure: researching for and reflecting on this book have brought me, in retrospect, full circle. Although I have published a number of books on pentecostal thought in the last decade, I have intentionally operated with a fairly "objective" stance as a theologian writing primarily for the wider academy.[8] Against the emerging popularity of confessionally rooted theological work in our late- or postmodern context, I have tried to strike a balance between assuming my ecclesial location within the pentecostal movement on the one hand, yet writing for both the church ecumenical/catholic and the theological and religious studies academy on the other hand. In order to address these latter audiences, I have had to maintain a levelheaded posture, one more fitting for the "proper" discursive approaches prevalent in these modernistic enterprises. In other words, I have had to soften, control, or altogether mute the more "enthusiastic" sensibilities that otherwise characterize my pentecostal commitments.

In this book, however, I am going to lay bare my pentecostal soul. In effect, it can be read as my personal *apologia pro vita sua*, at least insofar as such has unfolded across the last fifteen years of my work as a pentecostal theologian. This does not mean that I am going to simply take leave from academic integrity, formal argument, or scholarly documentation. It does mean that I proceed less as one detached from the ideas presented and more as one committed to, confessional of, even passionate about, what is at stake. Put another way, I grant here that I am working not only as a pentecostal theologian but as a pentecostal evangelist, and even a pentecostal missionary. As a pentecostal "missionary kid"—my parents came to the United States from Malaysia when I was ten years old to serve as pastors and missionaries to Chinese-speaking immigrants from Hong Kong to northern California—I have long realized that this is an inherent part of my spiritual DNA, and that it is time for me to explicitly claim and speak out of that identity. In some respects, readers can revisit my corpus of work produced to date in light of this book as an outworking of this missionary self-understanding and calling, even if I have been assiduous about avoiding such an explicitly missiological self-understanding.[9]

In this book I feel moved in my spirit to embrace that evangelistic and missionary posture. As we shall see, there are many other scholarly tomes and theologies of love on offer, and I would never claim that my book is an improvement on what has gone on before. Love is too complex, too beautiful, and too mysterious a reality for any one book to fully capture. But I do think that what I have to say makes some fairly important connections and leads us to helpful reconsiderations of love. And in the end, it is not just about understanding love better, but about knowing how to receive more of it and how to spread it around in redemptive ways. As Marx castigated the philosophical tradition for merely trying to understand the world rather than to mobilize its transformation, I here urge that any proper under-standing of divine love will result in embodying the mandate to change the world. We cannot be touched by the love of God, even in our intellect, without loving our neighbors. That is why the God who is love not only sent his only begotten Son into the world but also poured out his Spirit into human hearts so that she can help us make the world into a better place. It is this saving story and truth that the following pages are meant to explicate.

This missionary and evangelistic manifesto will unfold in three parts. Part I begins with the mysterious revelation of God as love, charting pneu-matological trajectories toward a theology of love from the theological tradition, in dialogue with the contemporary sciences, and via a mapping of pentecostal spirituality. Part II goes deeper into the grammar of pen-tecostal experience of God revealed as spirit, especially as the Spirit who baptizes in holy love, by tracing out the performative dimensions of this baptism of love, exploring its pneumatological explications, and revisiting the pentecostal canon-within-the-canon of Luke-Acts. Part III deploys the pentecostal and pneumatological hermeneutic developed in part II toward a constructive charismatic theology of love for the twenty-first century that registers also Pauline and Johannine perspectives. The last chapter presents a manifesto on a pentecostal and pneumatological theology of love in nine theses: I proclaim that the God who is love is also the God who gives love and loves unconditionally, in Christ and through the Spirit, for the sake of the world, and thereby empowers us to go and do likewise. This is perhaps a simple reaffirmation of the gospel, but it is no less profound for that. I hope the following pages unfold both the simplicity and the profundity of the mystery of such a gracious God who is both love and spirit.

• • •

Acknowledgments

A s usual, I am deeply indebted to many who have had a hand in this book, in particular Matthew T. Lee, Margaret M. Poloma, and the referees for the generous Flame of Love Research Project grant, funded by the John Templeton Foundation that underwrote my research; deans Michael Palmer and Randall Pannell for supporting my research and writing in so many different ways; Patty Hughson and her interlibrary loan staff at the Regent University Library; and my colleagues who have given me feedback on a draft of this manuscript (although they should not be held responsible for anything that follows): Craig Boyd for his comments on the Aquinas section in chapter 1; Margaret M. Poloma for reading chapter 3 and for challenging me to go further than I did in the first draft of my epilogue; Martin W. Mittelstadt for comments on the entire manuscript, although focusing his biblical studies expertise particularly on my chapters 6–8; Frank D. Macchia for thoughts especially on parts II and III; Timothy Lim Teck Ngern (my graduate assistant) for a careful review of the draft; Henry H. (Hal) Knight III for his encouraging thoughts on and reactions to the full manuscript; and Thomas Jay Oord, whose careful reading and recorded comments—sent via CD!—have left imprints across the manuscript, but especially the first two chapters. Last but not least, I am grateful to Vincent Le, my current graduate assistant, for helping with the indexes.

Thanks are due to Carey Newman at Baylor University Press for his enthusiasm for this volume in particular, his professional and expedient support of my work as a whole, and his wit and humor that have brought smiles to my day on many an occasion; two anonymous reviewers of the manuscript for their encouraging comments and for helping me strengthen the argument at various places; and Coleman Fannin, Diane Smith, and others at the Press for their copy-editorial and production work that has transformed this manuscript into a book.

I am also grateful to the Division of Christian Education of the National Council of the Churches of Christ in the U.S.A., for permission to quote from the New Revised Standard Version Bible, copyright © 1989 (all rights reserved).

Most important, though, I must thank my wife, Alma: this book will appear in the spring of 2012, right before we celebrate our twenty-fifth wedding anniversary. Alma, you have not only patiently shared your husband with a computer for most of your married life, but you have been unflagging in your support in so many ways big and small. You have endured the challenges that life has brought our way because you have believed in the God who loves us and who works all things together for our good. Nothing I do would be possible without your love, expressed daily in smiles, hugs, and deeds that energize me and help me to envision and dream of reaching higher and farther than I would have dared to on my own. The following pages do not even begin to do justice to the love you have shown, to me and to our children. For a man who otherwise has many words for his books, you leave me speechless, except to say: thank you Lord for this undeserved blessing who is my wife, and, Alma, I love you.

PART I

• • •

GOD IS LOVE
The Theology and Science of Love

CHAPTER 1

• • •

The Spirit of Charity

Toward a Theology of Love

One should not be surprised to hear that a great deal on love and theology of love has been published over the centuries and Werner Jeanrond's 2010 volume, for example, not only is the most recent installment of a long line of illustrious books on the topic but also provides an excellent overview of the state-of-the-question on these matters.[1] In addition to the more theological oriented approaches of Jeanrond and his predecessors are a wide variety of historical studies as well as philosophical analyses.[2] This is not to mention the emerging and even exploding field of scientific research on love, some of which we will discuss in the next chapter. All this to say that of books on love there is no end, and that the mysteries of love have perennially called forth authors who have attempted to communicate, if always in partially successful ways, about love's power, reality, and elusiveness.

This opening chapter will certainly not pretend to provide any overview of previous efforts. In fact, I will reproduce some rather one-sided perspectives, and concentrate on three main sets of ideas about love: Augustine's, Aquinas', and Tillich's. This rather narrow explication, however, is designed to fulfill very specific purposes related to the constructive arguments in the next two parts of this book. In particular, each of these theologians of love can be said also to have been a pneumatologian of love; that is, in each case, theology of love has been intimately connected with theology of the Spirit (pneumatology). As we survey the terrain charted by their reflections, various facets of the interrelationship between love and the Holy Spirit will come into focus, and critical engagement with their ideas will help to lay much needed groundwork for our quest for a (pneumatological) theology of love.

Augustine: The Spirit and Divine Love

We begin our discussion of St. Augustine's (354–430) theology of love where Augustine himself began, at least in his earliest extant writings, on "the happy life" (*De beata vita*).[3] These ruminations launched Augustine's philosophical and theological quest, one that would persist through much of his later writing.[4] Framed as a dialogue involving his friends and his mother, early on it is Monica who observes that happiness involves not just getting what one wants, but wanting and getting good things (*HL* 10). But good material things can be lost or they fade away, and those who have such goods often are unhappy because they fear losing what they have (*HL* 11). Hence the ultimate good that brings happiness must be everlasting. Put positively, then, happiness derives from desiring and having God, and doing God's will; put negatively, happiness includes being free of unclean spirits, and this involves living chastely (*HL* 12, 17–19). Thus the happy person desires not the material things of the world that will eventually perish but the spiritual wisdom that will last forever.[5] Those desirous of the former are the foolish, and they will be perpetually fearful, disappointed, and unhappy, while those who pursue the latter will come to see that what they are after is nothing less than the wisdom of God. This is the wisdom of the Father, incarnate in the Son, who is truth (*HL* 34). With this, we are led to the happy life of contemplation on the trinitarian God. Monica therefore exclaims at the end: "Cherish us as we pray, O Trinity[.] This is without doubt the happy life, and that life is perfect toward which we can, we must presume, be quickly brought through solid faith, lively hope, and burning love" (*HL* 35). Inevitably, the quest for happiness leads to God, to God's love, and to loving God.

I now shift to the more mature Augustine, picking up on his discussion on happiness in *De Trinitate* and his homilies on 1 John, both of which were finalized in all probability in the mid-410s.[6] Book 13 of *De Trinitate* expands upon the major themes of *De beata vita*, in particular the connection between happiness, the good, the incarnation, and the wisdom of

God.[7] Earlier in *De Trinitate*, Augustine had returned to unfold the interwoven character of the knowledge, goodness, and love of God. If in *De beata vita* the question was how human beings would recognize happiness if that involved desiring after eternal things and divine realities (which are not usually on our list of wants), then in *De Trinitate* the question is how human beings could recognize the divine Trinity sufficiently in order to desire or pursue after God. The epistemological problem is how we could wish to know the unknowable, or seek after the good that is transcendent, or desire after the love of God. How can we know that the God we think we love is no more than our projection? It is this challenge that leads Augustine at the turning point of the volume to reflect on the biblical witness "in a more inward manner" (*T* 8.1), since it is in and within ourselves that we can learn about these matters.

Thus we can only recognize the goodness and love God if we previously have experienced some form of goodness and love. And Augustine believes that in general we are capable of recognizing these in others since we all have some sense of what it means to be treated justly and to feel loved (*T* 8.9). In that case, "Let no one say 'I don't know what to love.' Let him love his brother, and love that love. . . . This is the love which unites all the good angels and all the servants of God in a bond of holiness, conjoins us and them together, and subjoins us to itself. . . . And if a man is full of love, what is he full of but God?" (*T* 8.12). In short, the human experience of love provides the analogical bridge for us to recognize God as love, to receive God's love, and to love God in response.

It is also here, in this part of *De Trinitate*, that Augustine draws on Scripture, in particular the first Epistle of John, to elucidate his point. Citing variously from the fourth chapter (especially verses 7-21) leads to the following line of reasoning: that we know not only what it means to love our neighbor but that we have an obligation to love our neighbor since we ourselves wish to be so loved; that to genuinely love our neighbor is to love our neighbor with the love of God since "God is love" (1 John 4:8, 16); and that thus to love our neighbor is also to love God. Perhaps at about the same time as he was completing *De Trinitate*, Augustine was preaching and teaching through 1 John.[8] This sustained engagement with the first Johannine Epistle produced the following exegetical insights:

- that those who keep God's commandments to love are perfected in God's love (*TH* 1.9; 1 John 2:5);
- that "Two loves there are: of the world and of God: if the love of the world dwells in us, the love of God can find no entrance. The love of the world must depart, the love of God come in to dwell" (*TH* 2.8; 1 John 2:15);[9]
- that "there is nothing to distinguish the sons of God from the sons of the devil, save charity" (*TH* 5.7; 1 John 3:10);
- that "the Holy Spirit's work in man is to cause love and charity to be in him" (*TH* 6.9), and if we love our brothers and sisters then we do so only because the Spirit of God dwells in us: "There can be no love without the Spirit of God" (*TH* 6.10; 1 John 3:24);
- that if God is both spirit (John 4:24) and love (1 John 4:8, 16), then "in love is the Holy Spirit . . . whom evil men cannot receive" (*TH* 7.6), which is consistent with the claim in *De beata vita* that happiness can only emerge after being rid of unclean spirits (cf. 1 John 4:1-6);
- that he can therefore admonish those who are born of and know God (1 John 4:7): "Love, and do what you will. . . . Let love's root be within you, from that root nothing but good can spring" (*TH* 7.8);
- that we can know God's love is perfected in us and both that we abide in God and that God's Spirit abides in us if we love one another (*TH* 8.12; 1 John 4:13);
- that, further, if "God is love" and we can only love in and through God's love, then so also is it true to say: "love is God" (*TH* 7.5-7, 8.14) and that those who love their neighbors do so with divine love and love God as well;[10] and
- that if the fear of the Lord prepares the way for charity, "when charity has taken up its dwelling, the fear that prepared the place for it is expelled. . . . The greater the charity, the lesser the fear; the lesser the charity, the greater the fear" (*TH* 9.4; 1 John 4:17-18).

In brief, these homiletical considerations deepened Augustine's existential and theological insights into human fears and happiness. They also strengthened both the connections between happiness and love on the one hand and between love and its negative relationship to unclean spirits and its positive relationship to the Holy Spirit on the other hand.

This brings us back to Augustine's considerations of love in relationship to the Holy Spirit in his reflections on the Trinity. It should be remembered that if Augustine's *De Civitas Dei* provides a history of God's saving works, *De Trinitate* gives us a glimpse into the "history" of the divine life itself, albeit in a manner that maps the Christian spiritual life as well.[11] Against this backdrop, a few summary considerations will suffice about Augustine's trinitarian theology of love. First, Augustine concludes that "brotherly love . . . is proclaimed on the highest authority not only to be from God but also simply to be God" (*T* 8.12). This is extrapolated from the Johannine witness that the presence of the love of God is manifest in nothing less than the love of others. Second, this economic understanding of love is consistent with Augustine's famous notion of God as lover, beloved, and love, a formulation that deserves to be quoted at length:

> What then . . . is this love or charity which the divine scriptures praise and proclaim so much, but love of the good? Now love means someone loving and something loved with love. There you are with three, the lover, what is being loved, and love. And what is love but a kind of life coupling or trying to couple together two things, namely lover and what is being loved? (*T* 8.14)[12]

Then later, toward the end of *De Trinitate*, Augustine asserts that since "this Holy Spirit is not just the Father's alone nor the Son's alone, but the Spirit of them both . . . thus he suggests to us the common charity by which the Father and the Son love each other" (*T* 15.27). While Augustine is sensitive to the difficulties of associating the person of the Holy Spirit specifically with love, he reasons that "in this triad only the Son is called the Word of God, and only the Holy Spirit is called the gift of God,[13] and only the Father is called the one from whom the Word is born and from whom the Holy Spirit principally proceeds. . . ."[14] If therefore any of these three can be distinctively named charity, which could it more suitably be than the Holy Spirit?" (*T* 15.29). It follows then, that, in light of the Johannine witness, the Holy Spirit "is the gift of God who is love . . . who fires man to the love of God and neighbor when he has been given to him" (*T* 15.31). Thus Augustine concludes,

> So the love which is from God and is God is distinctively the Holy Spirit; through him the charity of God is poured out in our hearts,[15] and through it the whole triad dwells in us. This is the reason why it is most apposite

that the Holy Spirit, while being God, should also be called the gift of God, and this gift, surely, is distinctively to be understood as being the charity which brings us through to God, without which no other gift of God at all can bring us through to God. (*T* 15.32)

Let us take stock here of Augustine's theology of love. I have suggested that it is best to understand his thoughts against the broader framework of the human quest for happiness. The happy life, which Augustine formulated soon after his decade-long quest for the truth and never abandoned, consisted in desiring and obtaining that which lasts forever. Such could only be the love of God, understood both in terms of receiving and experiencing God's love and in terms of responding to and loving God in turn. But how could human beings love God who they could neither know nor see clearly? At least in part in having been loved by and in loving others. But how might self-absorbed creatures love others? Through the Spirit of God who has been given to them. As Augustine said elsewhere, "without the gift of God—that is, without the Holy Spirit, through whom love is shed abroad in our hearts—the law may bid but it cannot aid."[16] In short, the possibility of the human experience of God and of human loving is itself an expression of God's love and God's gift. More to the point, God's love is given through God's gift of the Spirit—no other than divinity itself. "As then holy scripture proclaims that charity is God, and as it is from God and causes us to abide in God and him in us, and as we know this because he has given us of his Spirit, this Spirit of his is God charity" (*T* 15.37).

Here, however, we should note a curious inconsistency in Augustine's theology of love. If love is characterized by desire, then human beings may love God because humans desire God, but God cannot be literally said to desire or have affections for human beings. In Augustine's neoplatonic cosmology, desire characterizes the lower orders of creation, signifying the lack that exists at those levels such that only creatures have unfulfilled desires. If that is the case, can God be said to truly desire or love?[17] Yet God is clearly described as one "who desires everyone to be saved and to come to the knowledge of the truth" (1 Tim 2:4), and who gave of his Son in order to achieve this desire. This self-giving, I will argue in this book, is reflected not only in the incarnation but also at Pentecost. God's affectivity for human beings—the divine love writ large—is manifest in the sending of the Son and in the outpouring of the Spirit upon all flesh.

Aquinas: The Spirit and the Gift of Love

After Augustine, St. Thomas Aquinas (ca. 1225–1274) is regarded as the most important theologian in the church, certainly the most authoritative for the Roman Catholic tradition. By and large, Aquinas follows Augustine in linking love and the Holy Spirit, even if the ideas of the Bishop of Hippo were mediated to the former through the *Sentences* of Peter Lombard (ca. 1100–1160).[18] Thus, early in his massive and most important work, *Summa Theologica*, Aquinas affirms that "in God there is love, because love is the first movement of the will and of every appetitive power" (I.20.1).[19] (Of course, Aquinas understands all theological language analogically; the divine "appetites" are similar to but also ultimately different from, human appetites, so Aquinas can say that God is "moved" appetitively but only intellectually and not passionately, so as not to contradict Augustine; I.20.1.r2.) From there, after an exposition of other divine attributes, focus turns to the trinitarian mystery, during the middle of the discussion of which questions regarding the person and name of the Holy Spirit are taken up.

Aquinas differs slightly from Augustine in saying that the Spirit proceeds from the Father "through the Son" (I.36.3).[20] But the Angelic Doctor stands with Augustine in affirming both that Love is a proper name of the Holy Spirit and that Gift is also a personal and proper name of the Spirit. With regard to the former question, Aquinas answers, on the one hand, that "there are two processions in God, one by way of the intellect, which is the procession of the Word, and another by way of the will, which is the procession of Love" (I.37.1, see also I.20.1, as cited above), which justifies denoting Love as the proper name of the Spirit; and, on the other hand, that "when the term Love is taken in a notional sense, it means nothing else than 'to spirate love'. . . . As therefore we say that a tree flowers by its flower, so do we say that . . . the Father and the Son love each other and us, by the Holy Ghost, or by Love proceeding" (I.37.2), which justifies the view that the Father and the Son love each other by the love of the Spirit ("Love proceeding"). Hence the Spirit not only is Love but can and should be called Love.[21]

With regard to the latter question about Gift as a name of the Spirit, Aquinas engages in more sustained reflection than does Augustine. Building on the scriptural witness and the received theological tradition, the

Spirit can be understood as Gift in at least four senses: (1) as the eternal Gift of the Father to the Son, (2) as a Gift of the Father through the Son to the world, and since the Spirit also gives of herself, (3) as the Spirit's self-giving to the Father and the Son (eternally), and (4) to the world (in salvation history). The third sense involving the Spirit's self-giving (I.38.1.r1) in particular makes it appropriate to consider Gift as a personal name for the Spirit. The other senses of the Spirit as Gift involve the Spirit's procession or spiration from the Father (through the Son). Aquinas thus says, "As the Son is properly called the Image because He proceeds by way of a word, whose nature it is to be the likeness of its principle (although the Holy Ghost also is like to the Father), so also, because the Holy Ghost proceeds from the Father as love He is properly called Gift, although the Son, too, is given" (1.38.2.r1).[22] Consistent with the spirit of Aquinas' reflections, I suggest it is more appropriate to say that if the Son is properly called Image by virtue of his begottenness from the Father, then the Spirit is properly called Gift by virtue of her spiration from the Father to the Son (and through the Son to the world). Hence the Spirit not only is Gift but can and should be called Gift. By extension, if the gift of God and of the Spirit is gratuitous—and it is—then the Spirit of love is not only grace but can also and should be called grace. Herein is one of Aquinas' central contributions to the thesis of this volume.

I now turn to Aquinas' discussions of love in part II of the *Summa Theologica*, wherein he takes up questions regarding the moral and spiritual life, since it is here that, in my estimation, his most important and original contributions to theology of love are found.[23] Part II opens, as with Augustine, with a consideration of happiness, its nature, means, and attainability, and concludes that human happiness is fulfilled only with the beatific vision (I–II.5.1). But how then are human beings to pursue after such a telos? This leads to a discussion of human willing, including the intentionality, objective, and consequences of human actions. But beyond a merely intellectualist approach to human acting, Aquinas also recognizes that we are passionate creatures and that our choices and behaviors are driven in part by concupiscible appetites that desire the good (or things that are good for us) and irascible sensibilities that alert us to harmful (or bad) things.

For our purposes, the chief among our concupiscible appetites is love. Now Aquinas grants that there are various meanings involved: "We find four words referring . . . to the same thing: namely love [*amor*], dilection [*dilectio*], charity [*caritas*] and friendship [*amicitia*]. They differ, however, in this, that 'friendship,' according to the Philosopher, 'is like a habit, but love and dilection are expressed by way of act or passion';[24] and charity can be taken either way" (I–II.26.3). What is important for us is that human love is caused or attracted by the good and the true (I–II.27.1–2) and that love is the fundamental passion of the soul (I–II.27.4). As a passion, love is a passive potency that can be activated by objects, thus enabling lovers to suffer or be affected by the objects of their love.[25] Equally important is love as an active potency that effects union (between the lover and what is loved), mutual indwelling (here, Aquinas cites 1 John 4:16), ecstasy (here understood as experience transcending the self), and zeal (for the loved object), even as it supremely motivates human desires, behaviors, and actions (I–II.28.1–4, 6). In short, human actions are fundamentally shaped by love's desires.[26]

What if human beings desire something else besides the beatific vision? Remember that for Aquinas, human happiness is finally fulfilled only with the vision of or union with God, but it might well be that we are driven appetitively toward other lesser goods. It is thus in the latter half of Part II of the *Summa* that Aquinas turns to a discussion of the habits and inclinations that shape human action. There are certainly bad or evil habits—the vices—that cause human beings to act sinfully. Thus while human beings are created in the image of the Triune God, including the image of love that is properly called the Holy Spirit (for Aquinas), human love in the natural sense should not be confused with the Spirit but can become distorted if not directed toward the Spirit and the beatific vision.

However, redemption is possible since there are also good habits—the virtues—that can be direct toward the beatific vision and when properly oriented result in the sanctified life. Through God's gracious endowment of creation every person has a natural capacity for the basic moral virtues, the four most important of which are prudence, justice, temperance, and fortitude. More important, however, are the explicitly theological virtues, identified by St. Paul as faith, hope, and love (1 Cor 13:13). These are made available to human beings by virtue of God's gracious and redemptive work in the Incarnation and Pentecost. Human loves and appetites that are directed toward God order the will and the desire affectively toward the good, the true, and the beautiful. Here the concupiscible passions are redeemed and affectively inclined and habituated toward the love of God.

We would do well to remember that for Aquinas, the orders of nature (the moral, natural virtues) and of grace (the theological, supernatural virtues) are distinct but not disparate: "grace does not destroy nature, but perfects it" (I.1.8.r2). So also does the Holy Spirit impart gifts (Isa 11:2–3) that supernaturally grace and perfect the natural habits and tendencies of human hearts; more precisely, "the gifts perfect man for acts which are higher than acts of virtue" (I–II.68.1), and "so that he is ready to follow the promptings of the Holy Spirit" (I–II.68.4). This means that the moral virtues are perfected by the gifts of the Spirit, which in turn enable human beings to attain happiness (perfect union with God).[27]

This leads, finally, to Aquinas' discussion of the theological virtues. If faith perfects human knowledge (by gracing human minds with the divine truth) and hope perfects human hearts (by anticipating human desires being graciously fulfilled with the beatific vision), then love—understood in this part of the *Summa* as *caritas*, the love that is proper name of the Holy Spirit—perfects human willing (by gracing human actions with divine harmony and unity). Here we can only very briefly summarize some of the main points of Aquinas' extensive consideration of love, its object, order, and principal act (II–II.23–27). First, love binds us in friendship with God (II–II.23.1; here Aquinas draws on John 15:15), and by doing so, orders our affections—our inclinations and desires—toward and unites us with God (II–II.23.3). Second, "no true virtue is possible without charity" (II–II.23.7). Third, charity "can be in us neither naturally, nor through acquisition by the natural powers, but by the infusion of the Holy Ghost" (II–II.24.2; here Aquinas cites Rom 5:5), and that according to the mysterious ways of the Spirit (II–II.24.3, citing 1 Cor 12:11). Fourth, the object of charity should begin with God but extend from there to include our neighbors, ourselves and our bodies, sinners, enemies, and angels, but not demons (II–II.25).

Fifth, Aquinas charts a hierarchy of love, one that he believes will perdure in heaven in a more perfect form (II–II.26.1), according to this order (II–II.26): God first and foremost before all else, even before our neighbors and ourselves; ourselves, in terms of our participation in the goodness of God, before our neighbor who shares in this participation;[28] our neighbors, particularly those who are also more closely related to God and God's goodness, over others who are not neighbors; our parents, children, and then wider households, including those to whom we are related by blood, over those to whom we are not related by blood;[29] and our benefactors more than those we benefit. Sixth, we ought to love God for God's sake, wholly, and without measure (II–II.27.3, 5, 6). Last but not least, there is merit to loving our neighbors but only because we love them for God's sake (II–II.27.8). In all of this, of course, charity is the theological virtue imparted by the Holy Spirit to grace human nature so as to enable human beings to receive the knowledge, vision, and love of God and attain to final happiness.[30]

In sum, Aquinas, like Augustine, understands the love as the gift of God particularly in and through the Holy Spirit. What Aquinas adds is delineation of what might be called a medieval psychology of love that is pneumatologically understood. At one level, the human spirit has been naturally graced with concupiscible desires and loves which are part and parcel of our creational participation in the love of God that is properly associated with the Spirit and that leads the soul to seek after the good. At a second level, the Holy Spirit supernaturally graces these habitual, moral virtues with the theological virtues of faith, hope, and love.[31] The result is that human beings, although already naturally—even graciously— constituted in the love of the Spirit as creatures made in the image of God, are nevertheless also potentially open to being gradually caught up by the Spirit into the divine love and, if responsive to the specifically theological graces of the Spirit, are also enabled to enjoy the ultimate happiness that brings.[32] All of this is the work of grace, of the Spirit of love who is the underserving gift of a gracious God to the world.

The one question that arises for our purposes in Aquinas' pneumatology of love concerns its individualistic orientation. While the Angelic Doctor delineates a hierarchy of love that includes guidance for loving others, yet the presumed medieval faculty psychology, while helpful in terms of identifying the affective nature of charity, still oriented much of the discussion toward enabling the soul to access the Beatific Vision. The whole nature and grace framework undergirding Aquinas' theology is designed to consider how the soul can ascend to fully experience and inhabit the love of God. While this is an important topic, our own theology of love suggests that the journey of the soul toward love is not undertaken apart from others. Instead, it is precisely in benefitting others that love is experienced, so that the most pronounced encounter with love is not only in receiving but giving it on behalf of others. Thus, Aquinas takes us only halfway there in saying that the Holy Spirit graces human nature in order to enable human reception of the knowledge, vision, and love of God; rather, from a pneumatological perspective, Aquinas should have said that the Spirit's gracing of human nature empowers human reception of the love of God in and through the love of others. We will develop this extension of Aquinas' theology of love in the rest of this book.

Tillich: The Spirit and the Power of Love

If Augustine was one of the first Christian theologians to make explicit the connection between the Holy Spirit and love, and Aquinas developed that connection in terms of the Spirit's gift of love for the sake of the moral and spiritual life, then Paul Tillich returns to ground love not only at the center of the spiritual quest but also at the heart of being itself. As with the other two doctors of the church (although I realize that Tillich's "doctoral-ecclesial" credentials will be disputed by some), there is much that can and even should be said about Tillich's theology of love that will have to be omitted because of space constraints. The following focuses primarily on select sections in Tillich's three-volume *Systematic Theology*, highlighting along the way how the shift toward pneumatological categories invites "a new conception of the structure of the whole," a reconsideration that Tillich himself recognized and suggested (III.4).[33]

We begin by noting that the most sustained discussion of love in the first volume of the *ST* begins by saying that, "Love is an ontological concept. . . . But God is love. And, since God is being-itself, one must say that being-itself is love" (*ST* I.279). These claims get us into the thickets of Tillich's philosophical theology and ontology. For Tillich, God is not merely *a* being—to say such would be to reduce God to a creaturely status—but is rather the ground of being itself (*ST* II.235–41). More important, being itself is fundamentally whole, and hence there is but one reality from out of which existence flows. Love, then, as divine, permeates being itself and is woven into the fabric of primordial reality.

Creation and history represent the existential rupture of being, resulting in estrangement and alienation. Creatures thus live with and amidst anxiety,[34] even as finite and historical existence is caught up with ambiguity. Human anxiety in particular is precipitated and exacerbated by either "un-love" (the lack of faith or belief that separates humans from God as the ground of being) or by selfish love (concupiscence, a self-centeredness that ignores and does not love others) (*ST* II.47–55). Yet love, as the primordial force and foundation of being, conquers non-being through reuniting what is separated and by taking non-being up into itself. As Tillich notes, "The divine love is the final answer to the questions implied in human existence, including finitude, the threat of disruption, and estrangement" (*ST* I.286). If sin is at the heart of the existential estrangement of creatures from their ground of being, "Love as the striving for the reunion of the separated is the opposite of estrangement. In faith and love, sin is conquered because estrangement is overcome by reunion" (*ST* II.47).

Like Aquinas, Tillich recognizes different types of love: "Love as *libido* is the movement of the needy toward that which fulfils the need. Love as *philia* is the movement of the equal toward union with the equal. Love as *erōs* is the movement of that which is lower in power and meaning to that which is higher" (*ST* I.280). But *agape* is divine love that is universal, transcendent over all yet unconditionally immanent within and available to all.[35] In at least the first two volumes of the *ST*, Tillich remains within an existentialist ontological and philosophical frame of reference. Love is at the heart of being itself, and at work amidst the vicissitudes of creation and history in order to heal the separation of finite realities from their primordial source.

In the third volume of the *ST*, however, Tillich takes a pneumatological turn and comes to see love as a creation and "an ecstatic manifestation of the Spiritual Presence" (*ST* III.137). Elsewhere I have argued that part of the reason for Tillich's turn to pneumatology, besides the fact that it was only natural to devote this third volume to explicate the Third Article of the Creed, was motivated in part by his increasing realization that something more dynamic than the theology of the New Being articulated in the second volume was needed to bring about the reunion of being and existence.[36] What emerges then, complementing the Logos-christology of volume two, are a Spirit-christology and a Spirit-ecclesiology. Spirit, for Tillich, is understood as "the actualization of power and meaning in unity" (*ST* III.111). Hence, the Spiritual community is nothing less than the new form of inhabitation shaped by Jesus the Christ, the Spirit-anointed one, as the New Being that enables "the conquest of the ambiguities of life under the dimension of the spirit" (*ST* III.109).[37]

The key passage for our purposes is Tillich's discussion of both faith and love as "the manifestation of the divine Spirit in the human spirit"

(*ST* III.129–38). "Faith is the state of being *grasped* by the transcendent unity of unambiguous life—it embodies love as the state of being *taken into* that transcendent unity" (*ST* III.129; emphasis in original). Thus the Spiritual Presence manifest as love becomes the "blood" (*ST* III.134) or "moving power" of life that reunites the separated.[38] Love is neither merely an emotional feeling (liable to sentimentalization) nor an ontological abstraction (limited to being a speculative idea) but is also a concretely material, volitional, and relational aspect of creaturely existence. More precisely, *agape* "is the creation of the Spirit" that graciously urges finite existences toward reunion with their ground of being, and in that sense, love in all of its various senses—libidinal, erotic, philiac—is a gift of God that is "one and indivisible" (*ST* III.137).[39] Thus is pneumatology intertwined with the theologies of love and of grace; as Tillich puts it: "Theologically speaking, Spirit, love, and grace are one and the same reality in different aspects. Spirit is the creative power; love is its creation; grace is the effective presence of love in man" (*ST* III.274).

The love of God cannot be compelled by the human spirit, as the finite is simply incapable of imposing upon the infinite (*ST* III.112). However, the Spiritual Presence is continuously at work within the ruptures of nature and history to restore, reconcile, and reunite creatures with the ground of being. This requires, in effect, ecstatic manifestations, since in their finite state creatures prefer to be self-absorbed. It is thus the power of love that opens up creatures to what is beyond themselves, albeit in ways that do not destroy their centeredness and structure (*ST* III.116). Ecstasy is thus "the great liberating power under the dimension of self-awareness" (*ST* III.119), since finite creatures now remain distinct but no longer alienated from others. What emerges is the unambiguous life of the Spirit that simultaneously marks the Spiritual Community. *Agape* unites "the separated centers [of creatures] in the transcendent union of unambiguous life" (*ST* III.156), and in so doing makes manifest the healing powers of the Spiritual Presence.

How is the love of God related to the law, wrath, and judgment of God? Of course, Tillich recognized that the law was summarized both by Jesus and Paul as being fulfilled in love. Thus he affirmed that the law of love "is the ultimate law because it is the negation of law; it is absolute because it concerns everything concrete" (*ST* I.151). Similarly, "love cannot be commanded, because it is the power of that reunion which precedes and fulfils the command before it [the command] is given" (*ST* II.81). Therefore, love is above law, and, paradoxically, absolutely relative. This is because theonomous morality—morality lived under love rather than law—is applied not legalistically but, in wisdom, afresh in every new situation of ambiguous life (*ST* III.272–74).[40] Thus Tillich writes elsewhere, "Love alone can transform itself according to the concrete demands of every individual and social situation without losing its eternity and dignity and unconditional validity. Love can adapt itself to every phase of a changing world."[41]

But the primordial love of the ground of being is also intimately intertwined with divine justice.[42] Tillich puts it this way:

> [T]he justice of God is the act through which he lets the self-destructive consequences of existential estrangement go their way. He cannot remove them because they belong to the structure of being itself and God would cease to be God—the only thing which is impossible for him—if he removed these consequences. Above all, he would cease to be love, for justice is the structural form of love without which it would be sheer sentimentality. The exercise of justice is the working of his love, resisting and breaking what is against love. Therefore, there can be no conflict in God between love and justice. (*ST* II.174)

Similarly, the divine love is intertwined with divine wrath. The wrath of God symbolizes the power of love at the heart of reality that in effect suffers the estrangements of existence but does so precisely in order to heal and reconcile. Thus in the end, "The divine love stands against all that which is against love, leaving it to its self-destruction, in order to save those who are destroyed" (*ST* II.77).

For Tillich, then, love can be understood both as the ground of being and as the power of the Spiritual Presence. As the ground of being, love permeates and suffuses what is, but as the power of the Spiritual Presence, love strives to heal the fragmentation of spiritual existence in order to enable the emergence of the Spiritual Community. Simultaneously, love is normed concretely by Jesus the Christ, and it is the Spiritual Presence of the Christ, understood as the New Being, which finally reconciles finite creatures who are estranged from one another and from the God who is love. Put otherwise, love is the power of the New Being and of the Spiritual Presence at work in overcoming the alienation that marks finite existence among human creatures, so that the unambiguous life can be realized.

Although the erotic/affective and pneumatological aspects of Tillich's theology of love are clearly articulated, part of the challenge in appropriating the preceding set of ideas lies in the overall trajectory of Tillich's philosophical orientation. The Tillichian Ground of Being is certainly ontological, primordial, and essential to the healing of the rupture of existence, but is it sufficiently personal in accounting for the intersubjective experiences of human love, even of the interpersonal aspects of the human encounter with divine love?[43] Further, what about the teleological or eschatological aspects of love understood as benefitting others in anticipation of the coming reign of God? Yes, Tillich's is a profound consideration of the uniting power of love as enabled by the Spiritual Presence, but is this just a reconciliation with a primordial originality rather than a foretaste of the unity of many tongues, tribes, peoples, and nations in the eschatological reign of the Spirit? My intuition, to be followed in the rest of this book, is that Tillich's ontology places too much of an accent on the foundations of love but by doing so lacks a teleological orientation toward that divine love that is coming. In short, Tillich's Spiritual Community remains hopelessly fragmented and ambiguous apart from a more robust eschatological and pneumatological theology of love's graciously reconciling and healing power.

Conclusion

This chapter only scratches the surface of theologies of love in the Christian tradition. Our focus, however, has been on theologians who have linked love and the Holy Spirit. To be sure, a more appropriate historical overview would certainly have covered a number of other voices.[44] But our purposes are more theological than historical, and given these motivations, a critical retrieval of Augustine, Aquinas, and Tillich enables us to register a range of ecumenical perspectives toward a pneumatological theology of love.

In particular, our theological interlocutors have emphasized the centrality of love for the doctrine of God in general and for a trinitarian view of the divine nature in particular. Beginning with Augustine, love is linked both to theology proper and to the theology of the Spirit. If God is spirit and God is love and if love is God, then divine spirit is love and love is the divine spirit. But in this case, love is not merely of theological import but also has ontological ramifications. The latter are made most explicit in Tillich's theology of love wherein love is both the ground of being and the spiritual dynamic amidst the existential reality of nature and history itself.

It is Aquinas who helps us to see further the pneumatological, charismatic, and graced dimension of a natural world that is yet being elevated and remains to be fully perfected by God. The Spirit who is Love is also the Spirit who is Gift. Hence, the Spirit is the Gift of Love to the world, intended for its sanctification and eventual glorification. The world is thus graced with love in various senses: as the primordial creation over which the *ruach* of God hovered; as the natural realm that includes human beings who are graced by the Spirit with the moral virtues; and as the supernaturally endowed domain within which the Spirit redeems the desires of free agents so they might find fulfillment and happiness in relationship with God (Augustine), prepares creatures for union with God and the beatific vision (Aquinas), or heals, reintegrates, and reconciles creatures estranged and alienated from their ground of being (Tillich). From a pneumatological angle, the God who is love works through the unconditional Gift that is the Spirit of Love in order to lavish love upon creatures and draw creation back into the loving embrace of the Creator.

The preceding considerations take us to the brink of but do not bring us into the full flow of love's teleological and eschatological character. This is because for these thinkers dominated by classical theological and philosophical categories, even a pneumatology of love has a protological and primordial orientation, directed as it is toward union with God *before* the world, as it were. A more thoroughly pneumatological approach, however, will highlight an eschatological trajectory, one that emphasizes the edification and benefit of others in anticipation of the coming reign of God. Affectivity toward and activity on behalf of others is here teleologically normed according to the shape of the Spirit of the last days.

In the constructive portion of this volume (parts II and III), then, we augment the preceding sketch by drawing upon pentecostal theological resources to articulate a pneumatological and eschatological theology of love for the twenty-first century. Before doing so, however, we turn to thinking about love in dialogue with the social and natural sciences.

CHAPTER 2

• • •

Science and the Altruistic Spirit
Empirical Understandings of Benevolent Love

The preceding theological reflections invite us to understand love as woven into the basic structure of the cosmos that we inhabit. Beyond these ontological considerations, Tillich's theology of love also identifies its existential dimensions, especially love's role in healing and salvaging a fragmented world. Both of these aspects of the nature of love—the ontological and the existential—invite other, not strictly theological questions and analyses. Further, the long legacy left by the medieval understanding of theology as science (*scientia*) suggests that contemporary scientific perspectives may be fruitfully brought to bear on illuminating the phenomenon of love.[1] Might it be possible that the contemporary natural sciences could shed light on the ontological character of love while the social and human sciences could inform our existential experience of love?

I suggest that this is not merely an abstract question, especially in light of the conclusions of the preceding chapter. If the theological tradition has insisted not only that love is a gift of God but also that there is or should be a clear correlation between the love of God and the love of neighbor, then love is not only a vertical relationship between God and the world but also a horizontal relationship between creatures. If so, the latter suggests there should be an empirical dimension to love, one that focuses on altruistic human behaviors and on benevolent human activities that are measurable in some respects. The increasing interdisciplinarity of the theological endeavor makes possible today a dialogue with various sciences on this matter that would have been less plausible in previous generations.[2] My approach, however, is neither to seek legitimation of theology from the sciences nor to attempt any naïve correlation between them; instead, I advocate a theological approach to the natural world and a dialogical understanding of the relationship between theology and science in the conviction that all truth is God's truth and that Christian theological self-understanding can illuminate the natural world and contribute to the scientific enterprise in ways that do not undermine the integrity of science.[3]

This chapter therefore engages with what some scholars have called the "science of love."[4] Its three sections take up, respectively, the sociology, biology, and neuroscience of love, ordered in this way according to when each discipline began to produce research on altruism. We will see how these human and natural sciences illuminate the interrelational quality of love and its emotional character. More important, we shall also see how the contemporary sciences open up windows into what theologians call the love of neighbor precisely because they explore the tangible expressions of benevolent and altruistic behavior. But while each of these disciplines will provide an empirical perspective on the phenomenon of love, they also will suggest that love as an intersubjective reality is irreducible to the material domain. In other words, love may be biological, social, and historical, but the sciences nevertheless are not inimical to hypotheses regarding the inter- or trans-personal, and, by extension, the transcendental dimensions of love.

I need to register two caveats before proceeding. One is that I come to the "sciences of love" as a theologian rather than as a scientist. I am not unaware of the disputed and contested issues in these domains, but with both time and space constraints I have chosen not to delve into them. Not to mention that I am in no position to adjudicate between sometimes conflicting scientific hypotheses. More important, I do not claim to present merely an objective set of scientific accounts. But within the scope of our own investigation, there will naturally be certain data and findings that are more important for our purposes and others that can be left unmentioned. The following is a very selective discussion of what has unfolded in these scientific endeavors, one pertinent to the theological concerns animating this inquiry. I do not believe I have skewed the scientific data toward my nonscientific ends, although I am aware that there are other ways to interpret the data than as done here. The discerning reader will have to determine by the end of this book how helpful, or not, the following is for its overall argument.

Tapping into Love Energy? Sociology and the Search for Altruistic Love

We begin our conversation with the sciences by following explorations in the sociology of love. In this field, the mid-twentieth-century contributions of the Russian émigré to the U.SA., Pitirim Aleksandrovich Sorokin (1889–1968), remain in many respects unsurpassed.[5] By the time he completed his Ph.D. in sociology at the University of St. Petersburg in 1922, Sorokin was already a published scholar, but his opposition to the Communist regime led first to imprisonment and then to exile. He came to the University of Minnesota in 1923 and then shifted to Harvard University in 1930 as the founding chair of its Department of Sociology. His first two-plus decades in the United States led to a dozen or so books—a few multi-volumed, with these and many others very lengthy—on the sociology of revolution, sociological theory, sociocultural mobility and causality, and the sociology of war, among many other topics.

Having lived through the Czarist and Bolshevik revolutions, the First World War on its eastern front, and then the Second World War (as an American), however, Sorokin began to turn his sociological gaze to the question of what, if anything, could be done for what he called "the reconstruction of humanity."[6] Part of the answer to this, Sorokin became convinced, was that human beings needed to nurture their altruistic capacities. This involved attending not only to the concrete material, social, and historical factors that led to war and other destructive human activities, but also to human ideals as manifest in their cultural, aesthetic, philosophical, moral, and religious sensibilities. When Sorokin's vision was caught by Eli Lilly, one of the cofounders of the Lilly Endowment fund, he was given a start-up grant which was used to establish the Harvard Research Center for Creative Altruism.[7] Over the course of the 1950s under Sorokin's leadership, the Center produced a number of important volumes on the sociology of love.[8]

The most important of these books, and for our purposes certainly the most noteworthy part of Sorokin's legacy, was *The Ways and Power of Love*, originally published in 1954. Notice, though, that for Sorokin the sociologist, love was not merely a sentimental idea; rather, as indicated by the subtitle of the book—*Types, Factors, and Techniques of Moral Transformation*—what was needed from social scientists was research conducive to a culture's or society's moral elevation. With neither time nor space for us to do a full review of this book, the following summarizes a number of Sorokin's most significant findings that are still relevant over half a century later.

First, although Sorokin recognized that there were many facets to love—religious, ethical, ontological, physical, biological, and psychological—his focus as a sociologist was on the social aspect. A working definition was that "on the social plane love is a meaningful interaction—or relationship—between two or more persons where the aspirations and aims of one person are shared and helped in their realization by other persons" (*WPL* 13). From this Sorokin postulated five empirically measurable dimensions (*WPL* chap. 2) of psychosocial love: (1) its intensity; (2) its extensivity; (3) its duration; (4) its purity; and (5) its adequacy. Love that demands more (i.e., gives a higher amount of what one has) is more intense. Love that involves or reaches a greater number of others is more extensive. Love that is perpetuated over time (i.e., like that of a mother) is more enduring or of greater extent. Love that is least motivated by selfish motives is most pure. And love that is most adequate is when the lover's intentions to benefit others (the subjective aspect) correlate with the actual consequences of such actions (the objective aspect). In addition, Sorokin affirmed, "objectively altruistic actions are possible mainly through the indivisible unity of goodness, truth, and beauty, and the possibility of their mutual transformation into one another" (*WPL* 18–19). In other words, the social aspect of love could not ultimately be completely divorced from the transcendentals (goodness, truth, beauty).

Second, Sorokin observed that the intensity and duration of love were dependent on an "inflow of love from outside the loving individual that replenishes his great expenditures of intense love energy" (*WPL* 25). Without such a source of revitalization, no energy would be available for sustaining love's activities. Beyond the reception of love energy from others, however, Sorokin had also by now been engaged in studies of exemplars of love[9] and had observed that both historically and on the contemporary scene there were altruistic personalities who were persecuted, hated, and even martyred, and for these, "no observable 'inflow of love' from outside" (*WPL* 26) was documented. Yet such "great martyrs of love, such as Jesus, or Al Hallaj, or Damien the Leper, or Gandhi . . . did not decrease the intensity of their love" (*WPL* 25). Sorokin concluded that "The most probable hypothesis for them . . . is that an inflow of love comes from an intangible, little-studied, possibly supraempirical source called 'God,' 'the Godhead,' 'the Soul of the Universe,' the 'Heavenly Father,' 'Truth,' and so on," and that, "This hypothesis is corroborated by the purely empirical statements of the martyrs of love who were surrounded by an inimical world" (*WPL* 26).

Building on this thesis, Sorokin further suggested that the structure of the loving or altruistic personality involves a supraconscious mentality, one that enables human creativity (even extrasensory perception; *WPL* 112) above and beyond what is accessible to normal experiential observation and conscious rationality. If the supraconscious elevates human intuition and achievement in mathematics, the sciences, technology, the arts, and philosophy, it also facilitates human interaction with and reception of the supraempirical source of love energy that empowers the benevolence or unselfishness manifest in the great martyrs of love. As Sorokin pointedly put it, "Like supreme creativity in the field of truth or beauty, supreme love can hardly be achieved without a direct participation of the supraconscious and without the ego-transcending techniques of its awakening" (*WPL* 125).[10] Much of the rest of Sorokin's book is hence devoted to an exploration of the various techniques—including Patanjali and other yogic techniques, monastic practices, and psychoanalytic and counseling therapies—that can awaken, produce, accumulate, and distribute such altruistic love energy in both persons and groups.

Last for our purposes (but not least in terms of Sorokin's lasting contributions) is the discussion of what is called "tribal altruism." Sorokin had observed that by and large, altruism did not extend much beyond the local "tribe," but this resulted in "tribal egoism." What was needed was the capacity to transcend such altruistic limitations in order to develop a "universal altruism." Only the latter could, finally, undermine the human tendency to hostility, violence, and war. Essential to such a universal solidarity was "Self-identification with the supraconscious as one's highest and truest self" (*WPL* 481). To the degree that human beings could foster such identification, to that same degree might it also be possible to nurture forms of altruism that transcended tribal egoism. As Sorokin put it, "only the sublime love, unbounded in its extensivity, maximal in its intensity, purity, duration and adequacy, inseparable from the perfect truth and blameless beauty meets all the requirements of the supreme moral value" (*WPL* 485).

By the mid-1940s Sorokin's integralism, derived from the Russian philosophical tradition,[11] had already had the effect of marginalizing his views within the sociological sciences. For Sorokin, human knowledge involved reference to a superorganic world of ideals and values (e.g., truth, goodness, beauty), and these also should be integrated in sociological inquiry. On the one hand, then, it was Sorokin's integralism that both allowed and motivated his explorations into love.[12] On the other hand, these same interests could not be easily accommodated in an increasingly empiricist environment. As the postwar period witnessed a shift toward a more positivist epistemological, ontological, and methodological paradigm for sociology as a discipline,[13] the result was that Sorokin's work on love fell on increasingly deaf ears within the social sciences. To be sure, there were some who recognized how difficult, even impossible, it was to proceed with sociological research apart from the questions regarding values that Sorokin repeatedly reminded his colleagues about.[14] But by and large, research in the sociology of love waned after funding for Sorokin's research center dried up in the late 1950s, and especially after he died in 1968.

Yet all was not lost in the quest for a sociology of love. Social scientific research into love began to resurface as research on altruism continued to develop in the neighboring fields of the biological and psychological sciences,[15] and in the 1980s sociologists such as Samuel Oliner picked up Sorokin's mantle and renewed the exploration into love.[16] More recently, theological ethicists such as Stephen G. Post have also found inspiration from Sorokin to engage in interdisciplinary research on love. Post founded the Institute for Research on Unlimited Love (IRUL) in 2001 with funding from the John Templeton Foundation,[17] and then the next year reissued (and wrote a new introduction for) Sorokin's *Ways and Power of Love* with the Templeton Foundation Press. By this time, the sociology of religion was practically wide open for a reconsideration of Sorokin's ideas.[18] The methodological positivism, not to mention religious and ideological atheism, which dominated the field before had now at least begun to tolerate a softer methodological agnosticism, even one involving theistic hypotheses that Sorokin had championed. We will return to pick up the story of the sociology of love in our next chapter.

Against All Odds? Biology and the Science of Altruism

We now shift from sociology to biology. There is much more ground to cover here, so we cannot be exhaustive.[19] But we will begin with Darwin and then move quickly to focus the bulk of our energies on developments since the time of Sorokin's research on love, since it is these that are most crucial for thinking theologically about love in dialogue with the sciences.

We know that Darwin himself was not oblivious to the question of how altruism could evolve. Put bluntly, if the evolution of biological creatures was based on natural selection and the survival of the fittest, with those more capable multiplying while others less capable, failing to perpetuate themselves as much, then how does altruism, understood as self-sacrificial and loving behavior, emerge? How could individuals who are willing to give themselves up for others successfully reproduce? Darwin's initial response was to point to overall group reproductive success enabled by sharing and unselfishness. Thus he wrote, in discussing the evolution of morality in the middle of his book, *The Descent of Man*, a passage that deserves to be quoted at length:

> Ultimately our moral sense or conscience becomes a highly complex sentiment—originating in the social instincts, largely guided by the approbation of our fellow-men, ruled by reason, self-interest, and in later times by deep religious feelings, and confirmed by instruction and habit. It must not be forgotten that although a high standard of morality gives but a slight or no advantage to each individual man and his children over the other men of the same tribe, yet that an increase in the number of well-endowed men and an advancement in the standard of morality will certainly give an immense advantage to one tribe over another. A tribe including many members who, from possessing in a high degree the spirit of patriotism, fidelity, obedience, courage, and sympathy, were always ready to aid one another, and to sacrifice themselves for the common good, would be victorious over most other tribes; and this would be natural selection. At all times throughout the world tribes have supplanted other tribes; and as morality is one important element in their success, the standard of morality and the number of well-endowed men will thus everywhere tend to rise and increase.[20]

If the question was then about how such altruists could survive in such a tribe to begin with, Darwin's response was that this happened by members seeing that benevolent acts to others will bring rewards, or praise, and that nonbenevolent acts might bring blame or condemnation. In short, the Darwinian paradigm already, from the earliest days, recognized that altruism could be accounted for only if natural selection occurred not only at the level of the individual but also at the level of the group.

Group selection, however, fell out of favor during much of the twentieth century. This was in part because the neo-Darwinian paradigm that emerged in the hundred years after Darwin focused in general on evolutionary processes at the genetic and genomic levels. Over time, then, evolutionary theorists shifted increasingly toward individual selectionist models undergirded by what has come to be known as a "gene's-eye view" of natural selection.[21] Within this trajectory of research, altruistic metaphors suggestive of self-sacrificial dispositions and behaviors have been inevitably subordinated to egoistic ones such as that heralded by Richard Dawkins' bestseller, *The Selfish Gene.*[22]

Within this evolutionary framework, altruistic behavior could only be explicated in egoistic genetic terms. Individuals only seemed to behave altruistically. In reality, however, such apparently self-sacrificial behavior serves self-interested purposes, perhaps not in or for the altruistic organism but certainly in or for either their relatives or others with a similar genetic endowment. Thus, theories that have been circulated, discussed, and disputed among evolutionary biologists include kin selection (behavioral strategies that, even if costly for an organism, increase the reproductive capacity of that organism's relatives), inclusive fitness (behavioral strategies that, although costly for an organism, increase the reproductive capacity not only of that organism's relatives but also of organisms of equivalent genetic makeup), reciprocal altruism (behavioral strategies that, while temporarily costly for an organism, in the long run potentially increase the organism's reproductive fitness in light of expected similar responses of recipient organisms), and indirect reciprocity (behavioral strategies that, while initially costly for an organism, expect in the long run to elicit similar benefit from the behaviors of other organisms within the group).[23] While there are important differences from one theory to the next, what unites them is the idea that while the self-sacrificial character of some acts of benevolence should not be minimized, many of these can also be understood simultaneously as self-serving, especially if we understand the "self" from the gene's perspective so that the end result is the propagation of the gene pool related or similar to that of the altruistic organism.[24]

Yet it was also undeniable that there are cases of human altruism conducted with regard to total strangers, at the cost of the lives of the altruists themselves, and thus without any hopes of benefitting from reciprocation later. While there are certainly cultural influences that shape such behaviors (about which the rest of this volume will propose one cultural-religious theory of explanation), biologists have been reluctant to concede that there might be certain types of behaviors—altruistic ones, in this case—without genetic correlations, motivations, or constraints. The result has been the reemergence of group selection theories, partly retrieving the major idea of Darwin's own constructive proposal, but now informed by the latest developments in the biological sciences. Group selectionists generally do not reject but incorporate other altruism theories (kin selection, etc.) while also suggesting that genuinely altruistic behavior directed toward strangers (rather than to kin or those genetically related in some way) could evolve if between- or across-group selection forces were stronger than within-group selection forces. In other words, altruistic traits would evolve if they benefitted populations as a whole even if they were selectively disadvantaged within a group.[25]

Even with the shift to group selection, however, the dominant paradigm is framed by self-interestedness and its selective mechanisms. As Jeffrey Schloss puts it, in the Darwinian and neo-Darwinian scheme of things, "Not only does love appear to fail as creation's final law, but it is legislated out of existence."[26] What is being suggested is that even if we replace the rather nonscientific notion of love with the much more scientifically amenable concept of altruism, such a change of nomenclature is driven by the (allegedly scientific) conviction that whatever else self-sacrificial behaviors are, they are at bottom expressions of selfish egos and self-seeking genes. From this perspective, of course, love and altruism would be anomalies at best, or phenomenological aberrations simply awaiting fully reductive explanatory accounts at worst. But what if egoism in all of its competitive dimensions was not the most fundamental biological reality? Or what if competition was only one factor and maybe not even the most dominant modality of nature's selective instruments?

In the last half-generation, driven at least in part by the quest to identify the biological foundations of altruism, the notion of cooperation has begun to emerge as a significant category among evolutionary theorists. By and large, most evolutionary biologists who have begun to explore this issue see competition or conflict and cooperation as, in effect, two sides of the same engine that drives natural selection.[27] Thus it is claimed that, "while competition may always be possible, intricate cooperation is *always* part of life, at all levels."[28] This is especially the case when thinking and talking about the role that punishment plays in the formation of altruistic tendencies and behaviors. In other words, altruistic personalities who are still fundamentally self-interested egoists in some respect will not ordinarily act in self-sacrificial ways unless the costs of not doing so are greater than those related to the risks undertaken in acting benevolently toward others. These costs of non-benevolent behavior are usually tied in with notions of the potential punishment that might have to be endured if one's behavior was perceived as being egoistical rather than concerned for the welfare of the group.[29] Within this paradigm, then, cooperative behaviors emerge out of the self-preservational instinct vis-à-vis the pressures of the social environment. And if this is the truth of the matter, the emergence of mutuality, benevolence, altruism, and love would still be, as the saying goes, against all odds.

But others have begun to question the reigning paradigm. If the selfish-gene approach essentially emphasizes genetic entitlement, competition, sexual conflict, aggression, deception, and survival of the fittest, might there be an alternative way of understanding the evolutionary history of humankind that highlights instead cooperation, teamwork, and mutuality? One of a growing number of voices taking such an approach seriously is Joan Roughgarden, professor of biological sciences and of geophysics at Stanford University.[30] Her most recent book presents a theory of social selection that is predicated ultimately on teamwork, honesty, and genetic equality.[31] What Roughgarden is advocating is not necessarily group selection—she thinks that individual selection provides a more adequate overall framework on this matter—but that individuals get ahead less by competing than by cooperating with others. Hence evolutionary success materializes when individuals engage in cooperative and coordinated activity in pursuit of team goals. Central to the argument is that while the neo-Darwinian theory of sexual selection presumes that conflict, competition, and trickery drive the evolutionary process, this ignores the growing mountain of evidence indicating otherwise.

Of course, Roughgarden's claims—both the empirical and the paradigmatic—have been contested, and there is no reason not to think that even if she were right, business will not go on pretty much as usual in the disputed fields, at least for the time being.[32] My point, however, is simply that even in the field of evolutionary biology there is an increasing realization about the need to think of cooperation as at the heart of the evolutionary history of the world, rather than as arbitrary and irrational (from a selfish gene viewpoint) aspects. As Matt Ridley, a zoologist by training, describes it, life "is about the billion-year coagulation of our genes into cooperative teams, the million-year coagulation of our ancestors into cooperative societies, and the thousand-year coagulation of our ideas about society and its origins."[33]

These recent developments suggest that there will be further windows opened by the biological sciences to considering afresh how cooperation and, by extension, benevolence, altruism, and even love, have been adapted into the evolutionary history of our world.[34] If we were to consider such research in dialogue with the social scientific framework charted by Sorokin, however, we might also ask about how this cooperation and mutuality paradigm might shed light on the circulation of love energy, at least in terms of exchanges between biological creatures. Might it be possible to think of the biology of altruism as involving the cooperative exchange of benevolent love that may hold the key to the flourishing of all, not just the "fittest"?

My Neurons Made Me Love? The Cognitive Sciences and the Emotions of Love

Even if we might be able to show that biological life presumes and thrives on cooperative rather than competitive behavior, does that provide us with a scientific basis for understanding human altruism? If from a commonsensical perspective altruism involves actions that benefit others at cost to oneself, do not genuine acts of benevolence require a psychological or mental component? In this last section of this chapter, I want to survey what the neuropsychological sciences are telling us about altruism and love. If we are biologically constituted for cooperation in some respect, might we also discover that we are neurologically fitted for acts of altruism or what we feel is love?

Let us be clear here about the issues involved. Early on in brain research on altruism it was realized that any cognitive analysis of benevolence would have to do more than identify and then explore the neural correlates of prosociality. Prosocial behaviors, even those which resulted in the increased wellbeing of others, could simply be the expression of certain personality types socialized according to certain norms or, at some level, could even be selfishly motivated.[35] The bottom line had to do with the fundamentally psychological dimension of human behavior: the intended outcomes of an agent's actions. If egoism were understood as "a motivational state with the ultimate goal of increasing one's own welfare," then altruism was "a motivational state with the ultimate goal of increasing another's welfare."[36] Once we are clear about the differences, then we realize that altruism proper involves analyses of the reasons, desires, and intentions of agents. We then also realize that while our reasons may be amenable to merely rational analysis, our desires often resist reduction to discursive formulation. This is because our desires, as we saw earlier in our discussion of Augustine, concern matters related not only to our happiness but also to our hearts.

Hence it is appropriate to pause for a moment to dwell on the significance of C. Daniel Batson's research on the psychology of altruism that has since established the framework for discussion. The thesis he set out to explore was "the possibility that empathic emotion evokes altruistic motivation."[37] But what was empathy? Batson surmised that "Empathy is an other-oriented vicarious emotion produced by taking the perspective of a person perceived to be in need."[38] In order to test this hypothesis, research was conducted on alternative egoistic theories—that human beings help others in order to avoid the arousal of negative emotions, so as to escape anticipated punishments for selfish behavior, or because they feel certain positive emotions in some situations of benevolent activity. While the science did not unmistakably clarify that these alternative explanations are never the case, Batson could comfortably declare in light of his review of the available studies up to that time that there is "no clear support for any of the three egoistic alternatives to the empathy-altruism hypothesis.... In study after study ... we find results conforming to the pattern predicted by the empathy-altruism hypothesis, the hypothesis that empathic emotion evokes altruistic motivation."[39] In short, "Altruism is not a moral prescription for what we should do; it is a motivation, a desire. As such, it does not demand that we care for others; it leads us to want to do so."[40]

To be sure, many critics remained unconvinced, but perhaps not surprisingly those most opposed did not seem to question the conflict and self-interested presuppositions prevalent in the neo-Darwinian paradigm.

Within that framework, of course, any other-regarding activities not only can but should ultimately be explained as expressions of self-regarding concerns. My point is only to emphasize that even after self-regarding elements are factored in—and there is even a theological reason to do so in light of the second great commandment which urges that we love our neighbors *as ourselves*—Batson's thesis deserves further consideration on two accounts: that altruistic love is motivated emotionally (through the emotion of empathy, specifically), and that such emotional motivation is informed, at least in part, by the capacity to feel and take the perspective of others.[41]

These aspects of the empathy–altruism thesis appear to have been vindicated in research on the neurobiology of morality since Batson's study. In particular, three sets of corroborative findings can be identified. First, research in the neurobiology of love has emphasized the role of attachment and bonding, particularly as these are formed initially in the face-to-face relationship between mothers and their children, and then expressed later in romantic relationships.[42] In other words, unconditional love received first from mothers forms the kinds of emotional and social bonds that later enable the possibility of other expressions of empathy, including benevolent and altruistic love for nonrelatives.

Second, recent developments in the cognitive sciences have led to a wide range of research on the emotional basis of human morality and even moral decision-making.[43] There are three strands to this research: (1) that there is a real sense in which we think not merely rationally but also emotionally, there being an emotional dimension to our discursive processes; (2) that our emotions inform our moral judgments indirectly in terms of motivating pleasurably relevant action related to our empathetic solidarity with others, rather than directly influencing or shaping the content of moral judgments; and (3) that the emotions are central to human morality given their role in fostering human care, compassion, sympathy, cooperation, altruism, etc., so that intuitions like "reciprocity, loyalty, purity, suffering—are shaped by natural selection, as well as by cultural forces."[44] It should also be noted here that the science of human compassion indicates that it is a richer notion than altruism: "An altruistic act may be done merely from habit or natural inclination or a sense of duty or to engender obligation . . . [but] a true act of compassionate love involves more cognition, more freedom, more explicit *choosing* than 'mere' altruism would imply."[45]

Last but not least, there is now also clear evidence regarding the neuro-biological basis not only for empathy but also, from that, for intersubjective perspective-taking. Research on mirror neurons in particular has shown how particular classes of neurons discharge (observable through brain scans in humans) when we act in certain ways, perceive certain stimuli, or feel and experience certain things, and then also when we see others acting in those same ways, perceiving the same or similar stimuli, or feeling and experiencing similar things.[46] Thus we are in effect neurobiologically wired to perceive and even feel to some degree the experiences of others, based on our own experiences.

The cognitive neurosciences have thus helped to identify the origins of empathy and to understand it as the intersubjectivity through which we participate emotionally in the feelings of others.[47] Put another way, and turning on its head Dawkins' selfish gene metaphor, "our genes have gone about achieving their selfish objectives by making *us*—human beings— *really, truly* care deeply about the welfare of our children," and the fact that this "very act of providing sustenance and nurturance will tend to acti-vate feelings that foster further acts of caring suggests a way to expand the domain of altruism."[48] In short, "while natural selection may have favored the evolution of sympathy because it motivated actions that led to long-term beneficial outcomes for the actor, the motivational state itself is *not* self-interested. Sympathy appears to be a genuinely other-regarding emotion, capable of eliciting behavior that should therefore be consid-ered truly altruistic."[49] Understood in this way, even if we were to retain some of the basic commitments of the neo-Darwinian paradigm, we can see how other-regarding sensibilities can and have evolved, once we factor into the equation that genetically constituted creatures are not merely self-interested calculators bent on self-preservation and reproduction but also emotional and empathetic agents whose self-fulfillment depends on empa-thetic interpersonal relationship with others.[50] In the terms of the preced-ing discussion, we might say that the cooperative tendencies uncovered in the biological sciences are here rooted in the emotional and affective domains of human empathy currently being explored by the neurophysi-ological sciences.[51]

So far in this chapter we began with the sociology of love and were led soon thereafter into the sociology of altruism. This led us into the thickets of research on the biology of altruism and, most immediately preceding, on the neuroscience of altruism. Along the way, love itself has been sub-merged under the category of altruism. It is not difficult to see why the sci-entific community has been much more engaged with research on altruism than on love: the former is measurable in some respects—or at least altru-istic behaviors are more amenable to quantification or observation—the latter less so. I would, however, caution against minimizing the import of scientific research on altruism. If love is the affective/emotional disposition toward and intentional activity that benefits others, then increasing our understanding of altruistic behaviors adds to our theology of love.

Still, there are other reasons for the neuroscientific elusiveness of love, in particular that it, like human emotions in general, not only cannot be localized to one part of the brain (so as to enable exact neuroscientific anal-ysis) but is a holistic human expression involving the interactions between the mind–body and its environment.[52] There are, in other words, too many relational and contextual variables for scientifically rigorous studies of the emotional and affective experience of love, at least in the traditional senses in which this is understood.[53] One might attempt to probe deeply into the brain and its neurophysiological and neuropsychological mechanisms, but in that case one risks missing out altogether on the subjective experience of what we call love.[54] Or one can take the more expansive route afforded by the discipline of psychology, but this opens up in so many directions, including ones that raise questions about psychology as a "science" (which is always questioned by those with a more "scientistic" bent), that anxiety emerges then about the demarcation between the human sciences and the humanities.[55] What we are realizing is that not only is the ability to receive and give love embedded deep in the evolutionary history of the brain and the physiology of the human body but that this bioneurological capacity to feel and experience love is fundamental to human thinking and living as a whole.[56]

All this is to say that we are only at the beginning stages of under-standing love in relationship to our brain and embodied minds. What is needed, then, is what Thomas Oord calls a multilateral approach to the sci-ences of love.[57] To be sure, our neurophysiological makeup both constrains our capacity to love and respond to love and shapes the character of our love. Yet our neurological "hardware" does not predetermine if and how we love. For that, as we have come to recognize, involves various other factors related to our environment, socialization, and religious formation, not to mention the choices that free creatures like human beings make. And if this is the case, then neuroscientific research might also shed light on the exchange of love energy, particularly in terms of the emotional experience in human beings of empathy—just as we suggested, at the conclusion of the previous section, that biological research could show how benevolent love could be circulated or mediated through cooperative mutuality between embodied creatures.[58] Beyond this, might brain research on human emotionality and affectivity also open up windows into how love energy is perceived supra-empirically, to follow up with Sorokin's proposal, so as to enable human beings to tap into the transcendent sources of love hypothesized in some circumstances?

Conclusion

We began our journey (in the Preface) with a working definition of love as the affective disposition toward and intentional activity that benefits others. The biological and neurological sciences, as we have seen, do not ask questions about psychological intentionality; yet our cursory explorations of the "sciences of love" have turned out to be nothing less than a whirlwind inquiry into altruism. Why and how, in a world with plenty of empirical evidence for selfishness, have other-regarding dispositions and other-benefitting activities evolved? Here we found that just as in the human experience of love, so also the scientific research on altruism, at least when viewed from a neo-Darwinian angle, reflects a paradox: on the one hand, cooperation and benevolence seem pervasive in nature (as does love in our experience), but their origins and explicability remain elusive (as love remains mysterious to us). However, when viewed through an interdisciplinary perspective, and without a lens that registers the primacy of conflict and competition, altruism emerges almost as a convergent and inevitable possibility in the evolutionary stream of things.[59] Genuinely other-regarding actions cannot be explained merely cognitively but are expressive of how embodied creatures like ourselves feel our way through the world, and do so precisely by connecting at the empathetic and affective level with others along the way. Thus we are motivated to seek out the wellbeing of others as we instinctively hope that others will also for us.[60] Yet within this framework, love turns out also to be not just a feeling but a central manifestation of our way of being in the world. Similarly, altruistic love is not just a predisposition toward others but expresses a deeply rooted sensibility that our success, comfort, and happiness are intimately intertwined with that of others. We love and receive love, in other words, as part of what we are.

Sorokin's research has also placed two other items on the agenda for love research that continue to percolate under the discussions. First, recall that for him, the purpose of research on love and altruism was to change the world and turn it into a better place with less hate, animosity, and hostility, and more mutuality, creativity, community. As we have worked through the biological and neurophysiological and neuropsychological sciences of love, we have noted that research continues to uncover love's mechanisms almost in a way as to suggest that our understanding it is less important than seeing what it has accomplished. This reminds us that fully engaging the topic requires not merely a cognitive articulation of love but its nurturance, accumulation, and distribution—precisely what Sorokin averred. We will return to pick up on this aspect of Sorokin's proposal specifically in our next chapter.

Sorokin also hypothesized that there was a type of love energy available to and even active in the world that couldn't be grasped merely empirically or rationally. The neo-Darwinian emphasis on the selfish gene is incapable of registering the imprints of such love energy, if it existed. But what if, as Roughgarden (among others) is proposing, we adopted a cooperative or teamwork paradigm of inquiry instead, one that sees human mutuality not only with one another but with living creatures in general, the cosmic environment as a whole, and, if God existed, with divine powers that are graciously directed toward creatures as well? This overall orientation has implications at least at two levels.

First, it may be suggestive for one of Sorokin's major concerns, that the extensivity and duration of other-regarding love almost always is not sustained beyond the tribe to the out-group. The cognitive sciences of morality do suggest that given the neurophysiology of emotional empathy, it is possible for human beings to perceive the neediness of nonrelatives, that is, strangers, and be motivated to act benevolently even at great personal risk.[61] Even in that case, how can theology, the "science" that is concerned about transcendence, lend a hand to what nature has already dealt? I can imagine that while we would affirm Aquinas' ideas about the order of love (discussed in the previous chapter), we would also then want to emphasize that the grace which perfects nature, also a central Thomistic doctrine, makes probable the kind of out-group altruism that nature merely makes possible. In a very real sense, the rest of this book presents an extended argument for such a theology of grace, albeit informed by the pentecostal tradition.

At a second level, if we also reflect theologically on the conviction that nature is revelatory in some respects of the divine power and glory, what do the sciences of altruistic love reveal about God, or at least about perceptions of God and the real consequences of such perceived interactions in the world? In other words, what are the implications of the sciences of love for theology in general and for the doctrine of God in particular? On the other side of this question, though, are queries about the implications of the discipline of theology for the social sciences as well. The questions in both directions, of course, were already implicit in Sorokin's research over half a century ago, but they have not been taken up systematically. This is not to say that there have not been initial efforts, including studies focused primarily on how nature's propensities toward others are expressions of divine or agapic other-regard as well.[62] I will be taking up these matters in the next chapter (and by extension in the rest of this book), but will do so by asking more specifically pneumatological questions in light of our preceding discussion (in chapter 1) about divine agape as manifest in God's gracious gift of the Spirit. Might it also be the case that the outpouring of the Spirit, who always points to the Father through the Son, also graciously empowers creatures and enables their deferential mutuality with others (what biologists call cooperation), their compassion, concern, and care for others (what the cognitive sciences call empathetic identification), and their edification of others (what Sorokin called benevolent altruism)?

CHAPTER 3

• • •

What's Love Got to Do with It?

Pentecostalism, the Holy Spirit, and Love

The major premise behind this book is that pentecostal perspectives can contribute something important to the formulation of a Christian theology of love. It is now time to introduce at least some aspects of the Pentecostalism behind the perspectives we will be drawing upon. As we shall see, pentecostal spirituality and practice does not seem to have much to say, at least explicitly and in recent historical memory, about love. But, as we shall also see, Pentecostalism does have a good deal to say about the Holy Spirit. Given that the Christian theological tradition has seen a very close link between love and the Holy Spirit, might it be that pentecostal insights into the nature of the Spirit might also provide resources for thinking "pentecostally" about theology of love? That is the major theological wager behind this project.

In this chapter we provide an introduction to Pentecostalism oriented toward our larger purposes. This means we begin by unfolding why Pentecostalism has been less a religion of love and more a religion of the Spirit and of power.[1] From there, we will reconnect to the sociology of love introduced in the last chapter and observe how the recent and ongoing Godly Love project on Pentecostalism inspired in part by Aleksandrovich Sorokin's legacy highlights some of the connections between the Holy Spirit and love. The third and final part of this chapter will then sketch a phenomenology of pentecostal experience that will go deeper into this interface between a pentecostal spirituality dominated by the Spirit and a pentecostal praxis motivated, I will then argue, by love. The goal of this chapter will be to lay the groundwork for the pentecostal contributions to a theology of love that will be elaborated on in part II of this book.

As before, an important caveat needs to be registered. Readers should not presume any exhaustive discussion of Pentecostalism in the following pages. I have written elsewhere at—some would say, exhausting!—length about modern Pentecostalism and here will presume much of this other material.[2] Our sights will be trained instead on those aspects of the pentecostal tradition that will be helpful for thinking about the theology of love the rest of this volume will unfold.

Pentecostal Love? Pentecostal Power!

When people think about Pentecostalism, the first thing that comes to mind is not love but power.[3] Part of the reason for this is that the central biblical text for modern pentecostal movements features the power of the Spirit: "But you will receive power when the Holy Spirit has come upon you; and you will be my witnesses in Jerusalem, in all Judea and Samaria, and to the ends of the earth" (Acts 1:8). Over the course of the last century, then, pentecostal spirituality, practice, and theology have come to center on this understanding of the gift of the Holy Spirit as empowering Christian life in the world. In particular, we focus on pentecostal views of the Spirit's empowerment as an avenue toward manifestation of the Spirit's gifts, as enabling power ministry, and as sustaining the missional mandate of the church.

What comes with the Spirit's power? Pentecostals are quick to see the wondrous signs of miraculous healings following in the train of the apostolic experience: "Now many signs and wonders were done among the people through the apostles. . . . A great number of people would also gather from the towns around Jerusalem, bringing the sick and those tormented by unclean spirits, and they were all cured" (Acts 5:12, 16). As was promised to the apostolic believers, "And these signs will accompany those who believe: by using my name they will cast out demons; they will speak in new tongues; they will pick up snakes in their hands, and if they drink any deadly thing, it will not hurt them; they will lay their hands on the sick, and they will recover" (Mark 16:17-18).[4] While texts like these certainly have been susceptible to being taken in radical directions—for example, by serpent-handling Pentecostals in the Appalachians[5]—what is equally clear is how the tradition has come to understand itself as constituted by power-ful signs.

In more mainstream pentecostal circles, the outpouring of the Spirit in Acts followed by the sign of tongues or of other miraculous wonders has been read in a more domesticated sense, at least in light of Paul's discus-sion of the gift of the Spirit as the doorway to the charisms of the Spirit, especially in the first letter to the Corinthians. The Spirit who enables con-fession of Jesus as Lord (1 Cor 12:3) is also the Spirit who gives freely and liberally of the spiritual gifts to the body of believers for the edification of all (1 Cor 12:4-11). Thus the Lukan view of the Spirit's infilling not only enables the apostolic experience of signs and wonders but also opens up the church to the possibility of the many charismatic gifts of the Spirit.[6]

Committed Pentecostals, however, insist that when fully enacted, the spiritual gifts lead to the manifestation of what some have called power encounter ministries. This includes power healing, the Spirit-enabled capacity to minister healing to the sick according to the model of Jesus' life and ministry; power deliverance, the Spirit-inspired facility to discern oppressive spiritual realities and exorcise them in the name of Jesus; and power evangelism, an approach to missional engagement with unbelievers which depends not only on words but on miraculous signs and wonders.[7] Other Christians have built on these foundations to advocate for strategic-level warfare mapping strategies through which the principalities and powers of any region are identified and then resisted through spiritual disciplines like prayer, fasting, and other techniques.[8]

In the end, though, many of these emphases on power connect with the pentecostal commitment to fulfill the Great Commission. The power of the Spirit, as the book of Acts clearly shows, carried the apostolic believ-ers to the ends of the earth. Similarly, for Spirit-filled believers of any era, the gifts of the Spirit are meant for the church to fulfill its missionary and evangelistic mandate. Power encounter ministries are designed to func-tion as contemporary signs and wonders so that unbelievers will be turned toward the gospel of Christ. As such the Spirit's power sometimes provides missionaries with ability to speak languages they have never learned in order that they can share the gospel with others;[9] more often, however, the Spirit enables missionaries to brave excursions into strange places, and emboldens them to share the good news of Christ in situations in which they might otherwise choose to be silent. The Spirit provides supernatural insight and knowledge that leads to precise, purposeful, and meaningful evangelistic activity. The Spirit heals those who are physically, psychologically, or otherwise afflicted and who do not have access to other healing technologies (like medicine). The Spirit delivers these oppressed by demonic realities and other principalities and powers. The Spirit brings about blessings—sometimes in the form of material and financial prosperity—in transforming the lives of believers. The Spirit sustains missionaries and evangelists amidst their challenging circumstances. The Spirit protects and empowers embattled and persecuted fledgling missional communities.[10] The Spirit makes a way when none seems possible. Is it any wonder that modern Pentecostalism became the greatest missionary and evangelistic force in twentieth-century Christianity?[11]

As should be clear from the preceding, spiritual gifts, power ministries, and missionary and evangelistic exploits are interrelated. Thus Pentecostalism is growing around the world, from this point of view, because it is a religion of power: powerful miracles and healings, powerfully transformed (and now visibly successful) lives, and empowered ways of living in and engaging the world.[12] To be sure, the emphasis on power almost never operates alone, and is often connected with the theme of purity. The Spirit of God sanctifies and sets apart the people of God for works of power. This is especially clear in terms of the intertwining of these scriptural motifs, and has always been central in the pentecostal tradition.[13] But what is also clear is that these twin themes of power and purity still have marginalized that of love.

The history of power manifestations gone wrong in pentecostal movements is a sorry one.[14] Some Pentecostals have embraced an elitist self-understanding that effectively defines non-pentecostal or non-Spirit-baptized Christians as second-class citizens among the people of God and this has exacerbated ecumenical relationships with other churches and denominations. Often there has also been inordinate emphasis on the power dimensions of the Christian life—signs, wonders, miracles, deliverance, healings, etc.—to the point that in some circles, those whose lives do not feature such characteristics but their opposites instead (i.e., sickness, disability, poverty) are marginalized as lacking faith or as being compromised by sin. Last but certainly not least, such a motif has also encouraged the elevation of the powerfully anointed "man of God" (there are fewer women), and this not only minimizes the role of the laity but also undermines the structures of accountability so important for successful charismatic leadership and healthy ecclesial life. In other words, as conducive as the baptism of empowerment has been for pentecostal missionary and evangelistic success, there have also been problems related to how pentecostal power has unfolded in the life of the movement.

This raises the question of this book. Where is love in the pentecostal tradition? Is it there, buried within the history of the movement in some way? Or has the emphasis on power completely overwhelmed the gospel of love and effectively subordinated and marginalized its presence? The good news is that love is available for retrieval, and the unexpected discovery is that help for such reclamation has recently emerged from an unanticipated source: the social scientific quarters of researchers studying the phenomenon of godly love.

Godly Love and Pentecostalism: A Sociological Assist

In 2002 the Institute for Research on Unlimited Love (IRUL), which we met briefly in the previous chapter, invited proposals for competitive grant monies to explore the topic of altruistic love.[15] One of the respondents was Margaret Poloma, an established social scientist and veteran scholar of Pentecostalism and the charismatic renewal movement.[16] Poloma had already been sensitized to the importance of altruistic ministerial outreach in the Catholic charismatic communities she had studied even as early as the mid-1970s, and sensed a genuine "love for the lost" among the missionary-minded Assemblies of God Pentecostals she researched in the 1980s. Yet love as an explicit category and focus of research had not emerged during this time, not to mention that it was difficult for a respectable sociologist during those decades to study religious experience, much less the phenomenon of love.

The opportunity to explore love in more sociological detail came in the mid-1990s when, having now already established her reputation, Poloma was drawn to the Toronto Blessing revival and was involved as an active participant-observer of that movement over a number of years. What she was able to investigate in depth and document as central to the Toronto experience was a palpable encounter with what Toronto Airport Vineyard Church pastor and revivalist leader John Arnott called "the Father's love."[17] As Poloma noted, "it is love—experiences of divine love that in turn affect human love—that is at the heart of the renewal."[18] More precisely, she concluded from her study that "The love experienced during the renewal is empowering, for mission and ministry is seen to be the love of Jesus himself."[19] In other words, the encounter with divine love served to motivate concrete expressions of benevolent service. Yet by and large, the major categories structuring Poloma's analysis of "the Blessing" (as it was known) were those derived from the historic study of mysticism, with her explicit thesis being that the Blessing produced mystical encounters with God which in turn did the work of, as the subtitle to her book puts it, "reviving Pentecostalism."[20]

Hence the pump had been primed for Poloma the sociologist to ask more explicitly if this mystical divine love encounter needed to be further explored. In response to the IRUL call, Poloma teamed up with recognized psychologist of religion from the University of Tennessee, Chattanooga, Ralph Hood (who also had experience studying Pentecostalism), and proposed to inquire into how the pentecostal-charismatic experience of God's love translated, if at all, into benevolent service. Over the next few years, the duo studied Blood-n-Fire (BnF), a pentecostal emerging church ministry in downtown Atlanta led by a charismatic visionary who believed he was divinely called to establish the kingdom of God in the city and that such was to be accomplished at least in part by loving and serving the homeless.[21] As it turned out, while the church organization had been active since 1991 and had developed a reputable ministry of providing shelter and meals, and had ran a rehabilitation program for those seeking to recover from substance abuses of various types, by the time Poloma and Hood arrived in 2003, the ministry had peaked and was about to take a turn for the worse. Besides documenting the tensions and dilemmas related to the ongoing institutionalization of BnF, the researchers also uncovered (an unintentional) classism and racialism that threatened to undermine the ministry. In general, members of the BnF "family" of ministers were white and from middle class backgrounds while the recipients of their acts of benevolence were homeless, poor, and mostly African American. By 2005 the ministry as originally envisioned had closed, pressured by a number of different factors. Poloma and Hood concluded that "despite the sincerity and genuine love that exists at BnF, that love is far from adequate in actually transforming either the lives of the poor or a large metropolitan area."[22] The result was that a project intended to further explore altruistic love became as much a sociological study of failed charismatic leadership.

Even with the ministry unraveling right before their eyes, Poloma and Hood were able to distinguish various forms of love operative at BnF. Without whitewashing the serious problems endemic to the ministry during the time of their research, they were able to show that the leadership was nevertheless driven by a form of *appreciation-love* that embraced and promulgated what was perceived to be a divinely given vision of egalitarian friendship and ministry, and that such a vision was communicated to others who in turn experienced a form of *union-love* that bound them together in common cause, and that this then generated *care-love* for the homeless population.[23] Along the way they also gathered data that supported a number of other Sorokin hypotheses, including the idea that love energy is generated in pentecostal emerging church contexts. Through both quantitative and qualitative analyses, Poloma and Hood concluded that "experiencing a loving God through Glossolalia and spiritual gifts that accompany it in turn empowers compassion and loving behavior," and that "Those who experience more of the charismatic gifts of the Holy Spirit are more likely to report higher scores for reported empathic feelings and altruistic behavior than are those who do not experience God's presence and power in their lives."[24] In other words, while not encouraging overall, given BnF's demise, the results of their study invited further research.

In 2006, partly as a follow-up to the BnF project, Stephen Post teamed up with Margaret Poloma to launch the Flame of Love initiative, with funding from the Templeton Foundation, to develop an interdisciplinary (involving both social scientists and theologians) research team focused on exploring godly love in the pentecostal tradition, broadly defined. The focus on Pentecostalism was motivated by the growing realization that members of this movement were increasingly engaged in works of benevolence,[25] and that pressed the question of what, if anything, their spiritual experiences might have to do with their altruistic activities. Within the Flame of Love framework, Poloma has coauthored two more books recently.

The first volume, written with Matthew Lee, Poloma's colleague from the sociology department at the University of Akron, introduced the godly love research model. Defining godly love utilizing what they called a "diamond model" as involving "the dynamic interaction between divine and human love that enlivens and expands benevolence" (see figure 3.1),[26] Lee and Poloma sought to probe further into Sorokin's hypothesis regarding how love energy was produced and distributed. Whereas *Blood and Fire* explored a pentecostal emerging church ministry, this volume reported on

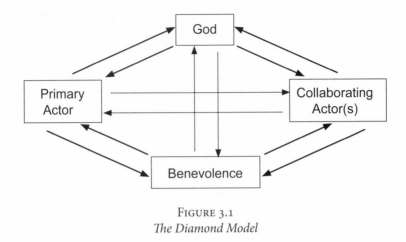

FIGURE 3.1
The Diamond Model

quantitative surveys received from and qualitative interviews conducted with 72 exemplars of godly love and 29 other collaborators in order to develop a grounded theory of benevolent service as arising unpredictably and variously from out of multifaceted and dynamic networks of people, institutions, and cultural resources (rather than just being the outcome of individual or personal characteristics).

Here are the highlights of some of their findings. First, a fairly positive correlation was found in both exemplars and collaborators (ECs) between their experiencing a divine call within a loving relationship with God and their benevolent activities. This call consists, of course, of a complex, dynamic, and "multifaceted process of interactions"[27] involving some understanding of the nature of the reign of God and various types of transformative spiritual experiences (such as what Pentecostals identify as being born again and receiving the baptism of the Holy Spirit, among others). Second, many ECs, as a result of their life experiences, shifted from a view of God as lawgiver to God as one who loved unconditionally and invited human beings into relationship. Similarly, evolving and dynamic images of God replace more or less static ones, and a more eclectic postmodern approach to cultural and ideological resources prevailed over earlier, more parochial and dogmatic mindsets. Last but not least, pentecostal benevolence takes on a variety of shapes: some ECs are involved in community service, some engaged in church revitalization activities, and a few are committed to working for social justice and positive structural change. Clearly emerging, however, was the connection between the two great commandments—the love of God and the love of neighbor—with both possible, even unavoidable, because of the prior experience of God's love. In other words, it was the unmistakable perception (for the ECs) that they had been touched by the love of God, which in turn drew forth their love for God and, by extension, led to benevolent works of love for others.

Lee and Poloma's assessment of pentecostal ECs provided a snapshot of lives viewed at a certain point in time. The perspectives on godly love thereby generated comparisons with the *Blood and Fire* study, which had the luxury of following one set of ECs and of observing the rise and fall of one emerging church ministry over the span of a few years. In contrast to these first two godly love volumes, Poloma's most recent book provides a more macro-level analysis, being a longitudinal study not just of a church but of the Assemblies of God (AG), an established pentecostal denomination with roots in the early twentieth century. Coauthored with John Green, her Distinguished Professor of Political Science colleague at the University of Akron, this study suggests that one key to the revitalization of the classical pentecostal tradition may be the experience of godly love.[28]

What would lead two social scientists to proffer such a thesis? The first half of the book sets the stage, documenting developments in the AG's handling of the tensions between charisma and institutionalization twenty years after the data had been initially presented and analyzed (in Poloma's *The Assemblies of God at the Crossroads*; 1989). Not much has changed, as the recent study reveals "the AG still to be at the crossroad between . . . the *primitive* and the *pragmatic*, though increasingly leaning toward the pragmatic" (*AGGL* 60, emphasis in original). What has changed is the landscape of the AG itself, now constituted by a variety of churches across a spectrum (*AGGL*, chap. 1): from traditional pentecostal-type churches at one end to alternative "seeker-friendly" churches at the other (with only minimal AG identity), and including more or less pentecostal-type churches that embrace supernatural or paranormal manifestations and practices in the middle (see figure 3.2, which reproduces these as ideal types, among which there is much overlap in reality). Within this broad context of a dynamic AG movement, what is revitalizing the churches are less denominational loyalties than various charismatic experiences of the Spirit that are shaping pentecostal attitudes and self-understanding and

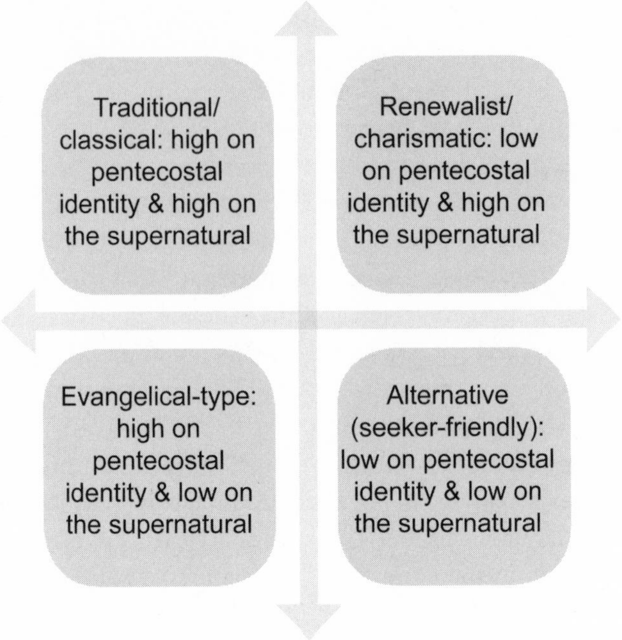

Traditional/classical: high on pentecostal identity & high on the supernatural	Renewalist/charismatic: low on pentecostal identity & high on the supernatural
Evangelical-type: high on pentecostal identity & low on the supernatural	Alternative (seeker-friendly): low on pentecostal identity & low on the supernatural

FIGURE 3.2
Typology of AG Churches

motivating benevolent action. Thus it is precisely the traditional/classical and the renewalist/charismatic types of churches (the top two quadrants in figure 3.2) through which some of the most dynamic currents within the AG are flowing, the former being experientially vibrant in part because of the growth of immigrant churches that fit this classification and the latter's experiential impulses partly related to the fact that many of these churches are actively and intentionally in a process of identity renegotiation.

For example, in Poloma and Green's quantitative surveys of 447 pastors and 1,827 AG constituents (from twenty-one congregations located across the typology of churches), the following are significant findings correlating pentecostal experiences, benevolence, and revitalization or renewal in the AG. First, glossolalics, more than nonglossolalics, were more likely "to report feeling God's love as the greatest power of the universe" (*AGGL* 114), and "glossolalia and other embodied manifestations were found not only to have a strong relationship with reporting of frequent experiences of the presence of God (the vertical divine-human link) but also to be statistically related to evangelistic outreach (the horizontal or interpersonal link)" (*AGGL* 118). Second, those who "frequently experience physical healing tend to be highly glossolalic, are more likely to experience a frequent sense of divine presence, and are more likely to be prophetic" (*AGGL* 128); thus, "Those who are highly prophetic are far more likely than those who are not to say they have been used to heal others" (*AGGL* 140), leading to the tentative conclusion that "the prophetic is not limited to human interaction with the divine; it also serves as a catalyst for 'divinely inspired' interpersonal interaction (i.e., benevolence)" (*AGGL* 142).

More important, Poloma and Green developed some multivariable measurements and analyses regarding the correlation between beliefs/ values, religious/charismatic experience, and benevolence. Conservative political, social, and moral values and doctrinal orthodoxy were found more in the traditional pentecostal and evangelical type congregations (those on the left side of the typology in figure 3.2), while more charismatic orientations were found in both traditional pentecostal and renewal-type congregations (those on the top two quadrants in figure 3.2). Two findings of particular interest emerged. First, "those who hold to more traditional values are significantly less likely to profess attitudes that are empathetic toward the needs of the poor and homeless. Those who pray in tongues and who experience an abiding sense of divine presence, on the other hand, are somewhat more likely to report pro-poor attitudes" (*AGGL* 166). Second, "those who demonstrate greater support for traditional Pentecostal values are also more likely to hold attitudes that disapprove of the AG cooperating with nonevangelical or [non]pentecostal churches. . . . Those who reported higher scores on prophecy were slightly more like to favor ecumenism" (*AGGL* 167). The statistical data thus suggest, as summarized by Poloma and Green, that "Those who scored high on the traditional Pentecostal values scale were no more or less likely to be evangelistic, to serve as healers, or to be more compassionate than those who were less traditional. However, measures of charisma—of experiences of the divine such as prophecy, a sense of divine presence, and glossolalia—consistently helped explain differences in benevolent behavior" (*AGGL* 168).

Similarly, with regard to engagement with public affairs and matters, three statistical correlations are significant. First, with regard to social views, while "religious experience is associated with the belief that Christians must work for a more fair and equitable society . . . traditional religiosity is associated with the opposite view" (*AGGL* 175). Second, in terms of overall congregational engagement with social activities and services, "religious experience is positively associated with congregational benevolence, while traditional religiosity shows the opposite pattern" (*AGGL* 176), and "religious experience influences attitudes toward congregational engagement in politics" (*AGGL* 177). Third, with regard to governmental social welfare services, "religious experience is associated with support for social welfare programs, while traditional religiosity is associated with opposition to them" (*AGGL* 179). I have only highlighted some of the conclusions from Poloma and Green's study that are relevant to our purposes in this chapter.[29] But they suggest that religious, even mystical, experiences of divine love, in particular that related to divine presence, prophecy, and healing, "are capable of producing seismic shifts in a person's worldview, core identity, and sense of purpose in life to a degree that few other life experiences seem able" (*AGGL* 206).

What seems also undeniable from the data is that the most vital congregations are the ones that nurture spiritual renewal in ways that allow for and invite overflow into the arena of engagement with socially benevolent activities, especially when these are directed to those outside the church. Thus there seems to be a positive correlation between congregational renewal or revitalization, religious/mystical experience, and social benevolence. This suggests that when studied across a movement as diverse as the AG, the following thesis appears to have sociological validation: "Central to the revitalizing process is Godly Love, a dynamic that is rooted in perceived experiences of the divine that deepen a person's love for God and in turn empowers acts of benevolence. . . . Godly Love begins with knowing the love of God and responding to that experience with acts of love and compassion" (*AGGL* 14).

Spirit and the Performance of Love: A Phenomenology of Pentecostal Spirituality

Two noteworthy observations, one methodological and the other theological, should be made from the preceding. The first is the perhaps ironic observation that it has been social scientists who have been involved in highlighting the centrality of love in the pentecostal movement. Even more incongruous is that these sociologists have not been content with merely exploring altruistic love among human beings but have boldly factored divinity into the equation. To the credit of Poloma and her colleagues, they have noted that their subjects are religiously committed and therefore, if their research were going to have any validity, it would need to take seriously the self-understanding of those who were being studied and to register their own explanations.[30] Thus the Godly Love project has been increasingly sensitive to explicitly religious and even theological variables, to the point of involving theologians in the construction of research hypotheses.[31] When we recall the fortunes traversed by the social sciences since the time of Sorokin's research on altruism in the mid-twentieth century, we can better appreciate how the methodological agnosticism of the godly love approach marks an important turning point for a discipline otherwise predisposed toward positivistic presuppositions. Thus perhaps we are only finally beginning to tap into viable modes of social scientific exploration of Sorokin's hypothesis about transcendent sources of love energy.

The more substantively theological point I wish to make concerns pentecostal spirituality. It may well be that the pentecostal emphasis on the Spirit's empowerment is the platform upon which its members have accessed and appropriated divine resources to carry out their evangelistic mission. However, it also may well be the case that their stress on divine power obfuscates the reality of divine love that is doing at least part, if not much, of the work of evangelical and charismatic transformation. What I mean is that, in light of the research of Poloma and her colleagues, perhaps pentecostal experiences of the Spirit are as much experiences of divine love as they are of divine power. What seems incontrovertible in the Godly Love research findings is that it is precisely charismatic experiences of the Spirit that have empowered benevolent service and ministry. In other words, encountering the power of the Spirit is at the heart of pentecostal mission. And if Poloma et al. are correct, such encounter of divine love is also central to the ongoing revitalization, revival, and renewal of Pentecostalism as a dynamic charismatic movement.

In the remainder of this chapter, then, I provide a phenomenological sketch of pentecostal spirituality in terms that highlight how experiences thematized in terms of charismatic power can also be understood as performative explications of encounters with divine love. My goal here is to note that underneath the explicit self-understanding of most Pentecostals is a set of sensibilities that are molded by the reality of divine love at the heart of the pentecostal experience. We can observe this phenomenology

of charismatic love, so to speak, in the pentecostal experiences of glossolalic prayer, praise and worship, and mission and evangelism.

We begin with pentecostal prayer since this provides us with another
window into the heart of pentecostal spirituality that revolves around the
experience of Spirit-baptism.[32] If articulation of this "distinctive doctrine"
has emphasized the filling of the Spirit as empowerment for witness, its
practical effects begin most immediately with the enabling of prayer. Pentecostal sensibilities connecting the Spirit and prayer not only attempt to
follow apostolic precedents—"When they had prayed, the place in which
they were gathered together was shaken; and they were all filled with the
Holy Spirit . . ." (Acts 4:31)—but also are motivated by apostolic doctrine:
"Likewise the Spirit helps us in our weakness; for we do not know how to
pray as we ought, but that very Spirit intercedes with sighs too deep for
words" (Rom 8:31).

We can gain further perspective on glossolalic prayer in Pentecostalism from two angles—the phenomenological and the performative. Phenomenologically, there is the fervency of prayer, the intensity of its mode
and delivery, the urgency of its expression, all of which manifest the cries of
the human heart longing for union with God, if not also for the interven-
tions of God.[33] Kinesthetically, prayer can be mediated through tarrying (at
the altar, in the classical pentecostal tradition), kneeling, hands raised or
palms open, or even lying down.[34] The last bodily form, also understood in
some circles as being "slain in the Spirit," is seen as reflecting the believer's
openness to the work of healing that God desires to accomplish.[35] There
are now also forms of what is called soaking prayer that combine tarrying,
being "slain," and resting in the presence of God.

What is going on performatively in pentecostal and charismatic prayer?
Most obviously, but nevertheless needing explicit articulation, Pentecostals
believe they are engaging God in and through the powerfully felt presence
and activity of the Holy Spirit. Their prayers, both linguistic and glossolalic, are expressions from the heart—for "Out of the believer's heart shall
flow rivers of living water" (John 7:38-39)—and such vibrant streams are
part of the work of Spirit. To be sure, at one fundamental level, pentecostal
prayers are expressions of desires, mundane as these may be, for God to
heal, deliver, and provide. At a deeper level, however, pentecostal prayer
reflects, in the Augustinian and Tillichian senses discussed in the first
chapter, the existential and ontological desire of creatures in relationship

with and in response to their Creator. From this perspective, prayer registers desires not really for the things that God might do or provide, but for God.[36] Glossolalic prayer, then, acknowledges that the God who is desired also escapes all rational or discursive formulation. More to the point, such prayer in the Spirit is in the end the only possible means of experiencing the rapturous love of God and, in turn, of "articulating" the incomprehensible and ecstatic character of this love.[37]

Consideration of pentecostal prayer leads seamlessly into pentecostal praise and worship. While these latter notions are technical terms that emphasize verbal formulation and heartfelt adoration respectively in "praise and worship" circles, we can treat them together for our purposes as representative of the corporate dimensions of pentecostal spirituality. Again, we can approach the phenomenon of praise and worship from two angles. Phenomenologically, there is the singing, clapping or raising of hands, enthusiastic swaying or dancing, kneeling, or exuberant celebration.[38] Performatively, however, praise and worship are modes of adoration of and surrender to God; they enable praisers and worshipers to rise above the challenges of life through the liminal experiences of the joy of the Spirit, which is and becomes their strength.[39] Corporate joy induces corporate laughter, which expresses not only the embodied character of pentecostal worship but also its deeply affective sensibilities.[40] These manifestations reflect pentecostal and charismatic avenues to the happiness that Augustine noted as being at the heart of the human quest.

If prayer manifests the affections of the human heart in longing for their Creator, then praise and worship unfolds the congregational or corporate affections of the church, understood according to the New Testament metaphor as the "bride of Christ," for their groom. A cursory review of two common songs reflects how pentecostal praise and worship articulates a desiring heart in response to the reception of divine love. A favorite at the Azusa Street Mission, the fourth stanza of "The Comforter Has Come!" provides a window into how the pentecostal experience of the Spirit also reflects an encounter with the love of God:

> O boundless love Divine! How shall this tongue of mine
> To wond'ring mortals tell the matchless grace divine—
> That I, a child of hell, should in His image shine!
> The Comforter has Come![41]

Thus the singing of such songs not only enabled the infilling of the Spirit but also the experience of the overwhelming love of God. Similarly, in a more contemporary vein, a widely sung chorus produced by Hillsong Music, a ministry based in a pentecostal megachurch in Australia, suggests that human love for God responds to divine initiative:

> Call me deeper into Your grace
> The river that flows from the Holy Place
> Wash over me cleansing me through
> My greatest love is You.[42]

Note the pneumatological allusions in this chorus, so that human desire is understood as shaped first by the purifying and cleaning activity of the Holy Spirit.[43]

Pentecostal prayer, praise, and worship certainly edifies the soul; but more than that, Pentecostals believe that these activities also empower Christian witness. In the end, the coming of the Spirit is not merely for the uplifting of the recipient's heart but for the propelling of his or her testimony in word and deed. My claim, though, is that the pentecostal mission and evangelism empowered by the Spirit is also energized by divine love, and that is because the Spirit of power is the Spirit of love. Thus, for example, pentecostal prayer and spirituality register sensitivity to felt needs which in turn inspire missional activity.[44] The Spirit who enables pentecostal prayers is also the Spirit who heightens pentecostal awareness and animates pentecostal mission. Put another way, the prayers that articulate a desire for the divine and the praises that express the surrender to and embrace of the divine translate into a passion for sharing the love of God with others. So while Pentecostals are right to say that the source of their boldness and courage is of the Spirit, it is also just as appropriate for them to say that they have been compelled by divine love.[45] The evidence of the Spirit is not just glossolalic utterance but the fruits of the Spirit, especially love, and their concrete manifestation in benevolent actions. Pentecostal missions thus involve the expectation that divine supernatural power will appear, although for some this is palpably felt not only in miraculous healings but in the feeding of the hungry, the clothing of those practically naked, the caring for the orphaned, and the ministering to the abandoned, oppressed, or marginalized of the world.[46]

What I have done in sketching this phenomenology of pentecostal spirituality—its prayer, praise, and missionary or evangelistic witness—is highlight its affective and performative dimensions. Later (toward the end of part II) we will return to explore how this spirituality maps onto the apostolic spirituality of the earliest followers of Jesus the Messiah. In the meantime, however, I wish to register the important point that the pentecostal encounter with the Spirit can be understood also as an experience of the heart whereby God is perceived to break through into the very depths of the human domain and awaken people's affections. Thus Pentecostals meet God not merely as rational creatures but as embodied, feeling, and desiring ones. And when the Spirit shows up, what happens is not just or even that Pentecostals come into new knowledge of God, but that bodies are touched, their emotions healed and liberated, their affections reoriented, and their ways of life transformed.[47] Baptism in the Spirit unpacked in this way shows how pentecostal prayer and praise can be understood as an overflowing response to the experience of God's love, and how pentecostal missional ministry then reflects a loving desire for others to experience, receive, and be transformed by the same.

Conclusion

This chapter has initiated our journey into Pentecostalism in search of pentecostal contributions to a theology of love. We began by observing how Pentecostalism has become known more as a religion of power than of love. However, we have also seen, with the help of social scientists in the middle part of the chapter, that pentecostal power is often seen and understood in terms of benevolent action and that this is also comprehended in relationship to the Spirit's empowerment for witness, and thus also to the church's renewal and revitalization. Given this impetus, we have broached a general phenomenology of pentecostal spirituality guided by the intuition that beneath the rhetoric of power lies a fundamentally transformative encounter with what is perceived to be the charismatically mediated and thus graciously endowed love of God. What we have found is that while the language of Spirit and power are at the forefront of pentecostal self-understanding, not too far beneath the surface is the presence and activity of divine love. Pentecostals may not talk much about love, but their love for others is manifest in their other-regarding activities. In fact, we might surmise that just as the Spirit points away from herself to the Father and the Son, so also does the experience of divine love not call attention to itself but invigorates those so touched to graciously love others in turn.

However, we are only at the beginning stages of considering the implications of pentecostal spirituality for theology of love. All we have identified so far are intuitive clues, perhaps phenomenological and performative gestures, to guide our reflection. Part II of this book builds on what we have gained so far toward a more robust pentecostal and pneumatological theology of love.

PART II

• • •

GOD IS SPIRIT
Pentecostalism, the Spirit's Gifts, and the
Resources of Love

CHAPTER 4

· · ·

Spirit-Empowered Transformation
Pentecostal Praxis and the Energy of Love

P art I of this volume provided us with first steps toward a theology of love, beginning with preliminary reflections from the theological tradition, moving then toward an interdisciplinary conversation with the sciences of altruism, and coming in the last chapter to identifying resources from within the pentecostal tradition for such an endeavor. What we have established is that there is a strand in the broader Christian theological tradition that has defined love in relationship to the Holy Spirit, and that the sciences themselves are not averse, with the appropriate methodological safeguards in place, to exploring what this may mean. Given our overall objective to contribute to a Christian theology of love from an explicitly pentecostal perspective, we have so far in a sense done no more than survey the landscape and find that there may be more potential for thinking pneumatologically and pentecostally about love than previously realized. So if part I can be understood as a quest for a theology of love that opened up to and invited consideration of a theology of the Spirit, part II provides a rejoinder by searching for a theology of the Spirit in anticipation that such may hold promise for a theology of love. This is the intuition that has guided our inquiry so far. On the one hand, a theology of love has led to pneumatology, and thus, for our purposes, to pentecostal spirituality; on the other hand, now we will attempt to complete the hermeneutical circle, by seeing how a pentecostal theology of the Spirit might enrich a theology of love.

The basic phenomenological and performative resources in chapter 3, however, are no more than pointers in the landscape about where we should be digging. In the next chapter, we will move explicitly from our phenomenology of pentecostal spirituality to first steps toward a pneumatological theology of love; here, however, our goal is to follow out our performative cues uncovered earlier. We observed that while thematized in terms of the baptism with power and the Holy Spirit, pentecostal experience can also be understood as an energizing and transformational encounter with divine holiness and love. What exactly does this mean for a theology of love understood performatively? In other words, what does holy love mean, not in the abstract discursive sense but in terms of how it shapes the living practices of a religious community?

This chapter attempts to answer this question through historical retrieval and reappropriation. We will go back to the pentecostal tradition and provide a thicker description of at least one of its major tributaries, that of the ethos and legacy of the Asuza Street Mission.[1] My claim is that pressing through pentecostal beliefs and practices will illuminate how the baptism of the Spirit is also the baptism of holy love, and that this in turn has had important performative implications both for the life of holiness and for pentecostal witness. The two strands of ethical consequences we will trace out will be pentecostal intuitions about ethnic and racial relations and the pacifist commitments of a pentecostal peace witness. Put in terms of the preceding discussion, pentecostal spirituality can be understood as tapping into what Sorokin called divine love energy, which members of the Azusa Street Mission understood simply as the transformative power of the "baptism of love."[2]

Empowered Holiness: The Pentecostal Baptism of Love

I begin with the Azusa Street Mission—"the Mission," for short—because it is here that some of the most fundamental impulses of modern Pentecostalism were set in motion. My argument here in no way depends on seeing the Mission as central to the origins of what scholars today call global Pentecostalism; this is a contested historiographical matter that I do not need to resolve.[3] What is important instead is that the Mission was founded by an African American man steeped in the holiness tradition, that it played an important role in the spread of Pentecostalism at least across the United States, and that the spirituality of the early pentecostal movement was thereby shaped by the distinctive gestalt of Africanist and holiness sensibilities and practices initially manifest at the Mission.[4]

My emphasis on the African American leadership of the Mission, of course, does prioritize the leadership of William J. Seymour over that of Charles Fox Parham. I have no intention of minimizing Parham's contribution, especially his role in the formulation of what is widely recognized as Pentecostalism's distinctive doctrine, the baptism of the Holy Spirit as evidenced by speaking in tongues.[5] My contention, however, is that while Parham made an undeniable contribution to the doctrinal self-understanding of Pentecostalism, he also rejected Seymour's ministry and the Azusa Street revival in no uncertain terms. In fact, Parham's reasons for rejecting the revival at the Mission were, to put it bluntly, racist, both in terms of his ideological views regarding white supremacy and in terms of his a priori rejection of the Africanisms featured at the Mission.[6] If this is true, then to acquiesce to the older (white) claim about Parham as the originator of modern Pentecostalism would not only be problematic theologically but also default uncritically to the modernist presupposition that religious movements are defined predominantly in intellectualist terms or according to their doctrinal distinctives (in this case, as revolving about the initial evidence teaching). But this would be to commit the fallacy of doctrinal reductionism, a typical Enlightenment tendency to minimize features of religious movements other than their doctrinal aspects.

I also have a theological reason for the choice of Seymour over Parham. Although Parham was also informed by the holiness tradition, as was Seymour, the former's legacy did not retain the full breadth and depth of the teachings about sanctification as did the latter's. In a real sense, white Pentecostals influenced by Parham's doctrinal heritage who came together to form the Assemblies of God in 1914 had by and large adopted what might be understood as a minimalist theology of sanctification viewed as a process culminating in eschatological glorification. This was due in large part to the influence of another white man, William H. Durham (1873–1912), whose teachings regarding the Finished Work of Christ included the rejection of the Wesleyan holiness view of sanctification as a second work of grace and insisted instead on its gradual achievement.[7] By contrast, Seymour was firmly rooted in the holiness tradition and thus accepted entire sanctification as a second work of grace subsequent to salvation (understood as justification),[8] and believed this to be followed by the baptism of the Spirit as the third work of grace. The baptism of the Holy Spirit was thus not denied as an endowment with power to witness, but such empowerment presumed rather than diminished the import of holiness and the sanctified life.

Seymour is important precisely for helping us understand the early modern pentecostal experience as an encounter with divine love. A few months after the revival began (in April 1906) Seymour began to publish his *Apostolic Faith* newsletter.[9] What seems to have been "lost in transmission" to later generations of the pentecostal movement has been this emphasis of the reception of the Holy Spirit as an infilling of the love of God. The initial issue of the newsletter thus noted a testimony of encounter with the Holy Spirit understood in terms of the presence and activity of divine love: "It was a baptism of love. Such abounding love! Such compassion seemed to almost kill me with its sweetness! People do not know what they are doing when they stand out against it. The devil never gave me a swet [sic] thing, he was always trying to get me to censuring people. This baptism fills us with divine love."[10] The author of this testimony is noted as a Nazarene, one whose understanding of the holiness experience of sanctification as, at least in part, an experience of perfect love,[11] would have resonated with Seymour's own views. As Seymour himself said later, "The baptism in the Holy Ghost and fire means to be flooded with the love of God and power for service, and a love for the truth as it is in God's word."[12] This reveals the continuity between the holiness and early pentecostal traditions: the Spirit's sanctifying grace was intimately connected with the Spirit's empowering witness.

In the second issue of the *Apostolic Faith*, another testimonial pointed to the intimate links between the baptism of the Spirit and the baptism of love:

> "Take my yoke upon you and learn of me." The Lord showed me that this yoke was the covenant of the new testament in His blood, and we put this yoke on when we are baptized with the Holy Ghost. This covenant is a marriage covenant. We are married, not for one day or year or life, but eternally married. When I got married to my wife it was settled for this life. So when I got married to Jesus Christ, it was settled forever. Hallelujah! Jesus and I are united. He baptized me with love.[13]

Here the author clearly understands the reception of the Spirit as yoking him with the love of Christ. The Jesus-centeredness of this statement is indicative also of the influence of the fourfold understanding of Jesus— Jesus as savior, sanctifier, healer, and coming king—at the heart of the holiness soteriology. What we see here both anticipates the addition of Jesus as Spirit-baptizer (resulting in the pentecostal fivefold gospel) and recognizes that this saving, sanctifying, and baptizing work of God can also be understood as the experience of divine love. Almost two years into the revival, the *Apostolic Faith* insisted in unmistakable terms that the full evidence of the Spirit's baptism involved nothing less than a life of love:

> What is the real evidence that a man or woman has received the baptism with the Holy Ghost? Divine love, which is charity. Charity is the Spirit of Jesus. They will have the fruits of the Spirit. Gal. 5:22. "The fruit of the Spirit is love, joy, peace, longsuffering, gentleness, goodness, meekness, faith, temperance; against such there is no law. . . ." This IS the real Bible evidence in their daily walk and conversation; and the outward manifestations; speaking in tongues and the signs following; casting out devils, laying hands on the sick and the sick being healed, and the love of God for souls increasing in their hearts.[14]

This view of the baptism of the Spirit as a baptism of love was certainly not limited to those in the Seymour's immediate circle. White Pentecostals in the South also testified to such an experience: "The baptism of the Holy Ghost does not consist in simply speaking in tongues. No. It has a much more grand and deeper meeting than that. It fills our souls with the love of God for lost humanity, and makes us much more than willing to leave home, friends, and all to work in his vineyard, even if it be far away. . . ."[15] One could multiply testimonies but the general point should be clear: that the pentecostal baptism with the Spirit was also a baptism of, in, and through the love of God.[16]

It should go without saying at this juncture that this baptism of holy love is also entirely gratuitous. This is the central point of a pentecostal theology of grace: that the reception of the Spirit of love depends not on human willing but on God's unconditional and unqualified desire to give of the divine self for the salvation of the world. Yes, pentecostal practices like tarrying are certainly what enables reception of the divine love. But this is not because tarrying merits God's grace but because tarrying removes the hindrances—sanctifies human vessels, to be more precise—that occlude full manifestation of the presence and activity of a holy and loving God. Hence, a pentecostal theology of grace emphasizes the redemptive gift of divine love, which is the gift of the Spirit, which is the gift of God.

The point that the pentecostal baptism of the Spirit is also a baptism of, in, and through the love of God also connects back with what I overviewed at the beginning of chapter 3: this pentecostal understanding of the Spirit's baptism of and in love has been gradually curtailed as the emphasis on the theme of power has come to center stage. Is this merely a difference of theological emphasis, or representative of an intra-pentecostal dispute with little relevance for the broader Christian theological conversation? What exactly is at stake, if anything?

The remainder of this chapter will argue that the Azusa Street Mission's understanding of the baptism of the Spirit as one of power *and* of love has important theological ramifications and especially ethical consequences. My claim is that it is the holiness tradition originating with Seymour that both emphasized this baptism of power *and* love conjointly, and worked to understand what this meant for pentecostal spirituality and Christian life. Put alternatively and more pointedly, it is in the holiness-pentecostal tradition of Seymour that we can most concretely see how the baptism of power is also the baptism of perfect love that has implications for the life of the church and its witness in and to the world.

Empowered Witness: The Reconciling Movement of Love

One way in which the empowerment of the Spirit manifested itself concretely at the Azusa Street Mission is summarized, as one early observer puts it, in the saying, "the 'color line' was washed away in the blood."[17] To be sure, as we shall see, this line reasserted itself quite quickly upon its initial blurring.[18] But there is also no denying that for a limited period of time during the early years of the revival, the Mission was what we would today recognize as a multiracial and multiethnic congregation, led by William Seymour, a black man. I suggest that this was possible only because the baptism of the Holy Spirit was understood at the Mission also as involving the sanctifying and perfecting love of God. Such a baptism of holy love was thus received as forming a new spiritual unity in the body of Christ, reconciling people otherwise divided by class, culture, language, ethnicity, and race.

The first issue of the *Apostolic Faith*, for example, reports that "Jesus was too large for the synagogues. He preached outside because there was not room for him inside. This pentecostal movement is too large to be confined in any denomination or sect. It works outside, drawing all together in one bond of love, one church, one body of Christ."[19] This led one contemporary writer to note that "The voice of the Holy Spirit . . . early Pentecostals believed, was accompanied by a new eschatological baptism of love that would unite Christians beyond denominationalism founded on such creeds."[20] Yet this non- or even antidenominationalism overcame not only ecclesial boundaries and divisions but also other perennial human divides based on class, language, and ethnicity. "Since then multitudes have come. God makes no difference in nationality, Ethiopians, Chinese, Indians, Mexicans, and other nationalities worship together."[21] We should recall, as historian David Daniels points out, that "nationalities" was the preferred early twentieth century discursive concept, not our contemporary rhetoric of "race."[22] Thus was it noted of the Mission that "All classes and nationalities meet on a common level."[23]

In short, one of the unique features of the Azusa Street revival was its multiethnic and multiracial character, unusual in the Jim Crow era, even on the Pacific coast of the U.S.A. It was precisely this mixing of ethnicities and races, not to mention the Africanisms manifest at the Mission, which repelled racists like Parham. But "William Seymour believed sanctification in the perfect love of God was necessary for Spirit baptism, essential to racial reconciliation and unity, and preparation for the return of Christ for a Bride without 'spot or wrinkle.'"[24] For him and the Azusa Street faithful, then, the baptism of the Spirit was an empowerment to love and a call to holiness, and this capacity enabled the crossing of human divides based on denomination, language, class, ethnicity, culture, and nationality. It was a baptism of holy love that enabled the inclusive acceptance of what was otherwise strange, and brought about, at least for a short while, the appearances of reconciliation among those who were otherwise far apart.

Seymour's vision of a church uniting black and white across the spectrum of cultures and nationalities was caught by one of his protégés, Charles Harrison Mason (1866–1961). Mason attended the Mission for five weeks in March and April of 1907, during which time he received the baptism of the Spirit, and then afterward returned to the South to spread the revival. For our purposes, what is important to emphasize is that Mason brought with him Seymour's mission for developing an interracial, ecumenical, and egalitarian fellowship.[25] Mason's organization, The Church of God in Christ (COGIC), facilitated an interracial pentecostal movement through the early 1930s by including whites within its congregations, by recognizing whites in high-ranking positions of leadership in the movement, and by ordaining whites as ministers both within the movement and to carry the pentecostal message beyond the formal confines of the reach of COGIC.[26] In so doing, Mason was doing nothing more than extending, even expanding, the mandate of the Azusa Street Mission to see the pentecostal baptism of powerful and reconciling love of God spread at least across the country, if not to the ends of the earth.

We should not underestimate Mason's resolve toward an interracial fellowship in the face of southern segregation during the first quarter of the twentieth century. Long after even Seymour had reacted defensively to white racism, paternalism, and antagonism—by revising in 1915 the Mission's *Doctrines and Discipline* to allow only "colored" leadership[27]—Mason continued to work with and include whites within the COGIC orbit. Throughout this early period, then, Mason's ministry wrestled in a very concrete manner with the potential of the pentecostal revival for reconciliation between classes, ethnicities, gender, and cultures. As noted more recently by COGIC historian and theologian Bishop Ithiel Clemmons, African American Holiness Pentecostals from Seymour to Mason and beyond did not view the pentecostal revival merely as a tongues movement as some whites would have it; rather, what they saw in the outpouring of the Spirit was the inauguration of a "prophetic social consciousness" such that "the Holy Spirit not only transforms persons but rearranges relationships and structures."[28] Thus within this pentecostal trajectory, "From the beginning, [the gift of reconciliation] was the very essence of the holiness pentecostal experience—not speaking in tongues."[29]

Yet as is well known, this interracial experiment was short lived, with cracks appearing within the movement already in the 1910s. While there is disagreement about whether the original formation of the Assemblies of God, drawing at least some of its ministerial constituency from the ranks of those ordained by Mason, was intended to secure a nonblack (read: white) organizational option for southern Pentecostals, there is no doubt that over the next half century,[30] the Assemblies of God came not only to be representative of white American Pentecostalism as a whole, but also to adopt a face that was racist at least in its activities and structures, if not also theologically. Thus if from its founding until the late 1930s the Assemblies of God viewed African Americans as simplistic or ignorant (as depicted in the fellowship's weeklies, for example) and clearly postured themselves in a paternalistic way toward blacks in the fellowship, in the next twenty plus years after that, there was a semiofficial policy of exclusion, including the refusal to credential or ordain blacks to the ministry.[31]

The climate began to change, of course, with the emergence of the Civil Rights movement in the late 1950s. Since then, white pentecostal groups such as the Assemblies have become increasingly sensitized to the institutionally embedded dimensions of racism in their midst. What I find intriguing, however, is that it is predominantly white groups like the Assemblies who, in following various aspects of Durham's Finished Work theology in distinguishing the doctrine of Spirit baptism from a more robust theology of sanctification, are the ones who have not retained the close connections between the baptism of power and of love.[32] Perhaps it should not be too surprising, then, if it is such groups who have not seen that the power of gospel involves the kind of reconciliatory vision long espoused by the African Americans in the holiness-pentecostal tradition. Equally noteworthy, then, is the fact that while other white Finished Work pentecostal groups have had similar track records to the AG in terms of their views regarding racial reconciliation, it has been the holiness-pentecostal organizations that did not sever the connections between sanctification, perfect love, and spiritual power who have been able to maintain interracial relations much longer, toward the end of the first and founding generation from the Mission.[33]

If it is the work of the Holy Spirit to always join together what human beings have put asunder, it also should not be surprising that the story of racial reconciliation within the pentecostal movement has not yet been concluded. To be sure, white Pentecostals have recognized that they can rightly be indicted for responding to the issue of racism only long after the sociopolitical climate and cultural exigencies necessitated activity on their part.[34] Yet such wider developments have also prompted some first steps toward racial reconciliation among Pentecostals. Most significant of these overtures was the disbanding of the all-white Pentecostal Fellowship of North America and its replacement by a racially integrated—at the leadership level as well—Pentecostal Charismatic Churches of North America at a historic meeting in Memphis, Tennessee, in October 1994. Observers recognized and have insisted since on the need for ongoing repentance that involves institutional restructuring, strategic expenditures of monies in a clearly interracial direction, revisitation of pentecostal statements of faith to reflect more inclusive commitments, involvement of other marginalized ethnic communities (in particular Latino/a Pentecostals), and full reconsideration of the role of women in classical pentecostal churches and denominations. In other words, much remains to be achieved in the work of the Spirit initiated at the Mission and revitalized at the so-called "Memphis Miracle" event: whites need to continue to come to grips with the reality of racism and its institutional, structural, and ecclesial effects, while blacks need to walk a fine line between projecting a posture of prophetic justice and working in solidarity with those who are willing to implement the difficult processes of repentance and change.[35] The challenges along this front indicate that Pentecostalism needs not just a historical pentecostal outpouring of the Spirit but ongoing baptisms of love in order that these "mountains" can indeed be moved.[36]

One way to foster an openness to the ongoing miracle of racial reconciliation is to retrieve the tradition launched, though not maintained, by Seymour, the leader of the Azusa Street Mission, who understood the baptism of the Spirit to be a baptism of holy love that had important implications for what it meant to be the church, the body of Christ. Chief among the accomplishments of the Spirit was a unity that transcended the divisions of its time and, by extension, could continue to do so anytime if there were willing hearts and lives. Experience of and encounter with the love of God in Christ through the Holy Spirit thus had practical and performative ramifications; exclusionary forms of ordering the people of God had to give way to mutuality, cooperation, and solidarity. The Spirit-baptized fellowship could thereby potentially be a sign to the broader church ecumenical, as well as to the world, of the reconciling power of divine love in the midst of hostilities, out-group indifference and hatred, and historic divisions.

Empowered Resistance: Spirit-Baptized Pacifism and the Ethics of Love

As should be clear from the preceding, the achievement of racial unity and the word of racial reconciliation are certainly not easily accomplished. But as recorded by Luke the evangelist, "What is impossible for mortals is possible for God" (Luke 18:27). And so also does this apply to the historic pentecostal peace witness, a strand within the tradition that most, even those within pentecostal circles, are oblivious to. But I will suggest here that if the Spirit's baptism of love worked, even against all odds, to accomplish a unity of the one body of Christ across its many divisions, then so also does the same Spirit empower, again against all odds, strains of a pentecostal pacific witness in a violent world. In this section, we examine the theological bases of pentecostal pacifism, again focusing especially on how this has unfolded in the holiness-pentecostal trajectory of the movement, in order to clarify further the performative, transformative, and evangelical aspects of Pentecostalism's distinctive missionary perspective on and engagement with the world.[37]

There is no denying that early Pentecostals' pacifism was informed more by their roots in nineteenth-century holiness movements,[38] among which were found various pacifist churches and denominations, than by their distinctively pentecostal experience of the Spirit. In that sense, this section will develop a more explicit pentecostal apologetic for pacifism than tease one from out of the history of Pentecostalism itself. Still, in order to appreciate the logic of a pacifist pentecostal theology, some historical perspective is in order. Again, we begin with COGIC.

The antiwar stand of the COGIC was no less shaped by the pacifist traditions of the Holiness, Quaker, and Anabaptist movements of the late nineteenth and early twentieth centuries. Early in its historical development, long before Mason had even received his pentecostal experience, the church had adopted an antiwar position on explicitly theological grounds: "We believe the shedding of human blood or taking of human life to be contrary to the teaching of our Lord and Saviour, and as a body, we are adverse to war in all its various forms."[39] If, upon formal declaration of war, the road ahead for white conscientious objectors was a difficult one to walk, it was twice as treacherous for blacks, especially those from religious movements that were not part of the historic peace churches who conscientiously objected to military conscription. As a result, during the latter part of 1917 and through much of 1918, many COGIC men and leaders, even Mason himself, were detained, interrogated, investigated, and subjected to surveillance for suspected acts of treason; after all, it was unfathomable to whites that blacks could object to the first World War for other reasons than either because they were sympathetic to the German cause or because they had been manipulated by enemy agents. As suspicions ran high, especially in the South, blacks were mobbed and beaten, and leaders such as Mason were almost continuously exposed to the threat of the mob. On at least one occasion, "Seeking to avoid a lynching, the local sheriff [of Lexington, Kentucky] arrested Mason for obstructing the draft,"[40] even while he was also jailed on other occasions—and then set free on bail—for inciting antiwar sentiments.

For his part, of course, Mason made clear that the COGIC's stance was fundamentally theological rather than political. On June 23, 1918, before a large congregation in Memphis, Mason preached a sermon entitled "The Kaiser in the Light of the Scriptures," in which he both approved the purchase of government war bonds (something those who were unpatriotic were accused of not supporting) and contrasted the Kaiser as an Antichrist who had come to kill and destroy with Jesus as the Prince of Peace who (quoting Luke 9:36) had "not come to destroy men's lives, but to save them."[41] None of the government's cases against COGIC men were upheld in court. But that did not mean that, as Mason himself understood it, they escaped persecution for their religious and theological convictions.[42] Many black Pentecostals still endured the harassment and discrimination, holding fast to their theological convictions about holiness vis-à-vis a life of nonviolent resistance.

Interestingly, at its founding convention, The Assemblies of God (AG) adopted a constitutional resolution regarding "the Actual Participation in the Destruction of Human Life."[43] Referring to "the principles of 'Peace on earth, good will toward men' (Luke 2:14)," among other scriptures, the council resolved that "we, as a body of Christians, while purposing to fulfill all the obligations of loyal citizenship, are nevertheless constrained to declare we cannot conscientiously participate in war and armed resistance which involves the actual destruction of human life, since this is contrary to our review of the clear teaching of the inspired Word of God, which is the sole basis for faith." The AG held to this position until 1967, when it deferred the pacifist issue to individual conscience. Much ink has been spilt regarding the historical, social, and ecclesial factors that motivated the AG to abandon its peace witness.[44] No doubt one factor was that there had always been members of the AG who served in the military, and that this number and percentage only increased throughout the twentieth century.[45]

Yet similar historical and social circumstances have not undermined the COGIC's pacifist commitments. Instead, a few years after the AG had revised its historic pacifist stance, the COGIC reaffirmed its identity as a pacifist church:

> We hereby and herewith declare our loyalty to the President and the Constitution of the United States and Pledge fidelity to the flag for which the Republic stands, but as God-fearing, peace-loving and law-abiding people, we only claim our inheritance as American citizens namely; to worship according to the dictates of our conscience. We believe that the shedding of human blood or taking of human life, to be contrary to the teachings of our Lord and Savior, Jesus Christ, and as a body, we are adverse to war in all its forms.[46]
>
> We recognize the existence of our nation's Selective Service Act and reluctantly submit to that [sic] provisions thereof only because the Scriptures teach us obedience to those over us (Heb 13:17 and 1 Pet 2:17). Accordingly, we accept induction into the Armed Services only as Conscientious Objectors; and as Conscientious Objectors, we submit to the bearing of arms only during basic training and oppose all advanced warfare training given to combatant soldiers. We will serve our country in non-combatant units where we will not have to engage in acts of war. Our Christian position rests upon the following scriptures: Matt. 5:9; 11[-]12; 5:21-22; 5:38-44, Exodus 20:13; Psalms 46:9; Isaiah 2:4; 1 Chr. 22:8; Psalms 68:30.[47]

What accounts for this difference between the AG's "defection" from pacifism and the COGIC's retention of it? Something should be said about the more accelerated "evangelicalization" of the AG when compared to the COGIC, although the latter has not been immune to such forces. Might it also be, however, that the African American and holiness ethos of the COGIC has minimized its uncritical embrace of American nationalistic aspirations and that this in turn has kept it from the seductions of worldly power?

Maybe there is one other consideration related to the holiness-pentecostal tradition that understood the baptism of the Spirit as a baptism of holy and perfect love. As Seymour and the leadership of the Mission had long emphasized, "Tongues are one of the signs that go with every baptized person, but it is not the real evidence of the baptism in the every day life. Your life must measure with the fruits of the Spirit. If you get angry, or speak evil, or backbite, I care not how many tongues you may have, you have not the baptism with the Holy Spirit."[48] This meant that the full encounter with and experience of God's empowering Spirit necessarily bore the fruits of the Spirit, including love, joy, and *peace*. Thus the COGIC has not denied the sign of tongues, but neither also has the church disassociated the baptism of power from holiness and its expressions of perfect love: "We believe that the Baptism of the Holy Ghost is an experience subsequent to conversion and sanctification and that tongue-speaking is the consequence of the Baptism in the Holy Ghost with the manifestations of the fruit of the spirit (Galatians 5:22-23; Acts 10:46, 19:1-6)."[49] Perhaps in a very real sense, holiness-pentecostal spirituality had never broken the link between sanctification and empowerment for witness, so that the missionization and evangelization of the world could only be accomplished through the Spirit of perfect love.[50]

Without a foundational spiritual experience and a strong theologically formulated rationale for a pacifist witness, churches and denominations are likely to be culturally adrift when pressured to support the government through, at least in part, military service. Thus, as has been noticed by almost all observers, the AG rationale to transition away from its pacifist identity was motivated almost entirely by pragmatic considerations. The scriptural references undergirding its original pacifist resolution were entirely missing in the 1967 resolution that replaced the article on pacifism by deferring to "the right of each member to choose for himself whether to declare his position as a combatant, a non-combatant, or a conscientious objector."[51] Might a commitment to holiness as an expression of the Spirit's empowering baptism have made a difference in halting this slide?

There are also more explicitly pentecostal reasons for embracing pacifism that even the COGIC, much less the AG, has yet to formally consider. Here I would simply urge that Pentecostals follow their predecessors and return back to their canon-within-the-canon, Luke-Acts—as did both the COGIC and the AG originally, as noted above—to reconsider the theological basis for a peace witness.[52] In no particular order, I present three lines of reflection. First, the book of Acts, considered across its broad scope, is about the Spirit's empowerment of the people of God to share the good news of Christ as a Prince of Peace with the world; as has long been noted, it is inconsistent for Pentecostals to emphasize missionary witness and evangelization to the ends of the earth on the one hand and yet support military engagement that always involves innocent suffering and loss of life to the ends of the earth on the other hand.[53] Second, the empowering of the Spirit includes the bearing of witness understood as martyrdom—this is, after all, included in the original Greek for "witnesses" (μάρτυρες—literally: "martyrs") in Acts 1:8; and this also is incompatible with taking up and bearing arms against one's enemies.[54] Third, pentecostal primitivism and restorationism, which led Pentecostals to embrace the apostolic experience as their own, should involve not only tongues as an apostolic evidence of the Spirit's baptism but also the moral perfections—the fruits of the Spirit—as apostolic signs of the Spirit's presence and activity.[55] Beginning down any of these scriptural pathways, however, would also accomplish a retrieval of the early pentecostal views of the baptism of the Spirit as the baptism of love, but now with emphasis placed on the love of enemies as well.

Of course, none of the preceding should be understood as advocating the kind of sentimental pacifism that is merely nonviolent in the face of injustice, oppression, and even war. As represented in the COGIC stance, pentecostal pacifism insists that there are many ways of supporting the causes of justice without bearing arms.[56] Further, on these matters, Pentecostals have much to learn from Anabaptist traditions that have developed proactive approaches to conflict rather than reactionary ones that default to justifying violence theologically.[57] In the end, though, I urge Pentecostals to simply return to their Jesus-centered piety that would highlight his peaceable witness and urge his followers to emulate the same.[58] It is such pacific witness that is truly in need of a new Pentecost, one that empowers those filled with the Spirit to courageous acts of witness that reconcile even enemies in the name of holy love.

Conclusion

This chapter has sought to explore the performative implications of the Spirit's baptism into divine love testified about at the beginnings of the twentieth-century pentecostal revival. The main interpretations of the pentecostal encounter with and experience of the Spirit involved an affective empowerment of gracious and holy love, one that energized pentecostal witness and other-regarding activity. We have observed how this pentecostal mission was borne, in all of its imperfections, both in the church and in the world. Ecumenically, the baptism of love made possible a unity in the Spirit that transcended human-made divisions: to be filled with the Spirit was to be filled with the unconditional love of God—a divine love energy, as Sorokin called it—for others, including those very different because of denominational, linguistic, cultural, ethnic, and racial factors and backgrounds.

In terms of the church's mission to the world, I have chosen to highlight its historic peace witness. Here my claim has been more indirect: that coming out of and being informed by the holiness tradition predisposed many, if not most, classical pentecostal churches toward a pacifist self-understanding which presumed that those filled with the Spirit of love could not and would not seek to harm or do violence to others. This is what might be called a performative theology of gracious love wherein those touched by the gift of the Spirit thus are sensitized and motivated to look out always for the edification of others, even putative enemies. Thus I have attempted to highlight the distinctive pentecostal reasons for a theological commitment to pacifism which are implicit and deeply embedded in pentecostal experience and piety. So if the holiness-pentecostal churches are right, then the baptism of the Spirit is also a baptism of love that not only sanctifies and perfects individual hearts but also produces a countercultural way of life and a transformational love energy that embraces the world, even those who are enemies of the faith.

So if pentecostal spirituality as rooted in the experience and piety of the Azusa Street Mission understands the Spirit's baptism of power also as a baptism of holy love, what are the implications for a theology of love? If pentecostal power involves, and cannot be detached from, reconciliation across human barriers, including that of race, according to the power of divine love, what else might be said about a distinctively pentecostal perspective on love? Last but not least, if pentecostal testimony involves, and maybe could even promulgate for our time, its historic peace witness according to the power of the Spirit-inspired Prince of Peace, as maintained by holiness-pentecostal churches like the COGIC, then how does this shape wider Christian considerations of the doctrine of love? The next chapter will take up and engage these more substantively theological questions.

CHAPTER 5

• • •

The Spirit's Baptism of Love
Pentecostal Spirituality and a Pneumatology of Love

This chapter is not only the middle of this section of the volume but also serves as the fulcrum upon which the entire argument of this book turns. The overall thesis being set forth is that there are untapped resources within the tradition of pentecostal spirituality for thinking afresh about theology of love. The entirety of part II is devoted to mining these resources and retrieving them for the constructive theology of love to be explicated later. The preceding chapter, it will be recalled, elaborated on the performative dimensions of pentecostal spirituality, arguing that its baptism of the Spirit can and has been understood as a baptism of holy love with ethical implications for the church and its missionary witness about a gracious God to the world. This chapter builds on the foregoing by moving from the performative to the explicitly theological level.

In brief, what drives the discussion in the next few pages has to do with how to understand this pentecostal baptism of love theologically. To unpack the theological issues and implications, we will engage primarily with three contemporary pentecostal theologians: Steven J. Land, Samuel Solivan, and Frank D. Macchia. Each will provide a very different set of windows—holiness orthopathy, liberative orthopraxy, and ecumenical orthodoxy, respectively—into pentecostal spirituality and pneumatology. Simultaneously, my reading of their work combined will show how the pentecostal distinctive testimony, long associated with the doctrine of

Spirit baptism, can be reconsidered anew toward a pneumatological theology of love. This means that we will understand love affectively in terms of its desires, hopes, and yearnings, effectively in terms of its impassioned and liberative practices on behalf of others, and cognitively in doctrinal terms, all of which are oriented toward the coming reign of God heralded by the eschatological Spirit of Pentecost.

So if in the last two generations or so the baptism of love has come to play second fiddle to the baptism for power in classical Pentecostalism, then this chapter is about the retrieval, reconstruction, and revitalization of the movement's theological self-understanding as it enters into the second decade of its second century, so that the ways and forms of love are more forcefully registered as being at the heart of pentecostal identity. Yet along the way, we shall see that Pentecostalism as a spirituality of love is oriented around pathic affectivity in ways that are consistent with what the sciences (as we have seen in chap. 2) tell us about the psychobiology of human benevolence. Hence more is at stake: if we are successful, we will also be poised to renew the conversations on theology of love in the wider ecumenical, academic, and interdisciplinary domains.

Yearning for the Spirit: Pentecostal Affections and Orthopathy

Steven Land, currently the president of Pentecostal Theological Seminary (affiliated with the holiness-pentecostal Church of God denomination headquartered in Cleveland, Tennessee), has long been at the forefront of pentecostal scholarship through his co-editorship of the *Journal of Pentecostal Theology* (1992–present) and its Supplement monograph series (which now includes about forty published volumes). The first book in the latter, *Pentecostal Spirituality: A Passion for the Kingdom,*[1] was a revision of Land's Emory University Ph.D. dissertation (1991). It broke new ground in launching the academic pentecostal theological enterprise by modeling the possibility of an authentically pentecostal theology, one that was deeply rooted in but yet neither uncritical about pentecostal faith nor unengaged with the wider academic theological enterprise. The following reviews the achievements of this work in light of our central concerns, therefore highlighting its basic structure and thesis (of pentecostal spirituality as trinitarian transformation), its theology of the affections, and its theology of love.

In brief, Land's argument is that pentecostal theology should revolve around pentecostal spirituality. Thus pentecostal prayer, praise, worship, etc., is recognized to be at the heart of the pentecostal theological task and self-understanding.[2] This means, then, "orthodoxy (right praise-confession), orthopathy (right affections) and orthopraxy (right praxis) are related in a way analogous to the interrelations of the Holy Trinity. God who is Spirit creates in humanity a spirituality which is at once cognitive, affective and behavioral, thus driving toward a unified epistemology, metaphysics and ethics" (*PS* 41). This interrelationship between orthodoxy, orthopathy, and orthopraxy thus leads to Land's trinitarian proposals, which are unfolded in at least three levels.

Soteriologically, pentecostal spirituality opens up to what the holiness-pentecostal movement has long identified as the three fundamental "works of grace": justification (regeneration of the heart), sanctification (perfection in love), and Spirit baptism (empowerment for service).[3] Theologically, this derives from the righteousness, loving holiness, and power of God's character. And last but not least, eschatologically with regard to the Holy Spirit and to the divine reign that the Spirit's outpouring inaugurates, Land points to correlations with the Pauline affirmation: "For the kingdom of God is not food and drink but *righteousness and peace and joy* in the Holy Spirit" (Rom 14:17, emphasis added; see also *PS* 125).

More precisely, given the prioritization of spirituality, "The personal integrating center of orthodoxy and orthopraxy is orthopathy, those distinctive affections which are belief shaped, praxis oriented and characteristic of a person" (*PS* 44).[4] Thus Christian salvation experienced pentecostally is constituted by an "affective integration" that "moves from experience to testimony to doctrine to theology and back again in an ongoing dynamic that is more implicit than explicit, more oral than written, more affectively-rational than principled-rational, more narrative than strictly propositional" (*PS* 46). Put this way, what drives pentecostal spirituality and theology are the affections.

There are at least four aspects of Land's theology of the affections that need to be highlighted. First, the "Christian affections are objective, relational and dispositional" (*PS* 134). The relationality of the affections points to their interconnectedness with beliefs and practices. Further, however, the objectivity of the affections and their links with beliefs mean that the affections are not merely fleeting feelings, passive passions, or subjective emotions but take an object. In particular, the Christian affections take God as their object and the reign of God as their telos. Finally, the dispositionality of the affections is intertwined with their teleological character: "Affections are abiding dispositions which dispose the person toward God and the neighbor in ways appropriate to their source and goal in God" (*PS* 136).[5]

Second, the distinctively pentecostal affections are those of gratitude, compassion, and courage (*PS* 139–61). Gratitude responds, often in the form of testimonial thanksgiving and praise, to God's salvific actions; compassion activates the wholehearted devotion, energized by holy love and longing for God, that enacts God's salvific presence in the world, especially toward the neighbor; and courage anticipates, through confident hope, the final victory of God over the powers of evil. Land does not claim that these three affections exhaustively define pentecostal spirituality, but only that they "are correlated with the view of God, the kingdom and salvation" (*PS* 138). I will comment further at the end of the next chapter about how these affections reflect also the spirituality of the apostolic followers of Jesus the Messiah.

Third, if the pentecostal affections are associated with the coming reign of God, then they have an apocalyptic character. By apocalyptic, Land does not mean world-denying as in the otherworldly emphasis in the classical pentecostal tradition. Instead, he intimates that pentecostal compassion and courage, which longs for reunion with God and the imminent return of Christ, is missionally engaged with the world and therefore lives paradoxically in anticipation and in actualization of the kingdom, simultaneously.[6] The imminence characteristic of Pentecostalism's apocalyptic eschatology, of course, is founded on the premillennialist understanding of the coming of Christ within a dispensationalist framework, widely accepted by many Pentecostals.[7] Thus the "apocalyptic affections" of Pentecostals "are constituted by [their] distinctive eschatological reality and vision" (*PS* 56), so that as "history drew nearer its proper end . . . everything had to change in light of the new direction, impetus and focus" (*PS* 69). Hence Pentecostals not only yearn for the liberation of the divine reign but also affectively embody and express the coming kingdom, and live toward its impending arrival.

Finally (for our purposes), the distinctively pentecostal affections are apocalyptic in part because they are also passional. In other words, the pentecostal affections are reducible neither to cognitive objectivity nor teleological praxis, but they are deeply rooted aspects of what Wesley understood as heart religion. As Land puts it, "This longing for the Lord to come, for the Holy Spirit and for the kingdom of God are part of the same thing: it is one passion. And for Pentecostals it is a passion that can change everything" (*PS* 66). Or, from a pentecostal perspective, it is a passion born out of having encountered and been transformed by the living God. Thus the miracles, healings, and wondrous signs have ignited the passions and redirected the affections. "All gifts of the Spirit are eschatological, proleptic signs of a kingdom of joy where sorrow, death and sin are put down and banished" (*PS* 177). The chief of these gifts, signs, or miracles is love: "The heart of Pentecostal spirituality is love. A passion for the kingdom is a passion for the king" (*PS* 176).

This leads us to the theology of love embedded within *Pentecostal Spirituality*. As might be predicted, Land's pentecostal theology of love is reframed in apocalyptic and eschatological light: "This all-consuming love for God [is] finally a longing for the coming of the Lord" (*PS* 150).[8] But following in the footsteps of Wesley, who Land identifies as "the theologian of the love of God" (*PS* 42) and for whom "the love of God and neighbor was the heart of true religion without which one was not a Christian" (*PS* 132),[9] such eschatologically oriented love and longing for God necessarily involves a historically directed love for the neighbor. Thus the Christian and pentecostal affection of compassion is constituted by loving responses to those who are in need (*PS* 143–47), with Jesus being "the center and model of compassionate love" (*PS* 145). Fullness of the Spirit is thus evidenced ultimately by love,[10] even as empowered witness is also animated by love. "To speak of power without the integrating center of love is to run the risk of becoming a 'sounding brass and a tinkling cymbal'" (*PS* 203, referring to 1 Cor 13:1, New American Standard Version). Further, pentecostal soteriology is itself constituted by love: "to be saved is also to love" (*PS* 202). In the end, then, the missional passions and the apocalyptic affections coincide in love, since "Perfect love longs for all God's children to be home with the Lord, so that the Pentecostal vision of heaven is at once theocentric and anthropocentric" (*PS* 156).[11]

I wish to make two sets of transitional remarks regarding Land's orthopathic theology. First, Land frames his proposal as a trinitarian rather than pneumatological theology. This is not to say that the Holy Spirit is absent—far from it—but that pneumatological and christological components are equally emphasized in Land's transformative spirituality. As Land puts it, "Jesus Christ is the center and the Holy Spirit is the circumference of a distinctive Pentecostal spirituality" (*PS* 23). Hence Land's is less a pneumatological theology of love than it is a trinitarian, apocalyptic, and affectively formulated one. So while we will have to think further about the more specific pneumatological dimensions of a pentecostal theology of love, what we can say now is both that perfect love is central to the renewal of pentecostal spirituality, at least as understood from a holiness-pentecostal perspective,[12] and that such perfection in holy love involves an affective dimension. At the very least, the role of pneumatology will need to be central if a robustly trinitarian theology of love is to fulfill its promise; otherwise, trinitarian theology collapses into Christology or, at best, a binitarian theology of the Father and the Son.

Second, however, Land's orthopathic theology presents the affections both as the integrating center for orthodoxy and orthopraxis and as the heart of Christian spirituality, pentecostally considered. What is important to observe is how the affections both orient us to God and enable our empathy with others (our neighbors).[13] Land's preferred notion is compassion, signaling our affective and dispositional relationship to others. Christian mission in general and pentecostal testimony and evangelism in particular are ineffective apart from this affective integration and motivation.[14] This understanding of the affections is consistent with what we saw before (chap. 2) about benevolent service as funded by empathetic feeling. I mention this here not apologetically as if to legitimate pentecostal affectivity but only to make the following observation: if the affections do indeed motivate pentecostal praxis and inform pentecostal beliefs, then pentecostal spirituality may provide one window into how human beings tap into the divine love energy and through that enter into solidarity with others to the extent that such piety motivates benevolent and loving action. We will revisit this issue momentarily.

Liberation in the Spirit: Pentecostal Passions and Orthopraxy

Samuel Solivan says that he developed his notion of orthopathos "independently of" Steven Land.[15] If the latter is driven from a form of pentecostal praxis—that is, as expressed in pentecostal spirituality—toward a theology of orthopathos, the former is moved orthopathically toward orthopraxis. This is in part because, as a Puerto Rican theologian (currently on the faculty at Universidad Interamericana de Puerto Rico), Solivan is motivated as much by the Latin American theology of liberation as he is by pentecostal spirituality. The other major difference is his more explicitly pneumatological focus, as compared to Land's trinitarian scope. These will be our two points of entry into Solivan's work.

Similar to how Land affirms orthopathy as the integrating center of orthodoxy and orthopraxy, Solivan insists that orthopathos "is an attempt to bridge the gulf between orthodoxy and orthopraxis" (*SPL* 11). If the former's orthopathy denotes the affectivity at the heart of pentecostal spirituality, the latter's orthopathos

> points to and highlights the importance that should be given to a people's suffering, dehumanization, pain and marginalization. *Orthopathos* seeks to show how correct doctrine uninformed by a people's suffering often tends to be stoic, apathetic and distant. Orthodox approaches to suffering and pain are often allegorized or dealt with in the context of either the result of sin or slothfulness or a means by which one is tempered spiritually. These responses represent an aspect of the truth, but fall short of a holistic response that is present in the Scriptures. (*SPL* 12)

With this definition, Solivan's liberative emphasis is clear, but it should also be unpacked from at least three directions: historically, scripturally, and ethically.

Historically, orthopathos is fundamentally informed by the pathos of suffering, in particular the suffering of the Hispanic people. The experience of this people since the founding of the "new world" is characterized fundamentally in terms of suffering: from desolation and despair (*SPL* 26, 71), poverty (*SPL* 97), exilic homelessness (*SPL* 24, 137), and voicelessness (*SPL* 33), among other tragic aspects of Hispanic historical life. To suffer is to be subjugated under the regime of oppressors, with the result, usually, being the exploitation, marginalization, and victimization of the oppressed. These are constant themes in Hispanic theological discourse, much of which has been formulated within a liberation theology framework.[16] Hence from a theological perspective there must also be the possibility of pathic redemption. "The *ortho* aspect of *orthopathos* is rooted in the distinction between suffering which results in self-alienation, and suffering that can somehow be a source for liberation and social transformation" (*SPL* 61).

Scripturally, Solivan roots the liberative possibilities of suffering in the divine pathos reflected in the Bible. His primary dialogue partner on this front is the Jewish theologian, Abraham Heschel, in particular the latter's classic text *The Prophets*.[17] This work highlights not only the covenant-making but also covenant-keeping God who enters into and is involved with the history of the people of God, who seeks to accomplish what is just on their behalf, and who liberates the people of God from their plight in order to reestablish—redeem or restore—the relationship between creation and the creator (*SPL* 52–54). The Hebrew Bible prophets thus reveal a God who is attentive to the human situation, who "is touched by our suffering . . . [and] sympathetic to our condition" (*SPL* 74). God is neither removed nor unmoved, but "engages the situation of the Israelites' pathos by responding concretely to their needs" (*SPL* 76).[18] From the New Testament two further orthopathic themes are teased out: that God enters into "kenotic empathy" with humanity especially in the incarnation (*SPL* 77–86), thus not only identifying with human suffering but also redeeming and transforming it, and that human weakness, powerlessness, and suffering are occasions for the manifestation of divine strength (*SPL* 86–89). Yet it should be noted that contrary to the general trend in liberation theological discourse, Solivan does not privilege the category of the poor. Certainly, he does not ignore poverty and he grants that the impoverished are part of those who suffer. However, divine pathos is concerned with *all* who suffer and this includes but cannot and should not be reduced to the poor (*SPL* 149).

Ethically, of course, this work represents also a pentecostal contribution to and maybe even intervention within the field of liberation theology. Here Solivan is one of two pioneers, at least for those writing in the English language. His predecessor, Eldin Villafañe, had focused more on developing a Hispanic American pentecostal social ethic.[19] The major thrust of Villafañe's work focuses on the role of the Holy Spirit in the charismatic empowerment of the church's *koinonia* (fellowship), *liturgia* (worship), *kerygma* (proclamation), and *diakonia* (service), all of which were or should be directed toward the task of sociohistorical liberation as normed according to the twin scriptural and theological themes of love and justice.[20] In this tradition, Solivan is also concerned with liberative ethics and social transformation: "*Orthopathos* empowers sufferers for the long-term struggle with their present, and often long-term, conditions" (*SPL* 65). Orthopathos is thus liberating passion/pathos that empowers the movement from suffering to liberation (*SPL* 60, 61, 69). In concert with Villafañe, orthopathos is particularly a work of the Holy Spirit.

This pneumatological emphasis can be said to characterize the distinctively pentecostal perspective in Solivan's liberation thinking. For Solivan, orthopathos is "the power of the Holy Spirit in one's life that transforms pathos, suffering and despair into hope and wholeness" (*SPL* 27). Thus the *ortho* in orthopathos is also pneumatologically charged: "the proper or liberating appropriation of suffering (pathos) to encourage living as loving subjects [is] inspired by the Holy Spirit" (*SPL* 66). This is because "the Holy Spirit is the comforter charged by God and the son to empower orthopathetic transformation in our lives as we accept the gift of Christ as Lord" (*SPL* 60). Apart from the presence and activity of the Spirit, sufferers are alone in their desolation (*SPL* 101–2). Liberative transformation is therefore inherently pneumatic: "Hope, love and faith in the orthopathic liberating process are not psychogenic, rather, they are the work of the Holy Spirit, the Spirit of Christ reconciling us to God, to ourselves and to our neighbors" (*SPL* 110).

Beyond these more generic pneumatological motifs, Solivan's pneumatology of liberation is even more explicitly pentecostal than Villafañe's in retrieving and reappropriating themes from the Day of Pentecost narrative in Acts 2. On Solivan's orthopathic reading, the outpouring of the Spirit "upon all flesh" (Acts 2:17) represents not only an affirmation of the particularity (in the many languages) and universality of divine presence and activity but also of ethnic and cultural diversity. The preservation of the many "tongues" (γλῶσσαι) and "dialects" (διαλέκτῳ) suggests that God is interested not merely in humankind in the abstract but in the particularity of their geographic, ethnic, and cultural makeup (*SPL* 112–18).[21] The argument is laid out against the background of the multilingual and multicultural character of the first-century messianic movement (*SPL* 119) and should be understood amidst the similarly diverse and multiracial Hispanic world today (*SPL* 134). The pentecostal gift of many tongues thus calls attention to "an inclusive community of the Spirit" (*SPL* 141), one in which the "liberating power of the Spirit breaks down the old paradigms of racism, nationalism, classicism and ethnocentrism" (*SPL* 142).

We have said enough about Solivan's orthopathic pneumatology by now to identify a number of salient threads that connect to our purposes in this book. While it should be obvious that Solivan does not engage in substantive discussion about love, his discussion of liberative or orthopathos invites further development vis-à-vis a pentecostal and pneumatological theology of love. My suggestion is to extend what are conceived by Solivan as epistemological springboards toward orthopraxis in a more robust theological and anthropological direction. Orthopathos functions for Solivan first and foremost as an experiential and hermeneutical category that enables solidarity between agents of change and those who suffer: "*Orthopathos*—the hope-full suffering within the experience of being a non-person—as opposed to passion in a sexual or moral sense, depicts the ontological reality of those on whose behalf we are called to advocate" (*SPL* 68). In this sense, those who do not suffer acutely are nevertheless called to enter into the suffering of others, as God did and continues to do with the oppressed and marginalized, in order to effect liberative transformation. In this sense, and here drawing from the work of Korean theologian Jung Young Lee,[22] "pathos is compared to empathy . . . [and] is the entire complex of potentially destructive feelings, emotions and behavior that suffering people, especially the poor, experience on a daily basis as a normative pattern of existence" (*SPL* 54). Orthopathos, then, is the epistemological standpoint, or historical experience, in and through which the Holy Spirit enables the shared liberative praxis that confronts and counters the negative aspects of pathos.

I wish to make two points in response. First, at the theological level, pathos should be understood first and foremost in terms of the mutuality of the intra-trinitarian relations.[23] Respecting the qualitative difference between the Creator and the created suggests that human persons are also pathically formed not primarily in mutual relationality with God but in light of gracious divine activity. This means that whereas God can enter into the pathos of the human condition, it is precisely such pathic openness that enables reception of God's redemptive work. Thus, going beyond Aquinas (see chap. 2), the divine affections are both intra-trinitarian and enable God to feel with and be moved by the world, even as human passions are reliant on God's salvific initiative. To be sure, humans can be affected and moved by the sufferings of others, but orthopathic redemption relies on God's primordial desire to save the world.[24]

Second, then, and at the related anthropological level, the passions enable our formation in light of the saving work of God while also providing the engine that drives the project of human liberation. Here we do not need to get into the convoluted disputes about the relationship between the passions, the emotions, and the affections.[25] Suffice to say that, in Solivan's terms, orthopathos consists of the liberative work of the Spirit in enabling human emotional empathy, which in turn produces human solidarity and mobilizes human action.[26] Put in interdisciplinary terms, orthopathos involves kinesthetic perceptions, evaluative sensibilities, and affective feelings under the guidance of the Spirit. This means that the Spirit works through human physiology (the visceral and embodied aspect), psychology (the cognitive dimension), and affectivity (the emotional and passionate domain), each of which is deeply intertwined with the others, in order to save human bodies, renew human thinking, reorient human desire, and, ultimately, redeem human life. So on the one hand, and viewed from a pentecostal angle, what Solivan calls the passions and what Land calls the affections are the integrative bridges between orthodoxy and orthopraxy. On the other hand, and viewed in more generic theological-anthropological terms, the passions and affections are constitutive of a more holistic theological anthropology and soteriological vision, one that involves not just our bodies (and brains) and our minds (beliefs) but also our feelings and our hearts. With regard to the animating concerns of this book, the passions and affections register the import of human emotion, feeling, and desire central to any robust theological account of love.

Baptized with the Spirit: Pentecostal Love and Orthodoxy

To think more specifically about theology of love, we turn to the work of Frank D. Macchia, former editor of *Pneuma: The Journal of the Society for Pentecostal Studies* (1999–2009) and one of the most prolific and renowned of contemporary pentecostal theologians. We focus here on Macchia's *Baptized in the Spirit: A Global Pentecostal Theology*,[27] which moves from the "central distinctive" (part of the title to chap. 1 of his book) of pentecostal spirituality and theology—the experience and doctrine of being filled with the Spirit—toward a pentecostal theology of baptism in divine love. How does this argument unfold?

Macchia's presuppositions, argument, and thesis are succinctly stated, and deserve to be quoted in full:

> I am assuming throughout this book a Pentecost/kingdom of God correlation. As a pneumatological concept, the kingdom is inaugurated and fulfilled as a "Spirit baptism." God's kingdom is not an oppressive rule but the reign of divine love. Paul thus calls Pentecost an outpouring of divine love (Rom. 5:5). Before the book is finished, I will be saying that the highest description possible of the substance of Spirit baptism as an eschatological gift is that it functions as an outpouring of divine love. This is the final integration of the soteriological and the charismatic. (*BS* 17)

Two sets of comments, one briefer and the other more expansive, need to be made about this agenda before unpacking Macchia's theology of love.

The first concerns what Macchia intimates in the last sentence of the quoted material. What he is attempting to traverse is the bifurcation that has opened up in some pentecostal and evangelical biblical studies circles between the association of St. Luke with a charismatic pneumatology and of St. Paul with a soteriological pneumatology. This division of labor has historical roots in the pentecostal revival, especially but not only in the holiness wing of the tradition, which has long understood the baptism of the Spirit that empowers for witness as subsequent—logically and theologically if not experientially—to the gift of the Spirit that regenerates and constitutes the members of the body of Christ (1 Cor 12:12-13). Pentecostal scholars have thus not only worked hard to distinguish Luke's charismatic Spirit from Paul's soteriological and ecclesiological one, but also to insist that the Lukan writings, especially the book of Acts, be read and understood on their own terms rather than according to Pauline presuppositions.[28] On the other side, of course, evangelical scholars in particular, indebted as they are to a Reformation hermeneutical paradigm, have been reluctant not only to recognize Luke as having his own theological agenda distinct from Paul, but also to de-privilege the theology of the Pauline epistles, especially given their didactic nature, when compared with the primarily historical accounts of the Lukan material.[29]

There have certainly been efforts to bridge the gap between these two positions.[30] Macchia's strategy, however, is to reread the Lukan baptism of the Spirit both in light of the overall emphases in the gospels on the coming reign of God and against the backdrop of the rest of the New Testament witness regarding the eschatological work of the Spirit to arrive at his proposed synthesis. Here, of course, he works primarily as a pentecostal and ecumenical theologian, rather than as a biblical scholar. However, there is much to reconsider in his arguments regarding Christ as the Spirit-baptizing inaugurator of the divine reign and of the church as the body of Christ and the fellowship of the Spirit that manifests signs of and heralds the coming rule of God.

This leads to our second observation, regarding the eschatological framework of Macchia's theology of Spirit baptism. As with Land, the reign of God is also central to Macchia's proposal. However, the former focuses on the affections shaped by the expectation of the Parousia—thus the apocalyptic affections, in Land's words—while the latter's emphasis is much more on the already inaugurated aspects of the coming reign. This is not to suggest that Macchia minimizes the second coming of Christ or rejects the futuristic emphasis prevalent in the classical pentecostal movement. It is to say that, along with many other pentecostal theologians,[31] there is a clear distancing from dispensationalist and even premillennialist discourses as hindering rather than nurturing pentecostal theological reflection. Instead, Macchia suggests that the pentecostal baptism of the Spirit accomplishes the perfection of holy and powerful love in human hearts that anticipates "the final sanctification of creation" (*BS* 86). What exactly does this mean?

In order to understand Macchia's more cosmic theology of the Spirit's baptism in holy love, we need to briefly digress to his earlier work, a published dissertation on the nineteenth-century pietists, Johann and Christoph Blumhardt.[32] This father and son tandem were precursors for pentecostal spirituality in their embrace and practice of some of the charismatic or spiritual gifts, in particular that of healing, miracles, and exorcism. While the elder Blumhardt believed that such manifestations urged believers to persist in the groaning prayer "for the liberation of all of creation from bondage and suffering (referring to Romans 8:26),"[33] the younger Blumhardt gradually replaced such quietism with the view that these signs of the Spirit heralded the in-breaking of the reign of God into history.[34] What emerged, then, was a more socially expansive understanding of the Spirit's healing and miraculous work that wrought redemption and deliverance from oppressive political, economic, and social conditions. In dialogue with the Blumhardts, then, Macchia could propose: "Spirit baptism for Pentecostals is the experience that brings to realization personally what the eschatological latter rain of the Spirit brings corporately to an era of time" (*BS* 40).

In making this move, Macchia reinterprets what Pentecostals called the "latter rain revival"—from Joel 2:23, which because of the link between Joel 2:28-32 and Acts 2 was thought to be fulfilled with the early modern pentecostal revival—as exceeding a merely individualistic application. This is in part also because the baptism or infilling of the Spirit in the gospels, particularly in the life and ministry of Christ himself, empowers the proclamation of the reign of God and the accomplishment of its works and signs. For Macchia, then, the work of the Spirit is fundamentally eschatological, meaning that it inaugurates the coming divine rule in the life and ministry of Jesus initially, and of those who are filled with his Spirit subsequently, so that the works of the time to come can be achieved. If the baptism of the Spirit fills human hearts and transforms and renews human lives so that they can become the temple of the Spirit (1 Cor 3:16; 6:19), then the pentecostal outpouring of the Spirit cumulatively anticipates and even brings about the redemption of all of creation which has been designed ultimately for pneumatic or divine indwelling.[35] This is the groaning of which Paul spoke and to which Johann Blumhardt referred, in anticipation of when the creation would be subject to the God who fills all in all (1 Cor 15:28; Eph 1:23). Toward this end, "Spirit baptism is a baptism into the love of God that sanctifies, renews, and empowers until Spirit baptism turns all of creation into the final dwelling place of God" (*BS* 60).[36]

The final chapter of Macchia's *Baptized in the Spirit* is titled "Baptized in Love." Sandwiched between a lengthy discussion of the charismatic gifts in general, and of the gifts of tongues and prophecy in particular, is a discussion of St. Paul's theology of love in 1 Corinthians 13, and here Macchia argues that love is not only the greatest of the gifts but also central to their authentic functioning (*BS* 243). But Macchia goes further to insist that love is at the center of the pentecostal filling of the Spirit: "If the Spirit is poured out from the Father who gave the Son and through the Son who freely gave himself, divine love must be at the essence of Spirit baptism" (*BS* 258).[37] With the gift of the Spirit, then, comes not only God's greatest gift but, in effect, the person and reality of God: "Love is God's supreme gift, for it transcends all emotion, conceptuality, and action only to inspire all three. It gives us life and that more abundantly. Love is not only God's supreme gift, it is at the very essence of God's nature as well" (*BS* 259). Thus the reception of the Spirit is a reception of divine love that fulfills the life of faith and drives earnest and fervent hope in God's capacity to transform the world. As Macchia puts it, "the eschatological drama of Spirit baptism [suggests] that the Son is the bond of love between the electing Father and the expansive freedom of the Spirit's work in all of creation, so that all things spiritual proceed in a direction faithful to God's love revealed in Christ" (*BS* 265).

More than this, as a classical pentecostal, Macchia affirms that there is a sense in which the baptism of the Spirit remains subsequent to the gift of the Spirit at Christian initiation (*BS* 153–54), and this sense is best captured in terms of love's "second conversion" (*BS* 280). What this means is that "Spirit baptism fills us with the love of God so that we transcend ourselves and cross boundaries," and that "Spirit baptism as an experience of empowerment is not just renewed energy to do things for God. It is rather the power of self-transcending, self-giving love" (*BS* 281). If the first gift of the Spirit, at initiation into the Christian life, turns believers to God in Christ, then the second baptism of the Spirit turns them—converts them, even, however forcefully—back toward the world, not only to a world full of individuals but also to the world in all of its sociality, but now with the full panoply of spiritual gifts to bear witness in the power of the Spirit to the saving work of God in Christ.[38] We have already seen (in chap. 4) this boundary-crossing power in the Azusa Street revival, especially in how the Mission transcended social conventions, political correctness, and even ecclesial divisions. And we have also caught a glimpse of the potential of Spirit baptized love to empower a nonviolent way of life, one that is suggestive of the kind of love energy that might indeed be harnessed in the cause of promoting greater benevolence in an otherwise hostile world. Are these some of the altruistic behaviors motivated by charismatic experiences of the Spirit, as suggested by the Godly Love project?[39]

Hence the baptism into divine love can never ultimately be self-contained or self-sufficient; rather, it draws us into the divine life itself, thereby enabling our participation in its self-giving character. And the nature of love means that it will be at the heart of all we are and do—meaning that it is never merely a physiological or neurological response, although it will certainly have an passionate and emotional dimension; that it will also never only be manifest in our benevolent action, although that will inevitably be an expression of authentic love; and that it will also never be reducible to a cognitive commitment, although love always finally has a divine shape in the gift of the Son and the outpouring of the Spirit, and an affective orientation toward the coming reign. This helps us to see how a pentecostal theology of the gift of the Spirit understood as baptism into divine love is undergirded affectively by orthopathic love, motivated liberatively by orthopraxic love, and normed teleologically by a pneumatological, trinitarian, and eschatological love. It also enables us to make preliminary connections with the sciences of benevolence, in particular indicating how a baptism into love empowers self-denying and other-interested behaviors and actions, not only toward other individuals but also as directed to making a difference in the world in all of its social and even structural complexity and in anticipation of its cosmic renovation as the dwelling place of God.

Conclusion

What I do not mean to suggest, either here at the end of this chapter or in this volume so far, is any kind of natural theology that either intends to call on the sciences to justify pentecostal spirituality or presumes to provide a pentecostal apologetic through correlation with the sciences. As I have already noted (in the introduction to chap. 2 above), such approaches are not theologically viable. In the context of the interdisciplinary character of the contemporary theological landscape, I am thereby extending what has been called the "analogy of love" to think about the meaning of love in a wider scholarly and interdisciplinary field.[40] Thus science does not "prove" anything on the one hand, nor is there any need to validate pentecostal spirituality on the other hand. Rather, if pentecostal spirituality is deeply affective and embodied, as it has in fact been characterized, then empirical research should be able to shed light on at least some aspects of this phenomenon with analogical implications for theological reflection, as I hope I have shown.

More important, in this chapter my goal has been to plumb the theological depths of the pentecostal experience of the Spirit's baptism in holy love, as testified to at the Azusa Street Mission. To accomplish this, we have engaged in reflection with Steven Land's holiness-pentecostal spirituality of affective love, Samuel Solivan's Hispanic pentecostal experience of liberative love, and Frank Macchia's classical pentecostal theology of eschatological love. Of the three, Macchia's is the closest to what might be formally considered a theology of love, but even his is still formulated explicitly as a theology of Spirit baptism. Still, all contribute to a pentecostal understanding of love by showing us how affective passions are at the center of pentecostal spirituality and how loving solidarity with others is at the heart of pneumatology in particular and of pneumatological theology in general.[41] And together, our interlocutors open up windows into a trinitarian theology of grace, one which features the Spirit of God in Christ who graciously baptizes the world so that all creatures who are otherwise without merit can receive the gracious and redemptive love of God.

Let us briefly recapitulate our path so far. Our goal is to articulate a theology of love by drawing explicitly from pentecostal resources. Toward this end, we have discerned in part I that there is a tradition of thinking about love in relationship to the Spirit (chap. 1), and that there have been scientific research projects focused on altruistic love (chap. 2) that have also helped—especially in the discipline of sociology—to draw attention to love as a central motif in pentecostal self-understanding, although one that has been more neglected recently. So far in part II, we have sought to retrieve this pentecostal notion of love both historically, phenomenologically, and performatively (chap. 4), and theologically (this chapter), and in doing so, have seen that the pentecostal baptism of the Spirit has long been understood, although not proclaimed often enough, as a baptism in divine love, and that such a baptism has affective, practical, and theological consequences related to the Christian mission in the world. We are now poised to take up the constructive task of articulating a Christian theology of love as informed by these resources drawn from pentecostal spirituality and theology.

CHAPTER 6

• • •

The Spirit Poured Out on All Flesh
Aspects of a Lukan Theology of Love

So far in part II of the book we have attempted to mine the pentecostal tradition for resources to rethink a theology of love. The movement has been from the phenomenology and performative analysis of pentecostal spirituality in chapter 4 toward a pentecostal theology of love in the previous chapter. In the following pages, we will revisit the pentecostal canon-within-the-canon, Luke-Acts, in light of these considerations. We will look first at how the gift of the Spirit in Acts unveils divine love, then return to the Third Gospel to think about Christ's life and teachings as manifesting and initiating a charismatic theology of love, and conclude with a consideration of what we might call a pentecostal and apostolic spirituality of love. Our goal will be to tease out what might be called a Lukan theology of love, which I argue will be suggestive for thinking about love from pneumatological and charismatic perspectives.

The focus on Luke-Acts in this chapter should be no surprise for pentecostal scholars who have long recognized the central role of especially the book of Acts for pentecostal spirituality and theological self-understanding.[1] For those unfamiliar with the pentecostal tradition, however, two preliminary remarks are in order. First, as a restorationist movement, modern Pentecostalism has been oriented since its beginnings to recapturing the apostolic experience; hence the Lukan description of the earliest followers of Jesus as Messiah is not merely of historical interest but has functioned normatively for contemporary pentecostal spirituality. Second, then, Pentecostalism has long exercised what might be called a primitivist hermeneutic, one focused not merely on understanding what happened back then but on how the apostolic experience can be realized in an ongoing basis in the life of the church. It is especially the book of Acts, which has served to guide pentecostal practice and theological reflection by providing a lens through which the rest of the New Testament, as well as the Hebrew Bible, is read. This chapter thus enters through this pentecostal window into the scriptural witness, but we limit our focus more specifically to thinking about the theme of love.

If the preceding chapter was the pivot upon which the argument of the book turned theologically, then it has set us upon the constructive theological task that will occupy most of the remainder of our time. Central to this reconstruction will be a return to the scriptural narratives. This chapter is the first of three forays into the New Testament, each of which will wind as one strand of a threefold cord toward a pneumatological theology of love.[2] I locate this chapter here in part II because it continues the explicitly pentecostal reflections on love, albeit moving from the earlier more phenomenological, performative, and theological considerations to rereadings of Luke-Acts. Then, in the next two chapters we continue our biblical retrieval by looking at the Pauline and Johannine materials, respectively. While our exegeses in part III will not be guided by specifically pentecostal concerns, they will be informed by the ideas developed in this part of the book. But we are getting ahead of ourselves.

The Gift of Pentecost: Intimations of a Pneumatological Theology of Love

Earlier (in chap. 3) we noted that the language of love has played a minimal role in more recent pentecostal theological reflection. Besides the historical reasons outlined above for this neglect, a further explanation is related to the centrality of Acts in the pentecostal scriptural imagination, and the fact that the word "love" does not appear at all in this New Testament writing.[3] Actually, Barnabas and Paul are identified as "beloved" (ἀγαπητοῖς) by the apostles in their recommendation letter to the churches in Acts 15:25. But other than this, there is no mention of love. We know, however, the book of Acts is about the Holy Spirit, and that the gift of the Holy Spirit has been associated with the gift of love in the Christian tradition. Might we be able to reframe the narrative of the Day of Pentecost outpouring of the Holy Spirit as an expression of what the Christian tradition calls the gift of love and what many early modern Pentecostals called the baptism of love?

To be sure, the book of Acts is very clear that the Holy Spirit is nothing less than the gift of God.[4] Luke puts the "gift of the Holy Spirit" on the lips of Peter (Acts 2:38)[5] and associates the Spirit with gift elsewhere in his two-volume work (10:45; cf. 8:18-20 and 11:17 with Luke 11:13). And as the gift of God, the Spirit is thus also the gratuitous self-outpouring of God upon and into all of creation. Nothing requires, demands, or necessitates this self-giving—that is, in effect, the definition of the Gift, absolutely considered. In the Lukan case, such a gracious and unconditional gift of God is nothing less than the Holy Spirit of God herself.

But why is the Spirit given in the book of Acts? The most immediate explanation provided, in the Day of Pentecost narrative, can be extrapolated from Peter's reference to Joel (2:14-20; cf. Joel 2:28-32): that the gift of the Spirit is to enable prophesying by men and women, slave and free, to give dreams and visions to young and old, and, perhaps most importantly, to make it possible that "*everyone* who calls on the name of the Lord shall be saved" (2:21, emphasis added).[6] In a very real sense, these effects of the Spirit's outpouring provide insight into the purpose of the gift of the Spirit, which ultimately relate to God's desires to save all people, even the whole world, as we shall see played out in the rest of the book of Acts.

The universal scope of the redemptive work of God structuring the Acts narrative is highlighted in its first chapter, in a verse that also lies at the center of the pentecostal imagination: "you will receive power when the Holy Spirit has come upon you; and you will be my witnesses in Jerusalem, in all Judea and Samaria, and to the ends of the earth" (1:8). Whereas pentecostal interpretation has focused on the empowerment clause, I wish to emphasize the breadth of God's saving intentions instead. That the "ends of the earth" were always included in Luke's horizon is clear also in his first volume.[7] At the end of that book, it is recorded that Jesus instructed the disciples to wait in Jerusalem "until you have been clothed with power from on high" (Luke 24:49) so that they can be witnesses of the good news that "forgiveness of sins is to be proclaimed in his name to all nations, beginning from Jerusalem" (Luke 24:47). Even at the birth of Jesus, Simeon praised God that he had been privileged to have witnessed the divine salvation prepared "in the presence of all peoples, a light for revelation to the Gentiles" (Luke 2:31-32). The Acts narrative then unfolds God's redeeming work through the Spirit according to the geographical divisions laid out in 1:8. The apostolic testimony spreads from Jerusalem (2:1–5:11) through Judea (5:12–7:60) and Samaria (8:1-25), and all the way to Rome (chaps. 9–28), representative of the ends of the earth from the apostolic vantage point centered in Jerusalem.

Let us now return to the Day of Pentecost narrative in order to observe the effects of the gift of the Spirit in light of God's intended universal redemption. At the end of his explanatory sermon, Peter urges his audience, "Repent, and be baptized every one of you in the name of Jesus Christ so that your sins may be forgiven; and you will receive the gift of the Holy Spirit" (2:38). While salvation involves human repentance and baptism, it is nevertheless constituted by the person of Jesus, especially in the forgiveness of sins. This is significant for a number of reasons, including the fact that the forgiveness of sins was precisely what this original audience needed as those who were responsible, even if only indirectly, for the crucifixion and murder of Jesus (2:36). If Jesus himself had forgiven his persecutors and tormentors (Luke 23:34), then so also was forgiveness of sins available through those who were commissioned to proclaim the good news in his name (3:19; 5:31; 8:22; 10:43; 13:38-39; 22:16; 26:18). In this case, then, the gift of God could be understood not so much in terms of the reception of something tangible but as the overlooking of the fault accruing to human sin. But the divine gift of grace is not to be understood merely in negative terms; rather it is also to be seen as the positive capacity to receive forgiveness. Hence, God's gift results in a cleansed conscience and the removal of guilt.

In fact, this marvelous gift of forgiveness is not only made possible in Jesus' name but is interconnected with the gift of the Holy Spirit (2:38). One might say that the removal of sins (forgiveness) logically anticipates the outpouring (gift) of the Spirit. These are two sides to the one coin of God's redemptive work in human hearts and lives. Put alternatively, the Day of Pentecost outpouring of the Spirit upon all flesh is God's prevenient gift that makes possible the repentance of individuals hearts so that any who call upon the name of the Lord will experience for him- or herself the forgiveness of sins and receive the Holy Spirit. And make no mistake, "For the promise is for you, for your children, and for all who are far away, everyone whom the Lord our God calls to him" (2:39). In other words, the forgiveness of sins and the gift of the Spirit are not only available to the ends of the earth but also to the ends of time.[8] The universality of God's redemptive work has both synchronic and diachronic dimensions, covering geographic barriers while also overcoming temporal ones. This perhaps explains why Peter also says that both the forgiveness of sins and the "times of refreshing . . . from the presence of the Lord" (3:20)—arguably an oblique canonical reference to the reviving, reinvigorating work, and regenerating of the Spirit—anticipate "the time of universal restoration that God announced long ago through his holy prophets" (3:21).[9]

The immediate effects of the Day of Pentecost gift of the Spirit are described in a passage that deserves to be quoted at length:

> They devoted themselves to the apostles' teaching and fellowship, to the breaking of bread and the prayers. Awe came upon everyone, because many wonders and signs were being done by the apostles. All who believed were together and had all things in common; they would sell their possessions and goods and distribute the proceeds to all, as any had need. Day by day, as they spent much time together in the temple, they broke bread at home and ate their food with glad and generous hearts, praising God and having the goodwill of all the people. And day by day the Lord added to their number those who were being saved. (2:42-47)

Two sets of comments should be made in this regard. First, the charismatic experience of the Spirit graciously empowers altruistic benevolence. Those of means were willing to part with what they had for the benefit of others who were needy. Later, Luke also notes that "There was not a needy person among them, for as many as owned lands or houses sold them and brought the proceeds of what was sold. They laid it at the apostles' feet, and it was distributed to each as any had need" (4:34-35). What Luke records here is consistent with the findings of the Godly Love project (see chap. 3). More important, it communicates an important theological truth: that the gift of the Spirit generates other gifts, in this case, economic gifts for the common good. Divine grace is in effect self-perpetuating, precisely because what is given is not just any things but the very gift of the Spirit of God herself. The result is love in action, even if it is not love as usually conceived.

Second, the pentecostal outpouring formed a community of the Spirit, a fellowship—the Greek word in 2:42 is κοινωνία—affectively united by joy, practically bound together by generosity, and spiritually oriented in worship. If we understand the Day of Pentecost gift as a baptism of love, according to the argument of the last few chapters, then we can also see the resulting fellowship of the Spirit (cf. 2 Cor 13:14) as a gracious community of love. In this case, the love of God ignites love for God, expressed in the prayers and praises of the people directed to God, and generates neighborly love, seen in the generosity and solidarity of the people with each other, as well as with those who were added to the community on a daily basis. While I want to return to elaborate more on this theme later, for now we can extend the theological truth formulated at the end of the preceding paragraph: that the gift of the Spirit generates all kinds of other gifts, some in response to God and others in the formation of a community of love around the name and person of Jesus. In other words, a gracious God forms a gracious—a grace-filled—community, and that because of the divine gift of the Spirit of love. Is this not also a manifestation of the love of God, even if not explicitly called such here?

And that is precisely the main point I want to argue about the Spirit of Pentecost: that it is nothing less than the gift of a loving God to the world. This has both salvation-historical and individual dimensions. With regard to the former, the gift of the Spirit is God's response to those who were yearning for the restoration of the kingdom of Israel (1:6) and for the redemption of Jerusalem (Luke 2:38; cf. Luke 1:55-56, 68). What most first-century Jews did not expect, however, was that God's response to this cry of their hearts would also involve the salvation of the Gentiles,[10] so that the covenantal promise made to Abraham, that "in your descendants all the families of the earth shall be blessed" (3:25; cf. Gen 12:1-3), might be fulfilled. When set within a theology of love framework, then, the Day of Pentecost outpouring is God's excessive and universal gift of love to the world, in and through the gift of the Spirit of God. God's love for Israel is thus manifest not only in her renewal and restoration but in God's keeping of the promises of the covenant so that the love of God can be poured out upon and given to all flesh.

Thus this salvation-historical rendition of the gift of the Spirit of divine love also finds concrete individual fulfillment. The gift of God's Spirit is, after all, described as a "baptism" (1:5; 11:16; cf. Luke 3:16), an inundation of the heart and the soul with the living breath of God. Thus the gift of the Holy Spirit is also talked about as an *infilling*—as a *being-filled-with* or a *being-made-full-of* the Spirit (2:4; 4:8, 31; 7:55; 9:17; 13:9, 52)—connoting an overflowing of God into human lives so that they are no longer full of themselves but full of God. The God who gives graciously of the Spirit thus spares nothing that will hinder the excessive flooding of human hearts and lives. Of course, what is suggested is that the human vessels are "space" for the divine life. Equally, it suggests that God also yearns to be yoked with human creatures, longs even to be reconciled with them, and through Christ pours out the Spirit into men and women, young and old, slave and free—in short, all flesh—as an expression of this desirous love.

On the human side, the infilling of the gift of God can only be *received* (8:15; 10:47; 19:2). This is Aquinas' passive potency, denoting the capacity of human hearts to become the dwelling or resting place (Luke 2:25) of God. Thus do human beings "suffer" the divine gift that is dispensed liberally but yet mysteriously through the presence and activity of the Spirit of love, and in doing so are transformed into human receptacles of divine love. But divine love also waits patiently for human openness, thus also "suffering" human rebellion and resistance. And when hearts are finally turned to God, then, they are also ready to receive—to be impressed by and upon, to be impassioned with—the gift of God's love in the Spirit.

The Gift of Christ: A Charismatic Theology of the Great Commandment

I now want to turn from the book of Acts back to the Gospel of Luke. I say "back" not only because of the canonical alignment of the two books but also because of their sequence of composition, with the opening verse of Acts referring to "the first book . . . about all that Jesus did and taught from the beginning."[11] Unlike the book of Acts, the Third Gospel does mention love. Revisiting these references to love in Luke's Gospel will validate the early modern pentecostal sense that the gift of the Spirit was indeed a baptism of and into divine love.

Beyond this, the following discussion will also shed further light on the gift of, in, and through Christ as the charismatic, gracious, and loving work of the Triune God. The classical theological tradition has rightly focused a theology of grace on the incarnational work of Christ, but all too often neglected the essential work of the Spirit. What I want to emphasize is that the gift of Christ is made possible through the charismatic presence and activity of the Spirit of God; that the gift of grace in Christ rests on the Father's love of the Son in the Spirit; and that the gift of grace through

Christ is graciously empowered by the Spirit in the lives of Jesus' brothers and sisters.

I begin by noting that if in Acts the outpouring of the Spirit represents the gift of God to the disciples and the world, in Luke we might also understand the gift of the Spirit as a baptism of divine love specifically on the Son. Further, if in Acts the apostles are anointed with and empowered by the Spirit to bear witness to the good news of Christ, to offer the forgiveness of sins in his name, and to herald the restoration of Israel and the redemption of the world of the Gentiles, in Luke Jesus is the Christ, the prototype of these apostolic ministries as the one who received the Spirit of love. This refers not only to his conception by the power of the Spirit in the womb of Mary (Luke 1:35)[12] but also to his own reception of the Spirit. Arguably, the Spirit's coming upon and filling the apostolic believers in Acts is anticipated by the Spirit's paradigmatic descent upon Jesus, with the difference being that she came "upon him in bodily form like a dove" (3:22) while the Day of Pentecost arrival was "a sound like the rush of a violent wind" and in the form of "[d]ivided tongues, as of fire" (Acts 2:2-3).

What is made explicit about the gift of the Spirit to Jesus is announced in the voice from heaven: "You are my Son, the Beloved; with you I am well pleased" (3:22). The bodily form and presence of the gifted Spirit thus manifests the love of the Father for the Son. From another angle, the gift of the Spirit mediates the loving relationship of the Father and the Son. Going beyond the Father-Son relationship, the manifest love of the Father for the Son, represented by the Spirit as the dove, is also announced for the benefit of all the people (3:21). It is as if the people are also caught up in the love between the Father and the Son through the Spirit, thus anticipating the later baptism of the Spirit into divine love. So when we read in Acts about Jesus, who has been "exalted at the right hand of God, and having received from the Father the promise of the Holy Spirit, he has poured out this that you both see and hear" (Acts 2:33), we realize clearly that the Spirit not only manifests the Father's love for the Son but also mediates that loving relationship to all flesh.

From his baptism, of course, Jesus proceeds, "full of the Holy Spirit" (4:1) into the wilderness, undergoes his temptations by the satan, and then returns to Galilee, still "filled with the power of the Spirit" (4:14). Then the Third Evangelist records that in a Nazarene synagogue on a Sabbath day, Jesus reads from Isaiah the prophet:

> The Spirit of the Lord is upon me,
> because he has anointed me
> to bring good news to the poor.
> He has sent me to proclaim release to the captives
> and recovery of sight to the blind,
> to let the oppressed go free,
> to proclaim the year of the Lord's favor. (4:18-19; cf. Isa 61:1-2a)

If Acts 1:8 outlines the structure of that book's narrative, then Jesus' reading of and teaching from this Isaianic text here at the beginning of his public ministry sketches the main lines of the Lukan account of his life's significance.[13] Two points need to be emphasized for our purposes. First, Jesus' entire life and ministry is characterized as empowered by the Spirit. This is confirmed in Acts when Peter is recorded telling Cornelius about all that Jesus did and "how God anointed Jesus of Nazareth with the Holy Spirit and with power; how he went about doing good and healing all who were oppressed by the devil, for God was with him" (Acts 10:38). In other words, if Acts confirms that Jesus the anointed one, the Christ, does what he does by the power of the same Spirit who has now come upon and filled the disciples, then Luke announces that the messianic anointing consists of the abundant gift of the Spirit that bears and communicates the love of the Father for the Son, and that this gift of love anticipates the divine gift at Pentecost, which is now nothing less than the baptism of love for the restoration of Israel and the redemption of the world.

This means, second, that the Father's love for the Son communicated in and through the Spirit's descent and infilling of the Son began to inaugurate the restoration of Israel and the redemption of the world. The Isaianic text that Jesus self-identifies as framing his ministry makes this clear. The gift of the Spirit to the Son enables the salvific activities of the Son in proclamation, liberation, and healing, and also precipitates the "year of the Lord's favor," the long awaited year of Jubilee.[14] These redemptive activities thus reflect the extension of the Father's love for the Son to Israel in particular and, as extended within the wider Lukan corpus, to the world as a whole. So if the gift of the Spirit involves resting upon and filling the Son, then the gift of the Father through the Son to Israel and the world involves the gracious outpouring of the Spirit so that many hearts can experience the same infilling of liberative love and that the world can become a dwelling place of the Spirit and be fully inundated with the shalomic love of God's peace, justice, and righteousness.

It is against this backdrop that I wish to turn to Luke's presentation of the Great Commandment. This happens soon after the commissioning of the Seventy to heal the sick and herald that "The kingdom of God has come near to you" (10:9, 11). The Seventy returned in joyous celebration that "Lord, in your name even the demons submit to us!" (10:17), which in turn precipitated Jesus' rejoicing in the Spirit (10:21). Here we should not too quickly overlook that the authority of the Seventy over demons is no less than an extension of Jesus' Spirit-empowered authority over the satanic powers that oppose the arrival of the coming reign. If the gift of the Spirit of love to the Son enabled the exorcism of all powers of hatred, sickness, disease, oppressiveness, alienation, and destruction (4:33-37; 6:18; 7:21; 8:26-39; 9:37-42), then so also did the same baptism of divine love enable the Spirit-filled apostolic believers to deliver all who were oppressed by the devil and his minions (Acts 5:16; 8:6-7).[15]

It is in this immediate context of the success of the mission of the Seventy that the following conversation ensues:

> Just then a lawyer stood up to test Jesus. "Teacher," he said, "what must I do to inherit eternal life?" He said to him, "What is written in the law? What do you read there?" He answered, "You shall love the Lord your God with all your heart, and with all your soul, and with all your strength, and with all your mind; and your neighbor as yourself" [Deut 6:5; Lev 19:18]. And he said to him, "You have given the right answer; do this, and you will live." (10:25-28)

Following this, the lawyer sought to justify himself with the counter-question, "And who is my neighbor?" (10:29),[16] to which Jesus responded with the parable of the Good Samaritan (10:35). One of the practical outcomes Jesus sought appears to have been that the lawyer would "Go and do likewise" (10:37), according to the example of the Samaritan.

There is an extensive literature on the Good Samaritan, so we cannot hope to discuss this parable exhaustively. My goal, however, is much more limited: to understand Luke's version of the great or double love commandment within the broader context of Jesus' Spirit-filled life and ministry and the Day of Pentecost outpouring of the Spirit on all flesh.[17] The obvious point should be made first: that the love of neighbor should be expressed concretely in compassionate and benevolent deeds for any, even strangers, who are in need. The text says that the Samaritan was "moved with pity" (10:33)—that is, moved in his heart, or the inward parts of his being—by the one fallen on the wayside, enough so as to care for the man, put him on his animal, bring him to safety to be nursed to health, and pay for his care (10:34-36). This compassion is later seen enacted by those who were baptized in the Spirit of divine love in Acts 2–4. This is simply the outflow of having been touched by God's love so that human creatures are enabled both to love God in return, even with all that they are—heart, soul, strength and mind—and to love their neighbors as themselves (as did the Good Samaritan). This highlights one of the distinctive aspects of Luke's version of the Great Commandment: when compared with Matthew and Mark, Luke "combines them into a single unified command so that 'love of neighbor' has the same force as 'love for God.'"[18] In other words, God's gracious baptism of love enables the response of love to the baptizer—in effect, the lover—but also overflows with compassion toward the love of neighbor as part of that response. Love is no "objective" or dispassionate bystander; rather, love compels sympathy and brings about solidarity, even between those who are separated or divided in so many ways.

The second, almost-as-obvious point is that the love of neighbor includes the love of those who we might putatively identify as our enemies. The effectiveness of the parable presumes the enmity between Jews and Samaritans that is lost to most modern day readers.[19] The irony here is that if on the one hand Jesus rejoices with the Seventy that they have been enabled to triumph "over all the power of the enemy" (10:19), and if part of the vision of the restoration of Israel also included salvation from the hands of its enemies (1:71, 74), on the other hand Jesus also proclaimed through this parable the truth enacted by his Spirit-filled life: that the gift of God provided victory over "the enemy" in and through enabling benevolent service to them and solidarity with them. This message of love is consistent with the Spirit-filled ethics of Jesus, announced in the (Lukan) Sermon on the Plain in no uncertain terms: "Love your enemies, do good to those who hate you. . . . But love your enemies, do good, and lend, expecting nothing in return" (6:27, 35a; cf. Rom 12:17-21).[20]

More importantly, let us recall that the parable of the Good Samaritan was provoked initially by the lawyer's question about how to inherit eternal life. If in the Christian tradition, eternal life is God's supremely gracious gift to humankind, what we observe in this passage is how such an exceedingly wondrous gift of grace is made available to the world. Thus I want to highlight not necessarily the implication of this passage that salvation is available to those who merely respond in love to their needy neighbors. Rather, my emphasis is on the fact that the salvific deeds enacted are not just by a neighbor in the abstract but by a Samaritan stranger in response to a needy Jew in particular. The idea that salvation is available to Samaritans— to Gentiles, no less!—would have been especially troubling to Jews. But the Spirit who empowered proclamation of the reign of God through the Seventy is also the Spirit who led Jesus and his followers through Samaria and who prompted the castigation of James and John who sought to call down fire from heaven to destroy the unresponsive Samaritans (9:52-55). All the more provocative, then, were the words of this parable.[21] That the gift of the Spirit mediates the grace of God through the Samaritan suggests that all those who follow in his footsteps and who are recipients of his benevolence already participate in some respects in the eternal life of the Father and the Son.

So when understood against the broader context of the Lukan corpus, the interconnections between the Great Commandment and the parable of the Good Samaritan illuminate the Day of Pentecost gift of the Spirit. If the baptism of divine love was intended all along for any who would call upon the name of the Lord, those near and far away not only in space but also in time, then the point of the parable is at least twofold: that it is possible for any, near or far away, to respond to the saving initiatives of God in works of love, and that it is possible for those outside the Jewish covenant, specifically Samaritans and Gentiles, even their children and their children's children, to participate in the benefits lavished by God. In fact, it is precisely the outpouring of the Spirit on all flesh that makes it possible for even Samaritans and Gentiles, alongside Jews, to respond in compassionate benevolence. It is God who has first given eternal life, in Christ and the Spirit, so that all human beings, Jew, Samaritan, or Gentile, those even at the ends of the earth, can love God in return, and love their neighbors as themselves.

Luke and the Longing of Love: An Apostolic Spirituality of Love

It is now time to begin bringing part II of this volume to a close. Our efforts to draw from the wells of pentecostal spirituality for resources that can inform a pneumatological theology of love have led us in this chapter back through the modern pentecostal restorationist and primitivist hermeneutic to the apostolic experience, especially as recorded by Luke. We have reread the Day of Pentecost narrative and come to a fresh understanding of how the unrestricted outpouring of the Spirit on all flesh manifests God's gift of love to the world, and then returned to Luke's Gospel to see that this gift constitutes and even mediates—charismatically, through the presence and activity of the Spirit—God's universal love for the world through the Son. I now want to revisit the experience of the early church in the book of Acts to fill out the details of what could be understood as an apostolic spirituality of love.

To accomplish this task, I utilize as a lens what Steven Land calls the apocalyptic affections. Recall (in the previous chapter) that Land identified these affections—of gratitude, compassion, and courage—from out of a phenomenological analysis of the spirituality of the modern pentecostal movement. I suggest that these affective categories are helpful for mapping the apostolic experience. What I do not attempt is any direct correlation between Land's affections and early Christian affections.[22] Rather, what I hope to show is that the affections identified by Land can also make sense of the dominant apostolic practices as described in the book of Acts, in particular its spirituality of praise, empowered witness, and prayer. Doing so will also enable us to observe how contemporary pentecostal spirituality—sketched phenomenologically at the end of chapter 3 above—is understood by Pentecostals as simply a restoration of the practices of the early church.

For Land, gratitude reflects an affectivity oriented responsively and experientially to God's salvific actions. Gratitude is supremely a response to the realization of grace, not least for God's gifts in Christ and the Holy Spirit. Such gratitude is registered most palpably in the pentecostal testimony: look and see what the Lord has done.[23] In Acts, the more encompassing term is "witness." Yet this is an expansive notion. Within this rather all-inclusive category, however, is what is identifiable as gratitude. In particular, apostolic gratefulness manifests itself both in thanksgiving and praise, acts of glorifying God for what God has done.

We have already seen that the apostolic community was characterized by praise (Acts 2:47a; cf. 10:46).[24] God is praised for healing, saving, and restoring access to the divine presence (3:9),[25] and is thanked for the preservation of life (27:35) and for journeying mercies (28:15). Yet apostolic gratitude and praise was prevalent both in the so-called "good times" and amidst trials, tribulations, and threats (4:21). Indeed, God is praised not only for the extension of divine protection but for having counted mere "uneducated and ordinary men" (4:13) as "worthy to suffer dishonor for the sake of the name" (5:41). Even more important than what God had done *for* them, the apostles are thankful for what God was doing *through* them. Thus God is praised for astounding salvific actions having ramifications literally to the ends of the earth: that God "has given *even to the Gentiles* the repentance that leads to life" (11:18, emphasis added; 21:19-20). Even the Gentiles responded, upon realizing God's munificence, with praise for God's generosity and benefaction (13:48, 19:17).

Indeed, praising was an ancient rhetorical art, concerned with magnifying the righteousness and worthiness of the one being hallowed, particularly in response to the salvific power and accomplishments that are experienced. In Luke-Acts, praise is related to divine visitation, especially vis-à-vis the prophetic pronouncements about the redemption and restoration of Israel surrounding Jesus' birth (Luke 1:39-56, 67-79; 2:14, 29-32), his healings (5:26; 7:16; 13:7; 17:15-18; 18:43), and revelation of his identity as Messiah (10:20-23; 19:37-38; 23:47; 24:52). These praiseworthy events are implicit throughout the Acts narrative. In fact, the apostles bore witness in gratitude and praise to God's salvific and revelatory acts in Jesus Christ through the power of the Spirit.[26]

My point is that grateful praise is an affective response to the gift of God in Christ and the Spirit. This is the apostolic experience recounted by Luke. God is to be glorified because God has not forgotten the covenant promises made to Israel through Abraham. More astonishing, God is exceeding the letter of those promises since now the benefits of the covenant are being extended, not because they are merited, to Samaritans and all the Gentiles, even those at the ends of the earth. And God is fulfilling and extending the covenant through the gift of the deity itself, in the Son and in the Spirit. The former manifests the love of the Father for the world and the latter bathes, or baptizes, the world in the Father's love for the Son. Minimally, then, these outpourings of the divine love call forth affective, even passionate, replies of thanksgiving, praise, and worship. Reception of divine love compels affective expressions of love in turn.

If God's love calls forth affections of gratitude in response, then it also motivates the witness to love as a way of life. Land identifies this as the affect of compassion, by which he means the wholehearted devotion that energizes evangelism. This is also the compassion that Jesus characterizes as moving Good Samaritan-like acts of kindness, even for strangers and those labeled as enemies. In the book of Acts, however, such compassion is manifest obliquely, primarily in the communal fellowship and economic solidarity of the early messianic community. Yet the entire thrust of the Acts narrative can also be read as an outworking of the compassion of the apostolic believers, one that expressed their own amazement at being caught up in the baptism of love and thus being motivated to share that same baptism and its effects with others. So also did the Gentiles who later received the fullness of the Holy Spirit follow in the footsteps of those who received the Spirit on the Day of Pentecost: if the latter began to share what they had so that none had need, the former were also moved with compassion to respond to those among the "mother church" who were experiencing famine and "determined that according to their ability, each would send relief to the believers living in Judea" (Acts 11:29).

A window into this reading of Acts is opened up in Jesus' interactions with the sinner woman at the home of Simon the Pharisee (Luke 7:36-50). Simon objected perhaps to the erotic nature of the woman's washing Jesus' feet but certainly to her actions as a sinner (7:39). Jesus responded with a short parable of a creditor forgiving his debtors and then compared Simon's minimalist response to him with the woman's extravagant affections for him (7:44-46). And she did this, Jesus clarifies, because "her sins, which were many, have been forgiven; hence she has shown great love. But the one to whom little is forgiven, loves little" (7:47).[27] It is evident that this woman had previously encountered Jesus and received the forgiveness of sins.[28] And this heart of gratitude was expressed in an act of loving and affectionate witness.

My claim is that the disciples' own experience of the forgiveness of sins motivated not only their own affectionate response to Jesus in gratitude and prayer, but also their own heart of compassion for others. Thus did the baptism into divine love overflow into and even produce the apostolic life: the disciples became the "sent forth" ones who were in a sense empowered by the Spirit but in another sense driven by Spirit-filled hearts to the ends of the earth (as Jesus was into the desert and then into his ministry). And in this light it is no wonder that the central message of the gospel proclaimed by the disciples was the forgiveness of sins. If neither Jesus nor

God would hold it against the world that they had crucified the Son, then there would indeed be no sin that could not be absolved. Peter himself had experienced the forgiveness of repeated denial of Jesus, so that it was the baptism into divine love that empowered a boldness to witness that was absent before. Similarly, Ananias himself became a conduit for the infilling of Saul (later Paul), the one who had until just a few days before that zealously persecuted the followers of Christ (Acts 9:10-19). Hence were the disciples motivated to announce God's gracious forgiveness of sins to the world. Even if the world were not asking for forgiveness, or even if the world were unaware of its need for forgiveness, such was the gratuitous offer of God in Christ through the Spirit.

Thus the forgiveness of sins not only unites human beings with the love of God but also reconciles those otherwise hostile to or estranged from one another.[29] The good news of forgiveness brings with it the gospel of joy, communion, and peace (Acts 10:36; cf. Luke 7:50). This message of peace is also, of course, anticipated in the life and ministry of Jesus, the one sent "to guide our feet into the way of peace" (Luke 1:79). His coming brought with it the pronouncement of peace on earth (2:14), and his ministry brought about peace in the hearts and lives of those touched by him (8:48).[30] To be sure, the message of Christ would be divisive, setting off those who received it from those who rejected it (12:51). Yet it was peace that the gospel was designed to bring about, and this was the first message of those sent to herald the rule of God (10:5-6). How could it be otherwise, if the Spirit-anointed Messiah was indeed beloved of the Father and represented the Father's covenant faithfulness to the world? And how could it be otherwise if the Son thereafter sent the Spirit to baptize into a divine love that brought about and enabled the forgiveness of sins for all? No wonder, then, that the work of the Spirit and the enjoyment of peace are mentioned in tandem in the apostolic experience (Acts 9:31).[31]

Last but not least, the apostolic spirituality of love features not only praise and power but also prayer. This is my way of mapping the apostolic spirituality and practice in light of Land's apocalyptic affections of gratitude, compassion, and courage. Land means by courage the confident hope that anticipates the final victory of God over the powers of evil, and that lives out this assurance in missionizing the world. Here the practices of courage as an apocalyptic affection overlap with those of compassion. The distinction I would make, however, is whereas the affect of compassion moves human hearts to engage the world, the affect of courage is buoyed by the ongoing and dynamic relationship of prayer, which both is given in and invites repeated visitations of the Spirit who baptizes in divine love.

What I mean is that courageous hope is a Christian affection nurtured in the apostolic experience by the practice of prayerful relationship with God. Prayer was certainly a staple of the apostolic life (Acts 2:42b; 3:1; 10:9; 16:13; 22:17). The Pentecost event was itself precipitated by a prolonged period of prayer (1:14), and this may have initiated a regular practice of prayer for the gift of the Holy Spirit (8:15). The messianic believers also accomplished miracles, signs, and wonders through prayerful reliance on God's saving and healing power (9:40-41; 28:8), and many other major decisions and events in the life of the nascent Christian community were informed by prayer (6:6; 13:2-3; 14:23; 20:36; 21:5).

Most important for our purposes, however, is the persistent prayer of the earliest followers of Jesus in the midst of persecution. Even after imprisonment during the early days of the communal movement in Jerusalem, the apostles reconvened in worship and prayer (Acts 4:24), asking for divine power to proclaim the gospel, heal the sick, and perform miraculous deeds. The divine answer was swift and unmistakable: "When they had prayed, the place in which they were gathered together was shaken; and they were all filled with the Holy Spirit and spoke the word of God with boldness" (4:31). Later it was said of Stephen's prayers, even in the moments preceding his demise at the hands of his persecutors, that they were inspired by the fullness of the Holy Spirit (7:55, 59). But if the answer to Stephen's prayer was not his earthly salvation but instead his heavenly "promotion," the apostolic community nevertheless persevered in prayer throughout their times of trial and tribulation (12:5). This was no doubt in taking after Jesus as a model of prayer.[32]

There are two aspects of the apostolic practice of prayer that deserve further comment in light of courageous hope as a Christian affection. First, the courage of the apostles was not only informed by the manifest faithfulness of a covenant keeping God—for which they were grateful—but also by the conviction that the fulfillment of the divine promises had begun only in part and was yet still to come. This meant that prior experiences of the love of God remained in a sense incomplete and thus had an eschatological component. One could not rest satisfied with what God had done in the past but one could be hopeful, even courageously so, that what God had done was a sign that God would also bring to pass what had been prom-ised. Prayer thus was an expression of this ongoing relationship of depen-dence on the faithfulness of divine love. Hopeful affections were therefore also similarly informed by trusting a covenant keeping and loving God. Thus St. Paul, at his trial before King Agrippa, pointed to the "promise that our twelve tribes hope to attain, as they earnestly worship day and night. It is for this hope, your Excellency, that I am accused by Jews!" (Acts 26:7).[33]

Christian hope is also expressed and realized, in alternation, in the prayers that move the heart of God. The God who loves and who baptizes in love will not ignore those whose prayers cry out in love and for love (Luke 11:9-10). More precisely, as Jesus said, "If you then, who are evil, know how to give good gifts to your children, how much more will the heavenly Father give the Holy Spirit to those who ask him!" (11:13). It is not surprising, then, that the deepest of the apostolic affections, expressed most palpably in their prayers and cries, brings about not just a generic divine response, but another baptism of the Spirit into divine love (Acts 4:31). If prayer is the means through which the beloved of God express their love, longing, and hopes to God, even in times of trial, then the apos-tolic experience promises that the response involves nothing less than the further emboldening and empowering of the Spirit through a deeper bap-tism into divine love.

What I have attempted in this section is a correlation of Land's apoca-lyptic affections of gratitude, compassion, and courage with the apostolic practices of praise, empowered witness, and prayer. Praise and thanksgiv-ing are focused on what God has done, empowered witness is attuned to God's ongoing redemptive deeds, and prayer is oriented in hopeful desire for the coming reign of God.[34] In this way, we have been able to sketch the main lines of a charismatic and graced spirituality of love while enriching Land's analysis in light of the apostolic witness.

Conclusion

This chapter has attempted to flesh out what the early modern Pentecostals experienced and called the baptism of love by returning to the pentecos-tal canon-within-the-canon, the book of Acts particularly, but including the Gospel of Luke more generally. Our main strategy has been a retrieval of the Day of Pentecost narrative specifically, and the Lukan corpus as a whole, as highlighting the unqualified outpouring of the Spirit as a gift of divine love. These Lukan considerations bring us full circle, back to the biblical traditions at the heart of pentecostal spirituality, in pursuing what this part of the book has identified as resources from the pentecostal tradition for a reconsideration of theology of love. To be sure, our movement from the phenomenology and performativity of pentecostal spirituality through the second order reflections of pentecostal theology (chaps. 4 and 5) may be accused of framing our rereading of the Lukan material in a way that deforms rather than is faithful to the overt intentions of its author. I have two rejoinders in anticipation of this charge.

First, contrary to the claims of some who privilege the author's intent as normative for interpreting and understanding a text, I contend not only that there is no avenue to that intent apart from the produced text but also that there are meanings embedded within texts that authors may not have intended explicitly but would recognize as consistent with what was written when pointed out to them by readers.[35] So with regard to the Lukan texts specifically, on the one hand, I would affirm that there is no way around the hermeneutical circle or spiral, so that there is no a priori approach that eliminates the biases of readers in interaction with the intentions of authors mediated through texts; if there is no "objective" reading from nowhere, then there are only intersubjective engagements with texts, so that my pentecostal reading will have to assessed both with and against those provided by others. On the other hand, it is in the nature of texts to invite a pluralism of readings; this is not to say that all readings are equal, but it is to say that the pentecostal reading I have provided needs to be assessed on its merits, not dismissed merely because it consciously unfolds out of a pentecostal perspective.

Second, though, what is proffered in this chapter is only the first of a three-part effort to articulate what might be called a biblical-pneumatological theology of divine love. I suggest that when read canonically, especially in tandem with the Pauline and Johannine witness, the preceding delineation of Lukan theology of the outpouring of the Spirit understood as a baptism of divine love is not only all the more defensible but even unavoidable. The power of love understood on the Lukan register is the transformational mission of a people unconditionally filled with the Spirit. The most miraculous signs and wonders are not merely the astounding healings or even the resurrection from the dead but the vivifying of peoples and communities touched by the Spirit as the flame of love. Hearts are affectively ignited, hands are effectively empowered, and lives are radically transformed as the reign of the time to come and of the Spirit breaks into and turns the present world upside down (cf. Acts 17:6). Moving forward from here, then, we shall also see that this Lukan contribution can shed fresh light on the pneumatological dimensions of love explicated elsewhere in the Christian Testament.

PART III

• • •

GOD IS SPIRIT, GOD IS LOVE
The Gift of the Spirit and the Gift of Love

CHAPTER 7

• • •

Love and the Gift/s of the Spirit

A Pauline Pneumatology of Love

In this part of the book we build on the retrievals of part II—from pentecostal spirituality, theology, and biblical interpretation—toward a pneumatological theology of love, the overall goal of this volume. Our reading
of St. Paul and the Johannine material in this and the next chapter will be
informed by our theological commitments regarding the gift of the Spirit
as a baptism of love as well as our Lukan perspectives on God's excessively
abundant outpouring of the Spirit as a further expression of the Father's
Love for the Son. I want to stay fairly close to the biblical text in what follows both in order to bring Luke into discussion with other New Testament
voices and in order to provide a more secure scriptural grounding for some
of our more speculative claims in the last chapter, where I present a manifesto on a pneumatology of love in nine theses.

Of course, given our intentions, the following cannot hope to present
any exhaustive treatment of either the Pauline or Johannine selections or
even pretend to interact with the voluminous existing secondary literature.[1] In fact, as will be clear, we will be engaging only a few passages within
both corpora. Even with these limitations, we will still not be able to take
up all of the critical matters "behind" the text, much less the contested
rhetorical and literary issues within these texts. Our approach is strictly
thematic (circulating around the topic of love) and theological (motivated

largely by the gains made so far), and is intended to bring pentecostal perspectives to bear on the formulation of a pneumatology of love.

This chapter will focus on two sections of Paul's writings: 1 Corinthians 12–14 and Romans 5–8. The first section explores what might be called an ecclesiology of love, with love being at the heart not only of the spiritual gifts operative within the congregation of God but also as a gift of the Spirit to the people of God. The last two sections will then turn to the middle part of Paul's letter to the Romans and develop both a cosmology and a soteriology of love that is informed by the gift and work of the Spirit. What we hope to accomplish here is both a confirmation of the Lukan thesis regarding the gift of the Spirit as a baptism of love and an enrichment of that thesis in light of Paul's corrective admonishments to the Corinthians and his didactic instructions for the Romans.

The Greatest of These Is Love: An Ecclesiology of Love

There have been numerous studies of the spiritual gifts in 1 Corinthians 12 and 14 that have also commented on the centrality of love in chapter 13.[2] Inevitably, pentecostal readings of this part of St. Paul's first letter to the Corinthians have focused on his instructions regarding the spiritual gifts and their normative implications for charismatic manifestations in the congregation. Further, these charismatic gifts have been read also alongside other lists of gifts in the New Testament, including the charisms or grace-gifts in Romans 12:3-8. Although the charisms and spiritual gifts are certainly nothing less than manifestations of divine grace, my approach will be slightly different, informed by the preceding discussion. In particular, I want to talk about the spiritual gifts as specific expressions of the most fundamental gift of love, and of all gifts as constitutive of the gift of the Holy Spirit, who is love.[3]

I begin by noting that at least within pentecostal circles, concerns have usually revolved around curbing the abuses that often arise with the manifestation of the spiritual gifts.[4] As should be clear from Paul's own emphasis on the importance of order in the charismatic congregation (1 Cor 14:26-40),[5] that was also a major issue for the Corinthians. Part of the problem has to do with how the spiritual gifts sometimes manifest themselves powerfully or spectacularly—one of them is called, after all, "the working of miracles" or, literally, powerful or miraculous works (ἐνεργήματα δυνάμεων; 12:10). Regular or even periodic materialization of such phenomena will no doubt lead congregants, not to mention visiting outsiders, to "bow down before God and worship him, declaring, 'God is really among you'" (14:25). But such incidents will also nurture, if cautions are not in place, spiritual pride and elitism, as it surely did among the Corinthians, in particular many of its charismatically gifted leaders.

Undeniably Paul invoked love in relationship to the spiritual gifts in part to counter these tendencies in this charismatically inclined congregation, but he also says something else about the power dynamics of the gifts that needs to be heeded. Whereas on the surface it may be thought that the more gifts are present the more the power of the Spirit is at work, Paul actually insists that it is the less honorable, less respectable, and less presentable members of the body who or that are valued of God. In Paul's own words, "the members of the body that seem to be weaker are indispensable, and those members of the body that we think less honorable we clothe with greater honor, and our less respectable members are treated with greater respect; whereas our more respectable members do not need this. But God has so arranged the body, giving the greater honor to the inferior member" (12:22-24). This is consistent with Paul's repeated urging that whereas the Corinthians might think themselves strong, eloquent, wise, and powerful, God has actually chosen the weak, foolish, and despicable of the world to manifest the divine character (1:18-31).[6] It is also but an extension of Paul's own ministry experience and self-understanding: that even if he were perceived to be weak (2 Cor 10:10), it is precisely in his weakness that he is graced by the power of God (2 Cor 12:9-10). In short, "Spiritual gifts are to be understood as gifts of God's grace, not evidences of man's [sic] achievement."[7] That is exactly what the *charisms* denote: that they have a gratuitous character which is most powerfully manifest on or through those who are neither strong nor powerful in their own eyes but are dependent on the generosity of Spirit's gifts.[8] In this reading, the spiritual gifts are precisely charisms—gifts of grace—that are bestowed by the Spirit unconditionally upon undeserving creatures.

I have taken this slight detour in order to highlight how the gifts are less status indicators or marks of power conceived in worldly terms than they are signs of God's counterconventional *modus operandi*. The many parts of the body are all important because, to resort to a Lukan phrase, "God shows no partiality" (Acts 10:34). Paul puts it this way: that "it is the same God who activates all of them [spiritual gifts, services, and activities—12:4-6] in everyone" (12:6), and "[a]ll these are activated by one and the same Spirit, who allots to each one individually just as the Spirit chooses" (12:11). To put it pneumatologically, the Spirit is no respecter of persons; the gift of God in the Spirit is given freely to all, even to the "weakest" of all flesh, at least as understood from the world's perspective. Thus the fellowship of the Spirit is an egalitarian and democratic dynamic that breaks down human elitism, classism, and any other divisions that might be erected. This is part of God's graciously redemptive work by the Spirit.

This segues into our consideration of the famous love chapter of 1 Corinthians 13. Here I need to begin by saying the obvious: that Paul's exposition of authentic love is inserted in the middle of a discussion on the spiritual gifts, between their general role in the Christian congregation (chap. 12) and the outworking of the gifts of tongues and prophecy more particularly (chap. 14), and intended to address shortcomings he observes among the Corinthian Christians. In other words, what Paul has to say about love relates to his theology of the gifts; on the other hand, Paul's charismatic theology also can be extricated from his theology of love and from his pastoral concerns for the Corinthians.[9] So while our focus will be what Paul says about love that is accentuated when we approach this passage from a pentecostal, pneumatological, and charismatic perspective, we should always keep in the back of our mind the sociohistorical situation at Corinth. With this in hand, I will make three sets of comments, corresponding to the three basic sections of this love hymn or poem.

First, love is "a more excellent way" (12:31b). Eloquent tongues (evidently prized by the Corinthians, as chapter 14 makes clear) without love is just noise; prophecy and knowledge (also similarly valued by the church at Corinth) without love is merely data (in fact, Paul had earlier said: "Knowledge puffs up, but love builds up" [8:1b]); faith that moves mountains without love is nothing; self-sacrificial benevolence without love "gain[s] nothing" (13:3). Thus have commentators concluded that love "stands supreme as the more excellent motivation for the manifestation of spiritual gifts,"[10] or that love is or should be "the medium" for the expression of the charismata.[11] Beyond being the motivation or the medium of the charismata, love could also be understood as being at the heart of *the identity* of the truly Spirit-filled life.[12] If this is the case, then we find a Pauline correlation to the pentecostal baptisms of empowerment and of love: here, the charismatic life is powerful—for the Corinthians and for other Christians—precisely because it is fundamentally loving.

Yet the mystery of love is such that of the various descriptions (13:4-7), what we find there are both positive statements about love's character and negative ones about what true love does *not* do or is *not* supposed to be. Love is patient; love is kind; love rejoices in the truth; it "bears all things, believes all things, hopes all things, endures all things." But love is *not* envious, *not* boastful, *not* arrogant, *not* rude; it "does *not* insist on its own way; it is *not* irritable or resentful; it does *not* rejoice in wrong-doing" (emphasis added). In short, love is manifest in concrete action, but it is also no less palpably *inactive* in various respects. Hence there is a certain passivity with regard to genuine love, one suggestive of what Solivan calls orthopathos: a redemptive form of passion that perseveres through some kinds of experiences without reacting in the normal ways dictated by human conventions of power. This is the case even with regard to the positive descriptions for love, especially its capacity to bear under and persevere through all things. Put another way, *not* being or *not* doing certain things are passionate manifestations of redemptive love gifted by the Holy Spirit. Thus there is the submissive dimension of love's passionate reception of all things—one all the more important for an aggressively engaged Corinthian leadership—even as there is the active dimension of love's compassionate response in turn.

But, and this is my third comment, even not being or not doing what is not loving gestures toward how "Love never ends" (13:8a). This is both because love is not merely a thing but is a way of life,[13] and because such a path has an eschatological dimension oriented toward the final redemption and revelation of the God who is love. So for "a community torn by a spirit of factionalism,"[14] the apostle urges the way of love, one that remains and is even greater than faith or hope (13:13). This dynamic and eschatological character of love reflects the vibrancy and unpredictability of the Spirit of love, poured out in the last days upon all flesh.[15]

What then is the point of love as a central identifier of the charismatic or Spirit-filled life? That it consists of what might be called orthopathic or redemptive service. When discussing the spiritual gifts as dispersed among the members of the congregation, Paul writes, "To each is given the manifestation of the Spirit for the common good" (12:7). Thus the members of the body support one another, suffer with each other, and rejoice and encourage one another (12:26). Then, when discussing the manifestations of tongues and prophecy in the congregation, Paul repeatedly invokes the cardinal principle of discerning their appropriateness: "that the church may be built up" (14:5b), that their expressions are "for building up the church" (14:12), and that "all things be done for building up" (14:26b). He also puts it negatively: if tongues persist without interpretation, the tongues speaker "may give thanks well enough, but the other person is not built up" (14:17). In short, the major criterion governing the expression of the spiritual gifts is whether or not others are being edified. And if it is the common good that is at stake, then the love of the Spirit might even call members of the ecclesial "in-group" to break out of its tribalism and love those who are outside of the congregation.[16] This is why Paul presents what might be understood as a new paradigm of Christian life and ecclesial relations, one defined by love that challenges the Corinthian congregation's charismatic self-understanding.[17]

Of course, Paul named one other standard by which to identify the Spirit's charismatic activity: "no one speaking by the Spirit of God ever says 'Let Jesus be cursed!' and no one can say 'Jesus is Lord' except by the Holy Spirit" (12:3). Paul's christological norm here is consistent with the Lukan theology of salvation history. If the Spirit is none other than the Spirit sent by Jesus the Christ and Jesus is also none other than the man anointed by the Holy Spirit, then the Spirit will do nothing less than inspire confession of and action oriented to the lordship of Jesus even as the manifestation of the Spirit's manifold gifts, services, and activities is identifiable by the love of the Father for the Son. The body of Christ is most representative of Jesus when she charismatically embodies the Father's love for the Son, and the fellowship of the Spirit is most expressive of the anointed Christ when she charismatically enacts the love of the Father and the Son.

The preceding discussion proceeds from the fundamental theological premises that the charisms of the Spirit are related to the unconditional gift of the Spirit and that love is "nothing less than God's gift"[18] through the Spirit. The charismatic gifts are misguided when apart from love, even as love itself is most powerfully manifest when the Spirit's gifts are present and active, especially through those who are truly undeserving according to the world's standards, for the edification of others. If we are urged to "strive for the greater gifts" (12:31a) of the Spirit, then love is indeed the charism above all gifts, indeed, the greatest gift of the Spirit (13:13).

The Spirit Groans within Us: A Cosmology of Love

Turning from 1 Corinthians to Romans will help us see other aspects of love as the greatest gift of the Spirit, indeed as *the* gift of the Spirit herself. We proceed right to the climax of Paul's doctrinal reflections on why "There is therefore now no condemnation for those who are in Christ Jesus" (Rom 8:1).[19] The culmination of the argument appeals to the surety provided in the love of God in Christ:

> Who will separate us from the love of Christ? Will hardship, or distress, or persecution, or famine, or nakedness, or peril, or sword?[20] As it is written,
>
> > "For your sake we are being killed all day long;
> > we are accounted as sheep to be slaughtered." [cf. Ps 44:22]
>
> No, in all these things we are more than conquerors through him who loved us. For I am convinced that neither death, nor life, nor angels, nor rulers, nor things present, nor things to come, nor powers, nor height, nor depth, nor anything else in all creation, will be able to separate us from the love of God in Christ Jesus our Lord. (8:35-39)

This is a remarkable passage that highlights the invincibility of the divine love manifest in Christ that elects, foreknows, predestines, calls, justifies, and glorifies (8:29-32) all "those who love God" (8:28) in response.[21] Paul's rhetoric is unmistakable: not only are believers absolutely safe in the love of God but historical or experiential circumstances are incapable of undermining that security, just as cosmic forces "in *all* creation" (emphasis added)—anywhere, any-who, or any-how—are unable to do so. The love of God in Christ thus never encounters insurmountable barriers in accomplishing the work of redemption.[22]

Where is the Spirit in this hymn of God's unconquerable love? Implicit in the foreground to this specific passage but explicit in the background. Implicitly, first of all, the love of God is manifest in Jesus who was given "up for all of us" (8:32) precisely as the Spirit anointed Christ. (In fact, the Spirit is specifically denoted as being both *of God* and *of Christ* [8:9], which is consistent with the image of the dove that descended simultaneously with the voice that rang forth announcing the Father's love for the Son.) Second, the same Christ Jesus, "who died, yes, who was raised, who is *at the right hand of God*, who indeed intercedes for us" (8:34b, emphasis added) is the one who, we have seen Luke tell us, poured out the Spirit upon all flesh from that "right hand of God" (Acts 2:33). Third, in response to the rhetorical question that if God "did not withhold his own Son . . . will he not with him also give us everything else?" (8:32), the response inferable from the Third Evangelist, through the lips of Jesus, is that, "If you then, who are evil, know how to give good gifts to your children, how much more will the heavenly Father give the Holy Spirit to those who ask him!" (Luke 11:13). The Spirit is thus implicitly present in the gift of the Son and in God's gift of everything else to the world, gifts that express the Father's insuperable love for the Son.

The Spirit is also explicitly present in the backdrop anticipating this hymnic celebration of divine love. As pentecostal biblical scholar John Bertone has noted, while the Holy Spirit appears thirty-five times in the Epistle to the Romans, twenty-one of these references occur in the first twenty-seven verses of the eighth chapter.[23] Paul's theology of unassailable love is therefore intimately tied in with his pneumatology, in particular what might be called, in the first part of Romans 8, his eschatological theology of life in the Spirit. What the Spirit does is bring to fulfillment the redemptive work of God. This redemption involves four elements: first, liberty from the realm of sin and death (8:2) and deliverance from the sinful nature and its effects (8:4); second, enablement of a life of peace (8:6); third, resurrection from the dead, both for Jesus (8:11a; cf. 1:4; 4:24) and for the mortal bodies of human creatures (8:11b); and fourth, freedom from fear (8:15) through adoption as children of God (8:14-16). This is the salvation of God in Christ through the Spirit, what the Reformers emphasized as God's gracious gift to humankind, to be received not by works but purely by faith.

Yet these soteriological benefits are set within an eschatological horizon. This is most clearly signaled in the resurrection of Jesus, which is the proleptic event heralding the full resurrection to come. Thus Paul here operates within a partially realized eschatological framework, one that acknowledges that in the resurrection of Christ, we have entered into what Luke calls "the last days" (Acts 2:17). In this inaugurated eschatology, the Spirit's cosmic work is further evident in the groaning of creation as it awaits "the freedom of the glory of the children of God" (8:21) and yearns for "the redemption of our bodies" (8:23). More specifically, the Spirit is present to inspire creaturely prayer amidst the suffering, decay, and bondage of this age that is passing away (8:18-21; cf. 1 Cor 2:6b): "Likewise the Spirit helps us in our weakness; for we do not know how to pray as we ought, but that very Spirit intercedes with sighs too deep for words. And

God, who searches the heart, knows what is the mind of the Spirit, because the Spirit intercedes for the saints according to the will of God" (8:26-27). Herein also we find the characteristic Pauline theme of strength in weakness—in this case, the powerful presence of the Spirit is manifest in the unutterable groans, cries, and prayers amidst the suffering of creation.[24]

In another article, Bertone has argued—in dialogue with many advocates and detractors—that the "sighs too deep for words" in Romans 8:26 can and even should refer to glossolalia and that this therefore represents what might be considered the eschatological passion and prayer language of those filled with the Spirit.[25] In effect, such glossolalic sighs are yearnings for the glorious age to come, in some respects intoning here and now, in human speech that is broken and halting, about the glory that has already begun to be unveiled in the resurrection of the Son and the outpouring of the Spirit. When read in light of the remainder of this eighth chapter, however, I suggest that the already-but-not-yet work of the Spirit can be understood as interrelatedly eschatological and cosmic. This cosmic dimension can be unpacked at two levels.

First, note that our lives are bound up with the created order. Thus our sighs synchronize with the creation's moaning. Such synchronicity has both material and spiritual dimensions. Materially, the Pauline discourse captures the embodied, emotional, and affective dimensions of human passions and hopes,[26] thus denoting how entangled and intertwined we are as creatures of dust with the stuff of the world. In effect, we participate as embodied beings with the world's sufferings even as the creation as a whole cries out under the bondage of sin wrought by human disobedience. On the one hand, we are impacted by the anguish of creation; on the other hand, the creation is burdened by our sin and affliction. It is in this fallen condition that we cannot even begin to pray rightly, much less according to the will of God; but once again, the gift of God in the Spirit restores our relationship to a world otherwise alienated and estranged from us by sin. This reconciliation effects solidarity between the world and its creatures, thus transforming the cosmos from being a hostile wasteland into a home, even if that awaits final restoration. It also gives us the gift of prayer, even if this is expressible only as unutterable sighs that reverberate with the aching of creation. The Spirit is passionately intertwined with and testifies to and bears witness with our spirits (8:17), enabling our sharing in the sufferings and resurrection of Christ (8:17), given for the sake of the world.[27]

Even more, the Spirit inspires our hopes for salvation so as to echo the creation's yearning for liberation in anticipation of the final and future revelation of God. This cosmic liberation is thus a mirror image of the Spirit's redemptive aspirations. The elements that keep or attempt to keep the cosmos hostage to sin, suffering, and decay—the grip of sin, death, fear, and antagonistic hostility between creatures and between creation and its Creator—have been overcome by the Spirit of God in Christ. Creation and its creatures now can begin to hope rightly, to yearn correctly, and to desire to be caught up in nothing less than the full manifestation of the Father's love of the Son. It is because of the Spirit's cosmic liberation that Paul is able to insist that nothing in the cosmos can thwart the salvific outworking of God's love in Christ. The Spirit who binds human creatures with the life of the resurrected one is the same Spirit who redeems the world and overcomes the powers of sin, hate, and death.

It is this orthopathic movement of the Spirit, I suggest, that works transformatively to redeem the sufferings of the present time through a baptism of the creation into filial love of God. That love is capable of overcoming all obstacles opposing the union of the beloved with the Father's love for the Son, and is desirous of reaching beyond any chasm in order to fill the cosmos with divine love. God is thus at work orthopathically, touched by the suffering of creation, but thereby moved in the love of Christ to pour out the Spirit upon the world so that it can be sanctified, redeemed, and restored as the dwelling place of love.[28]

The Spirit Poured into Our Hearts: A Soteriology of Love

I now turn to chapter 5, which many scholars believe begins this part of the letter to the Romans that culminates with the love hymn at the end of chapter 8.[29] It is here that Paul makes a statement, almost in passing it seems, linking love and the Holy Spirit that has perennially resounded in the Christian theological tradition. I want to show how, in light of our argument so far, the central theological message of this Epistle, long understood as being primarily about God's gracious gift of justification, can also be comprehended as the Spirit's unconditional gift or baptism of divine love. I begin by quoting this introductory portion in full:

> Therefore, since we are justified by faith, we have peace with God through our Lord Jesus Christ, through whom we have obtained access to this grace in which we stand; and we boast in our hope of sharing the glory

of God. And not only that, but we also boast in our sufferings, knowing that suffering produces endurance, and endurance produces character, and character produces hope, and hope does not disappoint us, because God's love has been poured into our hearts through the Holy Spirit that has been given to us. (5:1-5)

The "therefore" that introduces this part of the Epistle alerts us to the foregoing argument, wherein Paul exhorts the Roman Christians to receive their justification by faith following in the footsteps of Abraham. Since this is God's way of salvation, the Romans can be at peace with God in Christ (5:1). This is the peace of God that overcomes all fears, so Paul repeatedly reminds his Roman readers that peace is their possession in Christ, a peace for themselves and for their relationships with others (1:7; 2:10; 8:6; 12:18; 14:17, 19; 15:13, 33; 16:20). This peace is based on hope amid suffering that cannot be disappointed because of the surety of the love of God given to us in the Spirit.[30] In short, this passage marks a transition: we have been justified by faith and given peace with God in Christ, so now let us live in faith and in peace through Christ by the power of the Spirit. Romans 5–8 presents an argument about how new life in Christ overcomes sin and death through the Spirit.

This new life is also a life of love, given in the Spirit, from which nothing can separate believers. "God proves his love for us in that while we still were sinners Christ died for us" (5:8). Not only has God revealed his love in Christ, God is now bound to us in love by the Spirit given to our hearts. This is therefore no external love, located merely in a historical figure from Nazareth. Rather this is the Father's love for the Son that is given to, shared with, and internalized within us. Now Paul does not talk explicitly in Romans about the gift of the Holy Spirit (although that language does appear in the wider Pauline canon: 1 Cor 6:19; Gal 3:14; Eph 1:13). Instead, God's gracious gift is in Christ (5:15; 6:23), a gift that dispenses with our works as the necessary condition for receiving God's salvation (4:4). The gift of Christ is effective for our salvation precisely because the Spirit has been poured out into our hearts. Hence, "we are slaves not under the old written code but in the new life of the Spirit" (7:6).

Of course, it is not that believers may not still struggle with sin or the fear of death. The internal struggle in human hearts simply is a microcosm of the cosmic struggle in all of creation.[31] Yet the weakness of our flesh in the present life is made strong through the Spirit who not only raised

Jesus from the dead "for our justification" (4:25) but also empowers mere human beings by indwelling them (8:11). Hence the love of God both is manifested externally and historically in the world in the life, death, and resurrection of Christ and illuminates our hearts through the Holy Spirit. If that is the case, nothing can separate us from the love of God in Christ because that love is not separate from us but has already been given to us—deposited in our hearts, to be more precise—in and through the unqualified gift of the Holy Spirit.

The Spirit that was given to us was also the Spirit given to the Son, coming with the declaration of the Father's love for the Son. For the same reason, then, we who now have the Spirit also have the love of the Father and of the Son. And if the Father loved the Son in the Spirit, so also does the Father now love those who have been given the Spirit. Thus Paul writes, "For all who are led by the Spirit of God are children of God. For you did not receive a spirit of slavery to fall back into fear, but you have received a spirit of adoption. When we cry, 'Abba! Father!' it is that very Spirit bearing witness with our spirit that we are children of God, and if children, then heirs, heirs of God and joint heirs with Christ" (8:14-17a). In other words, the Spirit who is the love of the Father for the Son is now the Spirit that is the love of the Father for all who are in the Son. Put another way, the Father who loves the Son in the Spirit now also loves all those who are in the Son by the same Spirit. Thus are the gift of Christ and the gift of the Spirit two sides of the one coin of divine love, the former reflecting and the latter expressing God's salvific passion for the world. And if nothing can separate the love of the Father for the Son because of the bond of the Spirit, then nothing can separate the love of the Father for the children of God because of the love of the Son and the Spirit's bond of love in our hearts.

What then are the ethical and practical consequences of this inviolable and excessive baptism of love? We are caught up in spiritual worship and urged to renew our minds according to the will of God (12:1-2). This renewal occurs at least in part, as Aquinas urged, through the charismatic or gracious endowments of the Spirit (12:3-8, which is a shorter version of what is explicated at greater length in 1 Cor 12). The Spirit's gifts open up to the normative life of love (12:9-21),[32] constituted by loving responses and relationships:

> Let love be genuine; hate what is evil, hold fast to what is good; love one another with mutual affection; outdo one another in showing honor. Do

not lag in zeal, be ardent in spirit, serve the Lord. Rejoice in hope, be patient in suffering, persevere in prayer. Contribute to the needs of the saints; extend hospitality to strangers. Bless those who persecute you; bless and do not curse them. Rejoice with those who rejoice, weep with those who weep. Live in harmony with one another; do not be haughty, but associate with the lowly; do not claim to be wiser than you are. Do not repay anyone evil for evil, but take thought for what is noble in the sight of all. If it is possible, so far as it depends on you, live peaceably with all. Beloved, never avenge yourselves, but leave room for the wrath of God; for it is written, "Vengeance is mine, I will repay, says the Lord." No, "if your enemies are hungry, feed them; if they are thirsty, give them something to drink; for by doing this you will heap burning coals on their heads." Do not be overcome by evil, but overcome evil with good.[33]

Then, after giving instructions for how to live in relationship to the political authorities (13:1-7), Paul continues, reworking the Great Commandment, "Owe no one anything, except to love one another; for the one who loves another has fulfilled the law. The commandments, 'You shall not commit adultery; You shall not murder; You shall not steal; You shall not covet'; and any other commandment, are summed up in this word, 'Love your neighbor as yourself.' Love does no wrong to a neighbor; therefore, love is the fulfilling of the law" (13:8-10). There is much to comment on in these passages, even as we are constrained by both space and time. Let me thus unpack the preceding in light of Paul's discussion of relationships between the weak and the strong in Romans 14–15.

The issue here has to do with those who were more mature spiritually versus those, particularly Jewish Christians, who were concerned that certain activities, such as the eating of meat, would undermine authentic faith.[34] The outworking of the principle of the Great Commandment meant that "If your brother or sister is being injured by what you eat, you are no longer walking in love. Do not let what you eat cause the ruin of one for whom Christ died" (14:15). What the Romans were called to, in other words, was not the life of law but the life of love. And the latter was nothing less than life in the Spirit: "For the kingdom of God is not food and drink but righteousness and peace and joy in the Holy Spirit" (14:17).[35] The Spirit's baptism of love means that followers of Jesus the Messiah are no longer bound to the letter of the law but that any edification of or peaceful overture to (14:19; 15:2) the neighbor—strong or weak, friend or enemy, altruist or evildoer, as delineated in the earlier passage on love in Romans

12—would be a fulfillment of the law. And it is, after all, the Spirit who gives to each believer, weak or strong, his or her measure of faith according to the grace (χάριτος) of God (12:3).[36] The result would be a fulfillment of Paul's prayer and desire for the Roman congregation: "May the God of hope fill you with all joy and peace in believing, so that you may abound in hope by the power of the Holy Spirit" (15:13).

I have suggested that we can understand Paul's theology of love in the Epistle to the Romans in relationship to the gift of the Spirit. In fact, Paul's theology of grace, and of God's gift of salvation by justification by grace through faith, is also intimately tied up with this pneumatology of love. In Luke the gift of the Spirit to the Son enabled the messianic activities of Christ but in Romans this same gift of the Spirit raises Christ from the dead "for our justification" (4:25).[37] The gift of the Spirit is the gift of God and of divine love, one that brings with it the many charisms that enable human beings to live in love amid the suffering, challenges, and toils of the present age. The Spirit gives God's love to our spirits, and in that way, freely dispenses the redemptive power of the coming age so that followers of Jesus can build one another up in love.

Conclusion

This chapter has presented St. Paul as a theologian of the love of God, intertwining his ecclesiological, cosmological, and soteriological reflections on the theme. The differences between Paul's ecclesiological and charismatic theology of love articulated in the first Corinthian letter and his more christological, cosmic, and soteriological considerations outlined in Romans should be noted. The genre of the former is more polemical while that of the latter is more didactic, related to the sociohistorical contexts of both congregations. The Corinthians were in need of correction, in particular related to their factionalism, elitism, and charismatic excesses; the Romans were perhaps under persecution, existentially troubled, and in need of encouragement. For the church at Corinth, then, Paul wrote sternly, with love functioning as a corrective charting a more excellent way of congregational life; for the church in Rome, however, Paul wrote an exhortation, calming the fears of the members and presenting the world as their home—in the love of Christ and the Spirit—rather than as a hostile environment. The Corinthians were, by and large, challenged to be loving as a community, while the Romans were, again in general, informed that they were loved and that their affective response should only be to rest in the peace of that love and then allow that love to overflow effectively in the Spirit for the benefit of others.

What should also be clear, however, is that for Paul, the gifts of the Spirit are but an extension of the gift of the Spirit, who is also the gift of love. In the Spirit, we have the divine love inundate our hearts, even our lives as a whole. Hence the charismatic and spiritual gifts are empowering precisely as the gracious gift of the Holy Spirit who is present and active amid the groaning of the current age. What for Luke is the baptism or infilling of the Spirit is suggested by Paul as the unconditional love of God shed within the very core of human life, transforming human community in the process. We shall see these themes unfolded, albeit with their own distinctive marks, in the Johannine literature.

CHAPTER 8

• • •

The Spirit and the Gift/s of Love

A Johannine Pneumatology of Love

We now turn from the Pauline to the Johannine materials. We will begin with the First Epistle of John and then spend the last two sections on the Gospel of John. Again, our hermeneutical guide through both the Epistle and the Gospel will be the interconnections between love and the Holy Spirit. In particular, we seek to articulate a Johannine pneumatology of love that highlights how love is a community-forming and life-affirming gift of the Spirit that overcomes the strife, hate, and hostility of a fallen world.

This chapter is the final of our threefold scriptural cord, following discussions of Luke and Paul in chapters 6–7, woven around the New Testament witness to love as the Spirit's gift. It also returns us to the starting point of our book, where we encountered St. Augustine's reflections on love in relationship to the Spirit prompted by his homilies on 1 John. The following gives us an opportunity to burrow deeper into the Johannine vision of divine love and to wrestle with some of the challenging questions about love that have emerged over the course of this study. We will be especially sensitive to the particularistic character of love, one underwritten by the sectarian character of the Johannine community, and will need to see how this can be understood in light of the pneumatological and pentecostal resources motivating our inquiry.

One caveat before proceeding. There is no scholarly consensus about the relationship between the first letter of John and the Fourth Gospel.[1] This lack of consensus pertains not only to the question of authorship but that of priority and dependence.[2] We treat them both together here, however, in part because amid all of the disputes about historical-critical matters, there is very little debate about the existence of a Johannine *community* or *tradition*, one responsible both for the final form of the Gospel and for reception of the three letters.[3] This is what allows us to read the Epistle in light of the Gospel and vice versa, even while our canonical commitments invite approaching the Johannine witness in dialogue with other voices in the New Testament. We will begin with the Epistle not because it was written before the Gospel (it may have been, but we do not know for sure) but because any quest for a biblical theology of love will see not only that love is the central theme of the first Johannine letter but that, with regard to the topic of this book, it also has "the last and most profound word to say in the declaration 'God is love.' "[4]

Abiding in Love: The Spirit of God and the Community of Perfect Love

Any approach to love in 1 John from a pneumatological perspective should begin by acknowledging that the Holy Spirit is mentioned sparingly in the letter. In fact, there is only one reference to "the Holy Spirit" (τό ἅγιον πνεῦμα), and it appears in a clause that has long been recognized as a later interpolation (1 John 5:7b). It may be that this minimalist pneumatology is due to "a desire on the part of the writer to combat 'enthusiasm' of the wrong kind or false claims made in the name of the Spirit by heterodox members of the Johannine community."[5] Beyond this point—to which we will return in a moment—even the few references to God's Spirit are ambiguous. For example, the assertion, "By this you know the Spirit of God: every spirit that confesses that Jesus Christ has come in the flesh is from God" (4:2), suggests that there may be multiple divine spirits, each recognizable by a christological confession.[6]

I suggest, however, that we dive right into the two most obvious references to the Spirit in the middle of the letter, references which turn out to be surprisingly similar and which, I will argue, play important roles in John's argument. Toward the end of his first discourse on love (the third chapter), John writes, "And this is his commandment, that we should believe in the name of his Son Jesus Christ and love one another, just as he has commanded us. All who obey his commandments abide in him, and he abides in them. And by this we know that he abides in us, by the Spirit that he has given us" (3:23-24). Then, later, in the middle of his second great discourse on love (4:7-21), John says, "No one has ever seen God; if we love one another, God lives in us, and his love is perfected in us. By this we know that we abide in him and he in us, because he has given us of his Spirit" (4:12-13). Both references highlight the Spirit as divinely given, similar to the Lukan and Pauline affirmations about the Spirit as the gift of God, and this will be crucial to the development of our Johannine pneumatology of love. For now, however, we observe that sandwiched between these two references is John's famous set of instructions about discernment of spirits (4:1-6). I suggest that this structure highlights two interrelated pneumatological themes in 1 John's theology of love: that of knowing love and of abiding in love. We will take these up in order.

The knowledge of authentic love, 1 John informs us, involves the witness of the Spirit. If 1 Corinthians 12–14 involves two discussions of the spiritual gifts organized around a poem on love, then 1 John 3–4 involves two discussions of love organized around an admonishment to test the spirits. The problem is that there are many spirits of false prophets (4:1) that are no less than antichrists (4:3). What distinguishes "the spirit of truth and the spirit of error" (4:6) is the confession of Christ's incarnation (4:2).[7] When read in light of St. Paul's insistence that "no one can say 'Jesus is Lord' except by the Holy Spirit" (1 Cor 12:3b), it suggests that the Johannine community would recognize the Spirit of God through the christological confession only because such confession is made possible by that same Spirit. And for a Johannine community fragmented, so it seems, by incipient Gnostic tendencies—which in minimizing the incarnational character of the revelation of the Son inclined the church toward a docetic view of Christ—this pneumatically-inspired acknowledgment of the historicity of Jesus was an important criterion for discerning the truth.

This pneumatological principle, which involves both the process of confessional enablement and the content of the confession, is anticipated earlier in the letter when the community is assured that "you have been anointed by the Holy One, and all of you have knowledge" (2:20) and that "the anointing that you received from him abides in you, and so you do not need anyone to teach you. But as his anointing teaches you about all things, and is true and is not a lie, and just as it has taught you, abide in him" (2:27). It is unclear grammatically that this anointing refers to the Spirit, but there are at least two reasons for this association. First, the anointing in both instances is χρισμα, which even if linked to Christ as the "Holy One" (2:20; cf. John 6:69 with Luke 4:34 and Acts 2:27) presumes the messianic charism of the Spirit. Jesus is the Christ precisely as the one who the Spirit anoints, which not only the synoptic gospels note but also the Fourth Gospel indicates occurred at his baptism (John 1:32-33). Second, the concern of the Johannine community had to do with seeking protection from falsehood. The charismatic anointing that teaches the Johannine Christians the truth about all things accomplishes what the Fourth Gospel identifies as the work of the Spirit: "But the Advocate, the Holy Spirit, whom the Father will send in my name, will teach you everything, and remind you of all that I have said to you," and "When the Spirit of truth comes, he will guide you into all the truth" (John 14:26; 16:13a). In short, the Spirit of Christ is the Spirit of truth who will keep followers of Christ from falsehood.

But the Spirit of truth is also the Spirit of love. Now we need to tread circumspectly here simply because while John clearly says "God is love" (4:8, 16) and "God is spirit" (John 4:24), he never quite says "the Spirit is love."[8] I am suggesting, however, that the anointing of truth is the Spirit of love because that anointing remains and abides in believers and this in turns enables believers to remain and abide in divine love. All of this is related to the quest for assurance at the heart of the Epistle. Love is, after all, the primary criterion for discerning not only truth from falsehood but what is of God from what is not. Love separates, for example, the children of God from the children of the devil (3:10), love distinguishes those who "have passed from death to life" from those who have not (3:14), and love divides those who know God from those who do not (4:8). In fact, the presence of love reflects God's abiding within believers. Just as important, though, the presence of love indicates that believers are abiding within God: "God is love, and those who abide in love abide in God, and God abides in them" (4:16b; cf. 3:17). In short, believers recognize both that God remains and abides in them (3:24) and that they remain and abide in God (4:13) as witnessed to by the Spirit of truth and love.[9]

Our analysis so far suggests that the Spirit is intimately involved in both knowing and abiding in love. It remains to spell out, then, what exactly such knowledge and abiding entails. The world hates and murders

(3:12-15) because it "lies under the power of the evil one" (5:19b). Johan-nine believers, on the other hand, are urged to live out their confession through benevolent deeds of love (3:17). Thus John not only urges his readers, "let us love, not in word or speech, but in truth and action" (3:18), and "Beloved, let us love one another, because love is from God" (4:7a), but he also insists more forcefully, "*this is his commandment*, that we should believe in the name of his Son Jesus Christ and love one another, just as he has commanded us" (3:23, emphasis added). In fact, put bluntly,

> Those who say, "I love God," and hate their brothers or sisters, are liars; for those who do not love a brother or sister whom they have seen, can-not love God whom they have not seen. The commandment we have from him is this: those who love God must love their brothers and sisters also. Everyone who believes that Jesus is the Christ has been born of God, and everyone who loves the parent loves the child. By this we know that we love the children of God, when we love God and obey his command-ments. For the love of God is this, that we obey his commandments. And his commandments are not burdensome. (4:20–5:3)

Love of neighbor is not an option, at least not for those who say they love God; love of neighbor thus becomes *the* criterion for measuring how peo-ple relate to God.[10] Pneumatologically, I might add that the Spirit assures the hearts of believers by bearing witness to God's abiding in them, and their abiding in God confirms this inward testimony through outward deeds of love.

I do not wish to make more of the Spirit in this first letter of John than the author himself. However, I also do not think that the scarcity of references to the Spirit in this Epistle means that there is little pneumato-logical purchase for thinking about divine love. Rather, a pneumatological perspective suggests a unique understanding of the letter's major theme. While there are many reasons given by the author regarding the motivation for this correspondence, toward the end he indicates, "I write these things to you who believe in the name of the Son of God, so that you may know that you have eternal life" (5:13). As Jesus responded to the lawyer's ques-tion about how he might attain eternal life by telling the story of the Good Samaritan, John urges his audience toward eternal life through receiving and dispersing the love of God. The Spirit's role in this process, as we have now seen, is at least threefold: (1) to enable recognition that the God who is love lives and abides in us, and through that recognition to love and abide in him by loving others; (2) to facilitate awareness that Christ who commands us to love others lives in us, and through that awareness to live in him by obeying his commandment to love others; and (3) to make possible our knowing and continuing in the truth of love that constitutes and leads to eternal life. And all of this can happen because of God's initial gift of the Spirit. In this letter, then, God's self-revelation constitutes his love initiative (4:19), first in the Son who was sent "to be the atoning sacrifice for our sins" (4:10b), and then in the Spirit who was given so that we might be assured of the love of the Father expressed in and through the Son.

I want to make one final set of comments before moving to the Fourth Gospel, which has to do with the reason initially given by John for this letter: "We are writing these things so that our joy may be complete" (1:4).[11] There is an affective dimension to this missive that highlights its perlocutionary effect. Whereas epistemic ambiguity produces anxiety, certain assurance produces peace and joy. The affections are further acknowledged in terms of the author's insistence that "There is no fear in love, but perfect love casts out fear; for fear has to do with punishment, and whoever fears has not reached perfection in love" (4:18). What the Spirit accomplishes is the presence of God, and through this the Spirit brings about the joy that overcomes despair and the love that triumphs over fear. The Spirit of love thus not only moves the minds of believers (to confess that the Christ has been sent to manifest the love of God) but also touches their feelings (overcoming fears), vivifies their hearts (inspiring joy), and empowers their hands (to express in turn divine love to others).[12]

Comforting Love: The Breath of God and the Power to Love

Much more is said about the Spirit in the Gospel of John.[13] As we viewed the Lukan corpus through the lens of the Day of Pentecost narrative of the outpouring of the Spirit, I would like to begin with the account of the giving of the Spirit in John 20 as a springboard toward a Johannine pneumatology of love:

> When it was evening on that day, the first day of the week [after Jesus' crucifixion], and the doors of the house where the disciples had met were locked for fear of the Jews, Jesus came and stood among them and said, "Peace be with you." After he said this, he showed them his hands and his side. Then the disciples rejoiced when they saw the Lord. Jesus said to them again, "Peace be with you. As the Father has sent me, so I send you."

When he had said this, he breathed on them and said to them, "Receive the Holy Spirit. If you forgive the sins of any, they are forgiven them; if you retain the sins of any, they are retained." (20:19-23)[14]

There have been perennial discussions about the connection between this "Johannine Pentecost" and Luke's account in Acts 2. While some pentecostal scholars suggest that the former prepares the disciples for the latter,[15] there is no scholarly consensus on this matter, with the trend in general being to read at least the Johannine account, if not also the Lukan version, as primarily theological explications rather than historical descriptions of actual events.[16] Adjudicating this question is not essential for formulating a theology of love in relationship to Johannine pneumatology. For this purpose, a few preliminary remarks are apropos.

First, note the two pronouncements of peace in this context (not to mention a third greeting of peace in Jesus' visitation of the disciples a week later; 20:26). We have now seen repeatedly the importance of peace in relationship to the Spirit. The reign of God proclaimed by Jesus was one of peace, even as for Paul, the kingdom consists of "righteousness and peace and joy in the Holy Spirit" (Rom 14:17). Thus also in the historic classical pentecostal context the Spirit's empowerment enables a peace witness. Here, we find the peace of God pronounced over the fearful disciples even as the Spirit is breathed upon them, and they are affectively touched to the point of rejoicing. The breathing of the Spirit here calls to mind the primordial breath of life (Gen 2:7) and the renewal and revitalization of Israel depicted by the prophet Ezekiel as a valley of dry bones (Ezek 37:9). We will return in the next section to pursue a related question about the extent of the Spirit's life-giving love.

Second, the gift of the Spirit here is often compared with the Lukan version that occurs over three chapters (Luke 24:36-49; Acts 1:1-8; 2:1-4) because it also includes both the commissioning and empowering of the apostolic ministry. In this text, however, the sender is Jesus, although the model of apostolic authority follows the sending of the Son by the Father.[17] In other words, the power of the apostolic authority derives from the Father's relationship with the Son. We have already seen in the Lukan account that this was a relationship of love, and this theme is emphasized even more strongly, as shall be clear, by the Fourth Evangelist. The Lukan corpus also highlights that the disciples proclaimed the forgiveness of sins in Jesus' name (Acts 2:38 and passim), and this is also registered as central to the apostolic mission by John.[18] What is noteworthy, however, is that there are no other explicit references to the forgiveness of sins in the Fourth Gospel, with the exception being Jesus' declaration about not condemning the woman caught in adultery in a pericope that most scholars believe is a later redaction (John 8:1-12). Thus, that the forgiveness of sins is the only specified aspect of the apostolic work in this text suggests that we should not minimize the coming of the Spirit and the Spirit's role in this regard.[19]

In the next section, we shall note the further significance of this power of forgiveness for a Johannine pneumatology of love. For now, however, we need to connect this giving of the Spirit to the message of love that makes its appearance elsewhere in John's Gospel. It is clear that Jesus' breathing of the Spirit upon the disciples has long been anticipated, particularly with regard to the Spirit's being sent as a replacement for Jesus after his departure (16:7; cf. 7:39).[20] Thus the Spirit is called the Paraclete—παράκλητον, also Counselor or Advocate—who will encourage the disciples in Jesus' absence (14:16), remind them of his teachings (14:26), testify of Jesus to and through the disciples (15:26-27), lead them into all truth (16:13), glorify the Son and the Father (16:14-15), and convict the world "about sin and righteousness and judgment" (16:8b). In fact, the coming of the Paraclete establishes the peace of Jesus—"Peace I leave with you; my peace I give to you. I do not give to you as the world gives. Do not let your hearts be troubled, and do not let them be afraid" (14:27; cf. 16:33)—thereby linking the promise of the Spirit and the post-resurrection giving of the Spirit to the disciples through Jesus' breath.

We do not need to be detained here by the scholarly discussions about the origins of the Paraclete idea.[21] What I would like to focus on, however, is the connection between the promise of the Spirit and the love commandment. The first promise of the Paraclete (14:16-18) is nested within a larger passage that urges the disciples to be faithful to Jesus' commandments as an expression of love for him:

> "If you love me, you will keep my commandments. And I will ask the Father, and he will give you another Advocate, to be with you forever. This is the Spirit of truth, whom the world cannot receive, because it neither sees him nor knows him. You know him, because he abides with you, and he will be in you. I will not leave you orphaned; I am coming to you. In a little while the world will no longer see me, but you will see me; because I live, you also will live. On that day you will know that I am

in my Father, and you in me, and I in you. They who have my commandments and keep them are those who love me; and those who love me will
be loved by my Father, and I will love them and reveal myself to them."
Judas (not Iscariot) said to him, "Lord, how is it that you will reveal yourself to us, and not to the world?" Jesus answered him, "Those who love
me will keep my word, and my Father will love them, and we will come
to them and make our home with them. Whoever does not love me does
not keep my words; and the word that you hear is not mine, but is from
the Father who sent me." (14:15-24)

I wish to highlight three aspects of a Johannine theology of love embedded
in this passage. First, the Spirit enables and helps believers to respond to
Jesus' love by keeping his commandments.[22] The Spirit is capable of doing
this "because he abides with you, and he will be in you" (14:17b). Thus
the Spirit empowers believers from within, rather than moves them from
without. This is a fulfillment of the Old Testament promises that the Spirit
would not just hover upon but be placed within the hearts of the people of
God (Ezek 36:27; cf. Heb 8:6, 9:14).

Second, however, the Spirit empowers the keeping not only of Jesus'
commandments in general but of what the other evangelists call the Great
Commandment and what John calls the "new commandment" in particular: "I give you a new commandment, that you love one another. Just as I
have loved you, you also should love one another. By this everyone will
know that you are my disciples, if you have love for one another" (13:34-35;
cf. 15:12, 17). The context of this giving of the new commandment is Jesus'
departure (13:31-36). In his absence, the world will still know of Jesus by
the love that the disciples have for one another. The Paraclete, therefore,
who is sent to remind the disciples about Jesus' teachings, here and forever
not only reminds them to love one another but realizes and actualizes their
love one for another.

Last but not least, the Spirit who keeps the disciples in the truth and in
obedience to Jesus' commandment—including the new commandment—
also makes possible their participation in the love of the Father and the
Son. The witness borne by Jesus throughout the Gospel is that there is a
mutual love between the Father and the Son (3:35; 5:20; 10:17; 14:31) and
that it is this love that is being revealed to the world.[23] Keeping the (love)
commandments not only allows for participation in the divine love but
also realizes the Father's indwelling love for the disciples in a unique way.

In a moment we will see that the Father loves the world in a general sense, but there is also a sense in which for those who love the Son and keep his word, "my Father will love them, and we will come to them and make our home with them" (14:23b; cf. 14:21; 16:27). In short, the Paraclete is the comforter and the advocate precisely by working from within the hearts and lives of the disciples in keeping them in the truth of Jesus' love commandments so that they can partake in and receive the love of the Son and come to experience the indwelling love of the Father.[24]

Forgiving Love: The Spirit's Measureless Gift of Cosmic Love

Yet the Paraclete is promised to encourage and advocate for the disciples because they live in tension with their surrounding world. Jesus warned them that

> If the world hates you, be aware that it hated me before it hated you. If you belonged to the world, the world would love you as its own. Because you do not belong to the world, but I have chosen you out of the world— therefore the world hates you. Remember the word that I said to you, "Servants are not greater than their master." If they persecuted me, they will persecute you; if they kept my word, they will keep yours also. But they will do all these things to you on account of my name, because they do not know him who sent me. If I had not come and spoken to them, they would not have sin; but now they have no excuse for their sin. Whoever hates me hates my Father also. If I had not done among them the works that no one else did, they would not have sin. But now they have seen and hated both me and my Father. It was to fulfill the word that is written in their law, "They hated me without a cause." (15:18-25; cf. Pss 69:4 and 109:3 for the sources of the Hebrew Bible quotation at the end)

What we see described here is just the opposite of what the Spirit is supposed to accomplish among the Johannine community. If the world consists of hatred toward the disciples, they are supposed to exhibit love for one another. The world's hatred is motivated by their rejection of Jesus and their ignorance of the Father, whereas the disciples' love is marked by their embrace of Jesus and their reception of the Father's love for the Son.[25] Hence the world sins through its hate—of the disciples, of Jesus, and of the Father—while the believing community keeps the commandments, especially the new commandment to love. But the fact of the matter is that times were indeed difficult and challenging for this besieged community.

Jesus admonished them that "They will put you out of the synagogues. Indeed, an hour is coming when those who kill you will think that by doing so they are offering worship to God" (16:2).[26]

Within this context, then, the work of the Paraclete is to enable the persecuted community to persevere through their trials and tribulations. The Spirit empowers testimony and confession of the truth toward the world but also secures a community of love among the disciples. Jesus himself urged that his followers should stand in solidarity with one another, loving and serving one another. The whole context of his teachings on the new love commandment and of his promises regarding the Paraclete was at the last Passover supper when he ate with his disciples: "Jesus knew that the time had come for him to leave this world and go to the Father. Having loved his own who were in the world, he now showed them the full extent of his love" (13:1, New International Version). This demonstration of love included his washing the feet of the disciples, after which Jesus urged, "if I, your Lord and Teacher, have washed your feet, you also ought to wash one another's feet" (13:14). Later in the evening, after introducing the new commandment and amidst his promises about the Paraclete, Jesus ups the ante: "This is my commandment, that you love one another as I have loved you. No one has greater love than this, to lay down one's life for one's friends" (15:13-14). Within the span of the discussion, then, Jesus not only models the full extent of his love by descending to the most intimate and interpersonal level of service but also challenges his disciples to follow in his anticipated footsteps as well: by laying their lives down for one another.[27]

What emerges amid the dynamics of the Fourth Gospel, however, is a certain "in-group" mentality characterized by love over and against an "out-group" of haters. Herein lies the dualistic worldview of the Johannine community in which those who love God are opposed by those who do not. The Fourth Evangelist thus starkly draws lines in the sand to urge his reader to side with the light against the darkness, with the divine against the demonic, with truth against falsehood, with life against death. This is primarily a moral dualism—between good and evil, love and hate—rather than a cosmological or metaphysical dualism.[28] Yet this is a powerful strand throughout John's account, one confirmed in the final prayer of Jesus for the disciples at the end of the last Passover meal:

> I am asking on their behalf; I am not asking on behalf of the world, but on behalf of those whom you gave me, because they are yours. . . . And now

> I am no longer in the world, but they are in the world, and I am coming to you. Holy Father, protect them in your name that you have given me, so that they may be one, as we are one. . . . I have given them your word, and the world has hated them because they do not belong to the world, just as I do not belong to the world. I am not asking you to take them out of the world, but I ask you to protect them from the evil one. They do not belong to the world, just as I do not belong to the world. . . . Righteous Father, the world does not know you, but I know you; and these know that you have sent me. I made your name known to them, and I will make it known, so that the love with which you have loved me may be in them, and I in them. (17:9, 11, 14-16, 25-26)

When set in pneumatological perspective, then, the gift of the Spirit in the Fourth Gospel seems to encourage only an in-group love, albeit a powerful one which brings believers in Jesus into the love of the Father for the Son and which deposits the love of the Father and the Son in their midst and into their hearts.

Yet as comforting as such a love may be for those persecuted by the world, this circumscribed love of God sits in tension with the doctrine of universal divine love and unconditional divine grace. The Lukan outpouring of the Spirit on all flesh and the Pauline insistence that there are absolutely no barriers that can thwart the cosmic scope of the Spirit's witness to God's love in Christ suggest that this reading of John's pneumatology of love leaves something unsaid. Even the natural sciences have uncovered, as we have seen (in chap. 2), evidences of genuinely out-group altruistic benevolence. Does not the Fourth Evangelist have more to say about the Spirit and love than what we have uncovered in the Paraclete texts?

From a pneumatological perspective, I suggest there are at least two lines of response to mitigate the concerns of Johannine moral dualism that delimit divine love, one going backward to the beginning of the book and the other one looking (again) toward the end. The former highlights that while the world is generally identified as being opposed to God's revelation in Christ—after all, as the author of the First Epistle notes, "the whole world lies under the power of the evil one" (1 John 5:19b)—there are also indications that this generalization does not tell the whole story. As Cornelis Bennema notes, although the world is generally hostile to and ignorant of God and persecutes the people of God, some do respond to God's offer of eternal life.[29] From the standpoint of the author's explicit reasons for writing the book—for example, "these are written so that you may come to believe that Jesus is the Messiah, the Son of God, and that through believing you may have life in his name" (20:31)—"it appears that John wants the reader to evaluate primarily the character's response rather than the character."[30] So the world is not essentialized; there is always the possibility that aspects of (individuals in) the world will respond favorably to God's revelation in Christ.

We should not underestimate God's gracious offer of eternal life to the world. Jesus himself is recorded by John to have said, famously, "God so loved the world that he gave his only Son, so that everyone who believes in him may not perish but may have eternal life" (3:16). This claim, which is a staple of the Johannine tradition as a whole,[31] appears in a conversation Jesus was having with Nicodemus, a leading member of the Jewish ruling council (3:1). At the beginning of the discussion, Nicodemus is told that inheritance of the reign of God comes from being born again, of water and the Spirit (3:5-6). And as difficult as it might be either to conceive of this new birth or to experience such a spiritual rebirth, "The wind blows where it chooses, and you hear the sound of it, but you do not know where it comes from or where it goes. So it is with everyone who is born of the Spirit" (3:8). So even if it may well be impossible for obstinate and ignorant human beings to respond to the divine love, perhaps it is the mysterious and remarkable work of the Spirit that accomplishes what is otherwise out of the question. This seems to be confirmed in the next pericope when in response to a complaint that there were people going over to Jesus to be baptized by him, John the Baptist reaffirms the subordination of his ministry to Jesus'. More precisely, Jesus' ministry comes from above, and in effect comes and is empowered through the boundless gift of the Spirit: "He whom God has sent speaks the words of God, for he gives the Spirit without measure" (3:34). It is this illimitable gift of the Spirit that flows through Jesus even to a hostile world, the very world that God loves.[32]

The second pneumatological rationale for countering an exclusively centripetal understanding of Johannine love leads us back to Jesus' breathing upon the disciples and giving the Spirit at the end of the Fourth Gospel. Recall here the connection between the gift of the Spirit and the forgiveness of sins: "If you forgive the sins of any, they are forgiven them; if you retain the sins of any, they are retained" (20:23). English translations, however, render an ambiguous Greek. Sandra Schneiders has noted, for instance, there is no evidence in classical literature for translating *krateo* as "retain," just as there would be a theological problem to do so since repentant sinners are forgiven by God regardless of whether those who have been wronged do so![33] She thus suggests instead this translation: "Anyone whose sins you forgive, they are forgiven to them and those [the forgiven] whom you hold fast [in the communion of the Church] are held fast."[34]

This reading highlights that the breath of Christ empowers the disciples not only to forgive but also to live out of what has happened in the past in redemptive and salvific ways. This kind of forgiveness which does not merely overlook or ignore the consequences of sins but rather does not hold the sins of others against them is central to the continual reformation of the community of believers as it seeks peace, accomplishes justice, and loves those who have hated and persecuted it.[35] In effect, it is Spirit-empowered love that enables the new commandment to be directed unconditionally outside the group, even to its enemies, as we have seen repeatedly mentioned elsewhere in the New Testament. In an almost paradoxical sort of way, perhaps the intense love generated within the believing community that forgives the sins of one another itself becomes the light and beacon to those in the world "outside" about the possibility that their sins (the sins of the world's inhabitants) are also forgivable. In this case, then, love may be, first and foremost, the glue that holds together those who believe in Jesus, but keeping the commandments of Jesus also has the power to bear witness of the unending and unlimited love of God for the world precisely by turning enemies into friends, and by transforming inversus out-group hostilities into communal shalom and solidarity.[36] If it is impossible for mere human beings to forgive their enemies, then he to whom the Spirit has been given without measure has not left his followers alone, but has chosen in turn to lavish his breath and bestow the Spirit upon the disciples that they might now be more than just a light on a high place but a living embodiment of the graciousness of divine love that is henceforth equipped to love and win over a hostile world.[37]

Conclusion

I do not wish here to pretend that we have resolved all of the difficulties around the sectarian claims of the Johannine tradition. There is no way to minimize the antagonism that the person of Jesus draws forth from those who have chosen to remain in darkness. What I want to emphasize instead is the hopefulness that a pneumatological hermeneutic engenders for a Johannine theology of love. God loves the world and sent his son to save the world; but now that the Son is no longer present, it falls upon the Spirit to bring the world into the love that the Father has for the Son so that the world itself can experience the full scope of the divine filial love. And that is exactly what God wishes for the world, that its creatures might respond to this overture of divine love manifest in the Son and breathed out on or poured out through the Spirit. The disciples, those who are the first to be convinced about the love of the Father in the Son and through the Spirit, are those who are now urged to love one another first, and through such love to gradually embrace the world as well. This represents the heart of the divine love, which graciously touches and transforms all human hearts and knows no cosmic bounds.

Read in this way, the Johannine pneumatology of love undergirds and enriches the Lukan and Pauline witness. In Luke the renewal of Israel under the Spirit-anointed one anticipates the restoration of the world under the ministry of the Spirit-empowered apostles; in that narrative, the promise to Abraham that, "in your descendants all the families of the earth shall be blessed" (Acts 3:25b), is being gradually fulfilled by those baptized in the love of the Father for the Son. In the Pauline epistles the Spirit of the congregation is also the Spirit who has been shed abroad in human hearts and who from that "space" enables their crying out and praying for the liberation of all creation. So here in the Johannine writings the divine love of God who is spirit and who gives of the Spirit through the resurrected Christ is always both particular and universal: particular enough to kindle human hearts and affections and redeem individual lives within any group, but universal enough also to go beyond any pre-established group boundaries to save the world within which human beings live, move, and have their being.

CHAPTER 9

• • •

The Power of Love in the Spirit
A Manifesto in Nine Theses

We are at the last leg of our journey into the mystery of love. This relatively brief chapter will summarize the gains made while setting forth the fundamental elements of what I have called in this volume a pneumatological theology of love. In the preface of this book I had set forth a working definition of love as the affective disposition toward and intentional activity that benefits others, and the argument in the preceding pages has been to transpose this into a pneumatological key. What follows in this final chapter, then, describes certain core characteristics of love as viewed from our pentecostal perspective, in light of our understanding of the Spirit as the undeserved and gracious gift of God. Our findings and proposals can be divided into three parts—on the anthropology, theology, and missiology of love—wherein they are summarized in nine theses.

The Gifts of the Spirit of Love: An Anthropology of Love

There are three interrelated levels to a theological anthropology of love in a pneumatological key: the biological, the affective, and the spiritual. Each level can be understood to be a gift of the Spirit, broadly considered. The latter two levels presume the former but cannot be reduced to it.

Thesis 1: An anthropology of love in a pneumatological perspective begins with the human encounter with love as embodied and enfleshed. There is certainly a theological dimension to this thesis, one that is rooted both in the divine creativity that brought forth material and embodied creatures and in the incarnational love that took on human flesh, both of which I will return to in a moment. Here, however, I wish to highlight the material and fleshly nature of human love. Human beings are conceived through acts of love, nurtured in love from the point of conception, and carried to full term and then brought forth into the world through acts of (sometimes selfless) love. From our earliest moments, as we have seen, we are neuro-physiologically "hardwired" to receive the love of our caretakers, usually parents, and to respond to and develop in love. We grow in love in our embodied interactions with other embodied persons.

Yet the charismatic gifts of the Spirit also highlight the material nature of our baptisms in divine love. We encounter the reality of the Spirit palpably through our physicality, whether in "tarrying in" or "being slain by" the Spirit, receiving miraculous healings in our bodies, feeling our heart "strangely warmed,"[1] or speaking in strange tongues. In other words, the works of the Spirit are never merely ethereal but they are concrete, kinesthetic, and even tactile. We meet the Spirit as we are, in and through our bodies, and the Spirit condescends to touch us, alight upon us, even enter into the very depths of our sinews, joints, and marrow (cf. Heb 4:12).

This is the root of the self-love that arms our self-preservational instincts, precisely what is assumed in the Great Commandment. It is also the basis for the erotic nature of love that Tillich identified, not the concupiscent dimensions of self-loving that can become misdirected and self-absorbed but the embodied nature of love as a materially energetic force that binds creatures of dust together within the symbiosis of divine creative love.[2] And embodied love is the foundation for all love, not only since it is supremely manifest in the incarnate Christ, but also since it is through loving others in their embodiment that we can even begin to countenance the possibility of loving God: "for those who do not love a brother or sister whom they have seen, cannot love God whom they have not seen" (1 John 4:20b).

Thesis 2: An anthropology of love in a pneumatological perspective embraces the affective dimensions of love as felt human experiences. Even early on, however, we learn that the love received through our bodies is tinged with affectivity. Remember that the affections include, even if they are not exhausted by, our passions, our emotions, and our desires. We feel love because it is impressed upon us—our bodies and our hearts—so that we are even impassioned by the bodies, emotions, and desires of others. We then connect with love emotionally, feeling with others and empathically entering into the experiences of others so that we can share their feelings, pains, joys, and hopes. Last but not least, we love together with others in striving for what we hope, long, and yearn for. As affective creatures, then, we are a nexus of loving trajectories: receiving love from many different directions, and yet also channeling more or less loving impulses, feelings, and actions outward to others and forward in expectation. This is perhaps what the scriptures gesture toward in referring to the apostolic fellowship (κοινωνία) of the Spirit (Acts 2:42) and the "communion of the Holy Spirit" (2 Cor 13:13).

Further, as affective lovers, we love both instinctively and intentionally. The latter is perhaps best captured by Jesus' teaching that "No one has greater love than this, to lay down one's life for one's friends" (John 15:13). By and large, Jesus' injunction is reserved for "within group" companions, and this undergirds Thomas Aquinas' hierarchy of love that begins with those closest to us and extends outward from there. The former, however, arises out of our formation in loving communities of the Spirit so that, having been shaped in docile submission to the Spirit, we might be habituated or inclined to act lovingly in various situations. And this is reflected in our giving up our lives not only for family members and friends but even for strangers who we see are vulnerable and threatened in ways that are perhaps unknown to them. Jesus' parable of the Good Samaritan highlights the nature of this empathetically oriented love, which scientific research on out-group altruism has long been attempting to unravel. The point is that affective love persists, sometimes even to the point of death, because it is not caught up in the self-rationalization that often accompanies reflection; instead, we are affectively bound up with other creatures in emotional, empathetic, and other ways so that there may be occasions in which benevolent deeds of love require self-sacrifices that cannot otherwise be rationally justified but are instinctively undertaken, as the spur-of-the-moment demands. These also are unconditional gifts of the Spirit—gifts that make us what we are as recipients of the affections of others and that enable our affective interrelationship with and commitment to others as well.

Thesis 3: An anthropology of love in a pneumatological perspective accentuates the spiritual aspects of love as transcending mere human capacities and deriving, ultimately, from God. Ultimately, we were created not only to love others but also to love God who is spirit. As Augustine put it, human happiness is most complete when we desire, have, know, and love God. Of course, we come to recognize that our hearts ultimately yearn for God through experiencing the love of others and loving others. Sorokin also recognized that love was guided ultimately by the transcendentals of goodness, truth, and beauty. In other words, human love knows no boundaries because it participates through the Spirit in the ideals of the good, the true, and the beautiful that are ultimately unified in God.

This is what charismatic worship identifies as the passion for God. Such passion is expressed most concretely in prayer, praise, and worship. Human beings as praying, praising, and worshipping creatures find their highest aspirations fulfilled in the Triune God and thus reserve manifestation of their deepest affections to the spiritual life.[3] Steven Land calls this the passion for the reign of God, wherein our gratitude, compassion, and courage find their source and goal in the divine life. It is this passion that not only allows but motivates us to "strive first for the kingdom of God and his righteousness," since we know that everything else will be given or added to us as well (Matt 6:33).

Of course, even this passion for the reign of God is a gift of the Spirit since it is nothing less than an expression of the longing of our hearts for our home in the divine life. So when the apostle Paul urged, "I appeal to you therefore, brothers and sisters, by the mercies of God, to present your bodies as a living sacrifice, holy and acceptable to God, which is your spiritual worship" (Rom 12:1), it is already presumed this is only possible "because God's love has been poured into our hearts through the Holy Spirit that has been given to us" (Rom 5:5). Nevertheless, here we see that the spiritual dimension of human worship includes its embodied aspect (involving our bodies) as well as that of the heart (reflected in our willingness to live self-sacrificially), as normed by the values of the coming rule of God, which is nothing less than "righteousness and peace and joy in the Holy Spirit" (Rom 14:17b).

The preceding sketch (and it is certainly nothing more than this) of a theological anthropology of love is pneumatologically infused. Our embodiment, our affectivity, and our spiritual aspirations—each of these are gratuitous endowments of the Triune God. They are also gifts of the Spirit, broadly understood, into which the love of God is poured out, through which divine love is manifest, and to which human loves are ultimately directed. Our subjective experiences of love—at the affective and spiritual levels—are dependent upon albeit irreducible to the specificity of our embodied encounter with love.[4] If this provides an overview of love from our anthropological and experiential starting point of the human encounter with and experience of the Spirit and her gifts, we now shift to a more explicitly theological register and attempt to thematize love as divine gift of the Spirit.

The Gift of Love and of God as Spirit: A Pneumatology of Love

There are also three interrelated levels to a theology of love in a pneumatological key: the creational, the incarnational, and the pentecostal. These, as theologians will recognize, follow in broad strokes the pattern of salvation history as revealed in the scriptures. Each level can be understood to be not just a gift of the Spirit but a gift of God the Spirit. More precisely, each level represents what might be called a kenotic outpouring of the Spirit, one through which the Spirit's identity is found precisely in and through that to which/those to whom the Spirit is given. Again, the latter two levels presume the former but cannot be reduced to it.

Thesis 4: A theology of love in a pneumatological perspective begins primordially with the Spirit's hovering over the face of the deep and giving her life to the creatures of the world. We might say that God's gracious gift of the Spirit to the world is the flip side of the saying that God so loved that God created the world.[5] Yet God's creating of the world proceeded through what the early Church called the two hands of the Father: that of the Word and that of the Spirit. My pneumatological perspective thus highlights the *ruach* of God's primordial hovering over all creation (Gen 1:2) as well as the *nephesh* of God given to all living creatures (Gen 1:30) and the *nishmah* or breath of life given to *ha adam* (Gen 2:7).[6]

Yet God's abundant gift of the Spirit to creation was one that empowered the creation to fulfill its potential.[7] If God's word commanded that there be light on the one hand, that same word also allowed and enabled the creation to respond and participate in the processes of cocreating on the other hand.[8] God's powerful love thus made possible creaturely cooperation and mutuality so that these are deeply embedded in the processes of the world rather than alien intrusions from without. Of course, sin has infected the world so that such cooperativeness has been distorted at best and overcome by alienation, greed, and selfishness at worst, and this is precisely why we are in continuous need of the discernment of spirits in order to combat that which is destructive, false, and ugly with that which is good, true, and beautiful. The Spirit can be grieved, even quenched, by human disobedience and rebellion. Yet if there are expressions of benevolent altruism, even in the natural world, these also are sparks of the Spirit's stubborn and persisting gift, remnants of the Spirit's irremovable and unconquerable presence, and impulses of the Spirit's persuasive and empowering agency in the midst of a fallen creation. So if the fall means that creatures proceed on their own strength against the designs and intentions of God, then the scriptural story of salvation-history involves the gracious renewal, redemption, and restoration of all things so that they might participate in the workings of the breath and Spirit of God in Christ.

This pneumatological thesis regarding the doctrine of creation is in part why I am not surprised to find love outside the Christian tradition, even in other religions.[9] Human beings who manifest the fruits of the Spirit (Gal 5:22-24) are not only recipients of the Spirit in a fundamental sense but also conduits of the Spirit's presence and activity to others. Some aspects of almost all religious traditions have glimpsed this dynamic of the Spirit—as has the Christian tradition, on its best days—and in that sense, have been gifted by the Spirit to make a difference in a fallen world. This does not mean that all religious traditions are fully salvific in the Christian sense (most do not have explicitly Christian aims—thus they are *other* religious ways and forms of life), or that all religions are fundamentally equal (they are not!). It does mean that discerning the Spirit among the religious traditions of the world is less complicated than some think. Whenever and wherever we find the affective disposition toward and intentional activity that benefits others, prima facie there is the creaturely participation in the loving presence of the divine Spirit intending to save and redeem the world.[10]

Yet the Spirit's loving embrace of creation also sparks creation's capacity to freely and liberally love and respond in turn. Perhaps most fundamental to the Spirit's gift to creation, then, is the creaturely freedom that is empowered by the breath of life. There is a spectrum of creaturely initiative and responsibility across the created order, with human agency being most extensive. What should be most clearly observed is that the creative work of the divine breath is subtle rather than obvious, immanent within the creation and its creatures rather than only transcendentally operative from without. Thus the gift of the Spirit to creation can be said to be the basis for a cosmic ontology of creativity and freedom. The Spirit does her work not to call attention to herself but to empower the integrity of the world and its creatures each at their own levels and in relationship to their environments.[11] And the magnitude of God's creative love for the world is thus manifest in God's making space for creatures that are free and who may, or may not, choose also to love one another and God in turn.[12] To be sure, rejecting the love of God or the love of others, or rejecting to love God and others, undermines the flourishing of human life, even if it may not eliminate the creative capacities unleashed by human ingenuity.

Thesis 5: A theology of love in a pneumatological perspective finds its most fundamental expression in the kenotic incarnation of the Son and his messianic anointing for the work of the reign of God. The true nature of the Spirit is most supremely, unsurpassably, decisively, indispensably, and uniquely revealed in the Son. This is why the criterion for discernment of the Spirit inevitably and ultimately revolves around confession of the Lordship of Christ (in the congregational context) or of the incarnational nature of God's revealing love (in the context of Johannine docetism and Gnosticism). At the same time, we also know that the Son is who he is as the Christ precisely as one anointed by the Spirit, conceived of the Spirit, and empowered by the Spirit to declare, inaugurate, and instantiate the coming reign.[13] The Son manifests the love of the Father for the world because the Son is the Father's beloved—and the Spirit is not only the dove that represents their mutual love but also the power of the Son's incarnational life and ministry.[14]

If the Spirit is most eminently revealed in the Son, she is also most uniquely revealed in the Son's kenosis, even to the point of death, for the redemption of the world. Much has been made, of course, of the Son, who

> . . . though he was in the form of God,
> did not regard equality with God
> as something to be exploited,
> but emptied himself,
> taking the form of a slave,
> being born in human likeness.
> And being found in human form,
> he humbled himself

and became obedient to the point of death—
even death on a cross. (Phil 2:6-8)

Yet my point is to highlight not only that the kenosis of the Son enabled his empowerment by the Spirit but also that, apart from the life-giving work of the Spirit in the death of the Son, the redemptive love of God would not have come to fruition. After all, it is the self-sacrificial and bloody death of the Son, "who through the eternal Spirit offered himself without blemish to God, [who purifies] our conscience from dead works to worship the living God" (Heb 9:14), that rendered judgment on sin on the cross and made possible the reconciliation between God and creation.[15] And then it is the resurrection of the Son in the power of that Spirit that not only justifies but also saves and gives life to all mortal bodies (Rom 1:4; 4:25; 8:11; cf. 1 Pet 3:18). In short, the kenosis of the Son succeeds because of what could be understood as the Spirit's kenosis: the Spirit's willingness to enter into the death of the Son and give life to the Son in the absence of the Father.[16]

What the Spirit-empowered kenosis of the Son reveals is also the truth that Jesus proclaimed: "I tell you, unless a grain of wheat falls into the earth and dies, it remains just a single grain; but if it dies, it bears much fruit" (John 12:24). That life comes out of death is possible because of the Spirit of life, who enters into the death of the world in order that resurrection, renewal, and redemption might come forth. In this sense, then, the redemptive power of the Spirit makes possible—against the competitiveness, greed, and selfishness of the fallen world—the altruistic activities of all creatures caught up in the Spirit's work, so that self-sacrificial benevolence can emerge for the greater good.

Thesis 6: A theology of love in a pneumatological perspective finds its most expansive manifestation in the Day of Pentecost outpouring of the Spirit given for the eschatological renewal of the world. If the incarnation reveals the kenotic power of the Spirit to bring life out of death, then Pentecost unveils the kenotic work of the Spirit to enable the flourishing of all forms of life, even and especially from out of death. Thus the God who gives the Spirit to the creation and to the Son also now gives the Spirit to the world of living creatures, especially human beings. Pentecost is the gift of the Spirit not for the Spirit's self-promotion or self-aggrandizement but for the empowerment of creatures to participate in the divine love and in turn lift up the Father of the Son and the creator of the world (Acts 2:11).

Thus the gift of the Spirit proceeds from the Son's inauguration of the coming divine reign and intensifies the eschatological time—the "last days" (Acts 2:17)—of God's redemptive work. The Spirit does this by coming upon all flesh, just as the Spirit came upon the Son; not only that, the Spirit does this by indwelling all flesh, just as the Spirit indwelt the Son. Thus all flesh—male and female, young and old, slave and free; the Spirit shows no partiality with regard to gender, class, or any other human conventional ordering (Acts 10:34)—is primed to receive God's unconditional gift of saving love in the Spirit. The Johannine community also recognized the universal scope of God's love in Christ as St. John, the author of the Apocalypse, who was "in the spirit on the Lord's day" (Rev 1:10a), saw the eschatological gathering as including people from "every tribe and language and people and nation" (Rev 5:9b; cf. Rev 7:9; 14:6; 17:15).

The divine gift of God's Spirit therefore signals the eschatological baptism of all flesh, even creational materiality itself, into the love of the Father and the Son. This is the redemptive love of God that enables human creatures to sigh and groan with the creation for the full overcoming of the alienation that plagues the world. This cosmic estrangement is now passing away because no power within it can hinder the primordial love of the Triune God indwelling, filling, and overflowing the world through the Spirit.

What I have sketched here is a pneumatological theology of love that accents the gift and work of the Spirit in the salvation history of God's gracious activity. Of course, the Spirit is involved in each facet of God's creative and redemptive achievements, not to the neglect of the contributions of either the Father or the Son—since according to the traditional formula, *Opera trinitatis ad extra sunt indivisa*, the works of the Trinity are undivided[17]—but precisely as revealing, communicating, and even expanding the love of the Father for the Son.[18] It is because of this extravagantly gracious and magnanimous outpouring of love in and through the creator and redeemer Spirit that we are now caught up, as embodied, affective, and spiritual creatures, in the life and mission of the Triune God.

The Spirit's Gifts of Love and Power: A Missiology of Love

Last but certainly not least, the preceding anthropology and theology of love opens up to a missiology of love. Again, we approach our topic pneumatologically, proceeding in three interrelated modalities: that of personal evangelism, that of witness to out-groups, including enemies, and that of engaging the structures or the principalities and powers. Each mode of missional engagement can be understood as graciously empowered by the gift-giving Spirit.

Thesis 7: A missiology of love in a pneumatological perspective begins with the Holy Spirit who empowers the disciples of Jesus to bear witness to the ends of the earth. There are many aspects to this witness, including the invitation to repentance, the declaration of the forgiveness of sins, and the baptism to Christian discipleship, among other elements. Yet chief among these is the introduction of the gift of God's love in Christ to the world, so that the world may also come to experience and participate in the love of the Father and the Son.[19]

It is here that the inseparability of the two sides of the Great Commandment, which not only lies at the heart of the Great Commission but also reaches back deep into the heart of the faith of ancient Israel, comes into clear focus: to love God does involve the loving of neighbors and vice versa. Further, it is also here that the unity of love that St. Augustine glimpsed through his teaching and preaching through 1 John should be affirmed. God is love, yes, but love is also divine since God loves us through the love of others and God loves others through our loving them.

We should not underestimate the affective dimensions of such witness. Oftentimes, Christian witness is propositionalized so that what is communicated is information. A pneumatological theology of missionary love, however, understands that faithful witness is not only accomplished by or within the head (and the words it generates) but motivated by and undertaken through the heart, and expressed with the hands. We bear witness not primarily because we have something to say but because we have someone to share. Those who have been caught up in the baptism of love want others to experience that love for themselves. As Brian Houston, pentecostal preacher and founder of the Hillsong megachurch network in Australia, says, the disciples of Jesus are affectively consumed by their relationship with Jesus, to the point that they are also "consumed with seeing people come into relationship with Jesus."[20]

Mission and evangelism in this register make no rational sense, just like falling in love makes no rational sense, although all of us can agree when someone tries to describe that feeling and ends up saying, "you know what I mean!" But that is precisely what the Spirit's baptism of love brings about: an affective reorientation of our passions so that they are ortho-pathically energized to point others in the direction of the coming reign of God. We are "compelled by love," in the words of pentecostal missionary Heidi Baker,[21] because of our gratitude for divine love, our compassion for others who may not have experienced such love in this way, and our hope that, somehow, it will indeed come to pass that nothing in all creation can separate even the world from the God who loves all in Christ. And it is precisely such an affective dedication and loyalty to others that leads us to the radical love that is our next thesis.[22]

Thesis 8: A missiology of love in a pneumatological perspective extends even to our enemies, even to the point of death. As the Johannine witness declares, those who have received the breath of Jesus are empowered to forgive the sins of others and to embrace them in the communion of divine love. This willingness to forgive sins, especially of those who have sinned against and are hostile toward us, is the other side of the coin of the power to declare God's unconditional forgiveness of sins for all sinners. If sins are what alienate free creatures from one another and from their Creator, then the forgiveness of sins overcomes this alienation and reconciles God and the world, as well as brings harmony back to the creation that is divided within itself.[23]

As important, and perhaps even more so for the following consider-ations, this capacity to forgive begins with us. If, as the biblical authors repeat, we are to love our neighbors *as ourselves*, then we can only forgive others to the extent that we have forgiven ourselves. This is the biblical basis for a healthy self-love that does not degenerate into a selfish egoism. Yet it is also central to living out the love of neighbor; one who has not for-given him- or herself has not yet learned how to love him- or herself and is thus in no position to either forgive or love others.

With self-forgiveness and self-love in place, then, Jesus' new com-mandment calls us to love not just our family and friends as ourselves, but even our enemies. As St. Paul indicated, "God proves his love for us in that while we still were sinners Christ died for us" (Rom 5:8). This would rep-resent the highest level of altruistic love that even sociologists like Sorokin have identified as central to the transformation of the world. The intensity of God's love was revealed in the enfleshment and then death of the Son; its extensivity is measured by its scope, that Christ "is the atoning sacrifice for our sins, and not for ours only but also for the sins of the whole world"

(1 John 2:2); its duration is reflected in God's eschatological patience, "not wanting any to perish, but all to come to repentance" (2 Pet 3:9); its purity is reflected in the selfless and kenotic character of the divine gifts in the death of the Son and the outpouring of the Spirit; and its adequacy is represented in the capacity of divine love to transform hostilities into solidarity. This incomparable divine love is nevertheless what followers of the Messiah have been baptized into, so as to be able to participate in and manifest and share it with maximal intensity, extensivity, duration, purity, and adequacy with the world.

The goal of the divine missions of the Son and the Spirit is to establish the Shalom of God's reign replete with its righteousness, peace, and joy. Our Spirit-empowered mission, therefore, anticipates the coming divine rule by embodying the nonviolent but yet powerfully subversive and resisting acts of the Christ who so loved the world that he gave himself for it. We thus turn the other cheek not in weakness but as a charismatic manifestation of the Christ's Spirit, the Spirit who is life and peace (Rom 8:6). If necessary, witness is borne even to the point of death—precisely the kind of witnesses unto martyrdom intimated in Acts 1:8 (where the word for "witness" is the Greek μαρτυρες, literally "martyrs")—as following in the footsteps of the one who emptied himself even to the extent of embracing death on the cross.[24] In this way, all of the enemies of God and all of the enemies of lovers of God will be overcome not by evil but by the gracious goodness of the Spirit of love (cf. Rom 12:17-21).[25]

Thesis 9: A missiology of love in pneumatological perspective culminates in the reconciliation of all things, even the powers of the cosmos itself. St. Paul indicates that in the end, "When all things are subjected to him, then the Son himself will also be subjected to the one who put all things in subjection under him, so that God may be all in all" (1 Cor 15:28).[26] Here this eschatological work of God is said to involve the destruction of God's enemies (1 Cor 15:24-26), although elsewhere it is also said that, "all things in heaven and on earth were created, things visible and invisible, whether thrones or dominions or rulers or powers—all things have been created through him [Christ] and for him," and that "through him God was pleased to reconcile to himself all things, whether on earth or in heaven, by making peace through the blood of his cross" (Col 1:16, 20).[27]

My claim, however, is that the eschatological outpouring of the Spirit upon all flesh portends the eschatological redemption of even the principalities and powers that structure creaturely and historical relations and conventions.[28] This means that we are empowered in the here and now to bear witness to the divine love that heals what is broken in the creation, that reconciles those who are otherwise set apart by the destructive social, political, and economic conventions of this world, and that enacts the peace, justice, and righteousness of the coming reign of God. Racial reconciliation, gender emancipation, socioeconomic justice, the abolition of hierarchicalism, elitism, and classism—each of these and others are fallen principalities that the followers of the Messiah are empowered to engage redemptively through the gifts of the Spirit.

Thus the love of the Spirit spans cosmic, natural, and human history. It involves the salvation of our bodies, the reorientation of our affections, and the restoration and restructuring of the various dimensions—political, economic, social, etc.—of our lives. The love of the Spirit salvages, as Tillich asserted, all of what currently constitutes our bifurcatedness (divided into soul and body, self and other, personhood and structure, etc.). This is because the Spirit who is the bond of love between the Father and the Son is also the bond of love between God and the world.[29]

Is it possible that there will be recalcitrant spirits that will resist this excessive, abundant, and unconditional love of God? Of course, in a world characterized by freedom, this is always possible. After all only enspirited creatures can be free to love, to receive love, and to reject love. Does this mean that such creatures have it within their power to refuse eternally God's gracious offer of love in Christ and the Spirit? Theoretically yes, although practically, I cannot fathom how this might be possible. Do love and grace then win? It seems that our answer must be yes, for a God who loves the world unconditionally in Christ and by the Spirit; but on the other hand, our answer may also be no, if we were to look carefully at creaturely gravitation toward hate and evil, even amid a world awash with the baptismal love of God's Spirit. So is the final answer negative? Perhaps not so long as we have the breath of the Spirit within us to announce to the world that it does not have to be that way, that God loves the world, and that God desires, in Christ and through the Spirit, that we can experience and participate in that love even now.

How Can This Be a Conclusion?

I do not know how there can be a conclusion to this chapter. We are "wired" and constituted by and for love because of the love of God that has created and is in the process of redeeming the creation. This is the love that also motivates us—"For the love of Christ urges us on . . ." (2 Cor 5:14)—to love one another, to love our enemies, to love the world that God has created, and through all of this, to love the God who first loved us. The Christian mission consists in nothing less than this, since we have received gratuitously of the love of God in our hearts by the Holy Spirit. What else can or should we do other than to live that love, even to the point of death, for others?

• • •

Epilogue

There is not much more that needs to be said, so I end by reiterating seven points—the first three of which are more directly related to the pentecostal aspects of the book's argument, the next three which are more theological and pneumatological in nature, and the last one presented as a question to the church.

First, now that we are at the end of this book, I hope my readers can see why the preceding represents, unequivocally, my *apologia pro vita sua*, at least to date. It captures my pentecostal passion and fervor unlike any of my other books, revealing that what I have done as a pentecostal scholar and theologian has been fueled by what Steven Land calls a vision "for the kingdom." I hope it is also clear, however, that the particularity of my pentecostal confession should not be read as opposed to my ecumenical commitments and even my enthusiasm for interreligious encounter, cross-cultural engagement, and the dialogue between theology and science. The gift of the Spirit of love who hovers over the face of the deep and who has been poured out upon all flesh mandates that the expansiveness of our vision of love and the comprehensiveness of our mission of love cross boundaries that we might not have otherwise been led to navigate on our own.

Second, however, I trust that the preceding illuminates the nature of Pentecostalism as a lived religion. I certainly do not intend to defend everything that occurs under the pentecostal banner, but I also surely hope that readers of this volume have come to a new or deeper appreciation for the movement's major gifts to the church catholic and ecumenical: its affective orientation toward God and the world, its passion for the reign of God and its message, its emotional and embodied spirituality. Pentecostalism and the charismatic renewal emphasize the felt nature of religious life; not that the cerebral dimension is neglected but it is not predominant. Instead life in Christ through the Spirit is holistic, engaging not just our minds but our hearts in all their richness, complexity, and volatility. Thus are pentecostal and charismatic hearts caught up in the love of God so as to love and desire after God in turn.

Third, the preceding has implications for the study of Pentecostalism and of pentecostal theology. The oral, narrative, and populist character of Pentecostalism has long meant that the pentecostal theological tradition, whatever that might mean, will be informed by what has emerged on the pentecostal ground. Thus it should not be surprising that our springboard into a pentecostal theology of love was provided by social scientists doing research on godly love in the pentecostal-charismatic movement. These sociologists have not only studied a religious movement and set of religious experiences, but taken even greater professional risks calling into question the scientific nature of their research by involving theological perspectives in the process. Pentecostal theologians need to begin not only paying attention to such social scientific research on Pentecostalism but also engaging their theological work in an interdisciplinary manner. Hence, pentecostal theology should proceed with one ear to the pentecostal ground—learning from the popular, oral traditions of the movement preserved in their booklets, cassette tapes, CDs, DVDs, and television programs—and with one ear to the broad spectrum of interdisciplinary data. I hope that the value of triangulating between pentecostal lived religion, scientific perspectives, and the broader theological tradition has been clearly registered. I hope that one conclusion we take from this discussion is that pentecostal theology does not just revolve around a theology of a charisms but that it is supremely about the Spirit of love and about the Spirit's love as the saving grace of God.

Fourth, I am optimistic that my readers, both within and outside of the world of pentecostal-charismatic Christianity, can see the benefit of mining this tradition of spirituality for rethinking a theology of love. What has emerged, as should be clear, is a new appreciation for love in relationship to the Holy Spirit. Such a pneumatology of love, as I have called it, belongs not just to pentecostal and charismatic Christians but to all who are followers of the anointed one from Galilee. In fact, authentic Christianity is nothing less than being captivated by the power of love manifest in the life of Christ and made available now to all of his disciples through the same Spirit who descended upon him as an expression of the Father's love for the Son. This Spirit is, of course, the one given unconditionally to the world, for its salvation, sanctification, and redemption. The world needs the saving love of God, regardless of how that is understood, expressed, or unfolded. This does not necessarily mean that the world needs to be "christianized" in any conventional sense, or that the church needs to be "pentecostalized" or "charismatized" as assumed by Pentecostals and charismatics in their mistaken triumphalist moments. It does mean that the church—those who have been caught up in the love of Christ by his Spirit—ought to live in ways that reflect this self-sacrificial and kenotic aspect of the Spirit's presence and activity.

Fifth, consider then how our pentecostal lenses have retrieved and spotlighted an important idea with deep roots in the theological tradition, that God is not just a gift-giving deity but the one who gives of the Son and the Spirit. This means that God gives who God is, not just something else that might be accumulated and discarded; it means that God gives primordially, freely, and unconditionally—there being nothing else to condition or merit God's giving; it means that God's gracious gifts can be repudiated, as unthinkable and incomprehensible as that might seem, but it also means that as God gives out of Godself there is no way to exhaust the plenitude of divine love that is presented in the Son and poured out in the Spirit. Hence the gift of God never ceases to circulate, and as befits the divinity of the gift, endlessly replenishes and invigorates those who receive it with gratitude while paradoxically judging and yet redeeming others simultaneously.

Sixth, our pneumatological theology of love opens up to and empowers a missiology of love. Again, such a missionary witness can take many forms: traditional evangelistic postures that invite others to make commitments to Christ, social activism or socio-political engagement that involve the quest for righteousness, justice, and peace, or even interreligious and cross-cultural dialogical interactions that enable further understanding and even self-transformation. That the baptism of love in the Spirit is now unconditionally and eschatologically available to all means neither that all are saved or that all are going to be saved, but it does mean that those of us who have been baptized into that love are in the position of heralding its accessibility and embodying its reality. Perhaps in these ways the world might indeed also come to know that the God who is spirit is also the God who is love.

Finally, then, I want to highlight the connections we uncovered above, particularly in chapter 4, not only between charismatic spirituality and benevolent ministry but the charism of prophecy more specifically and altruistic ways of life on behalf of the world. Where is the Spirit of prophecy? In some ecclesial circles the claim that God speaks prophetically through the Spirit is minimized or ignored; in other environments there are so many alleged prophecies that the force of these messages is dulled. One person's prophecy is another person's heterodoxy and it has become difficult to identify the voice of the Spirit. To be sure, the most important criterion for discerning the Spirit remains Christ, although we may not always be threatened by the same challenges confronting the Corinthians and Johannine communities. But another criterion must surely be love; may followers of the anointed one from Galilee pray for his prophetic Spirit of love that will challenge local injustices, edify specific groups of people, liberate people from oppressive principalities and powers, and transform embodied lives and communities who are hoping and desiring for something better. In all of these ways, may we prophesy love, so that the gracious and good gifts of the Spirit can accomplish the redemption of the world.

• • •

Notes

Preface

1   The nature of Pentecostalism has been contested. By and large, I will use "Pente-costalism" and its cognates inclusively, covering, e.g., what sociologists call clas-sical Pentecostalism (the group of churches related to or derived from the Azusa Street revival), the charismatic renewal movement (in the mainline, Roman Catholic, and Orthodox churches) since the late 1950s, and "third wave" or other indigenous charismatic type movements in the Euro-American West and across the global south since the 1970s. On occasion, to be more specific, I will insert qualifiers so that readers will be alert to when I desire to cast a narrower net. For discussion of these definitional challenges and categories, see my *The Spirit Poured Out on All Flesh: Pentecostalism and the Possibility of Global Theology* (Grand Rapids: Baker Academic, 2005), 18–22.

2   Throughout this book, I only capitalize "Pentecostalism" (the noun) and "Pente-costals" (referring to adherents and members of the movement) but not when I use to term "pentecostal" adjectivally.

3   This is close to Thomas Oord's definition: "To love is to act intentionally, in sym-pathetic/empathetic response to God and others, to promote overall well-being." Thomas Jay Oord, *The Nature of Love: A Theology* (St. Louis: Chalice, 2010), 17.

4   See my article, "A P(new)matological Paradigm for Christian Mission in a Reli-giously Plural World," *Missiology: An International Review* 33, no. 2 (2005): 175–91.

5   I will take the liberty throughout this book of using feminine pronouns in refer-ence to the Spirit, following the proposals of theologians across the spectrum, e.g.,

charismatic Catholic theologian Donald L. Gelpi, *The Divine Mother: A Trinitarian Theology of the Holy Spirit* (Lanham, Md.: University Press of America, 1984), and evangelical theologian Clark H. Pinnock, *Flame of Love: A Theology of the Holy Spirit* (Downers Grove, Ill.: InterVarsity, 1996). This is not because I view the Spirit as feminine but because there is grammatical latitude to deploy such imagery and because there is a need to develop theological discourse that overcomes the patriarchal bias of the Christian tradition.

6   David Coffey, *Grace: The Gift of the Holy Spirit* (Manly, NSW, Australia: Catholic Institute of Sydney, 1979).

7   Stephen H. Webb, *The Gifting God: A Trinitarian Ethics of Excess* (New York: Oxford University Press, 1996).

8   Besides the previously noted *The Spirit Poured Out on All Flesh*, see also my *Discerning the Spirit(s): A Pentecostal-Charismatic Contribution to Christian Theology of Religions*, Journal of Pentecostal Theology Supplement Series 20 (Sheffield, UK: Sheffield Academic, 2000), and *In the Days of Caesar: Pentecostalism and Political Theology* (Grand Rapids: Eerdmans, 2010), most pertinent among other books on pneumatological theology.

9   With the exception of my "turn to missiology" in my *Hospitality and the Other: Pentecost, Christian Practices, and the Neighbor* (Maryknoll, N.Y.: Orbis, 2008), which remains in parts of the book still at a fairly high level of theological abstraction.

Chapter 1

1   Werner G. Jeanrond, *A Theology of Love* (New York: T&T Clark, 2010), which succeeds, in reverse order of publication, Gary Chartier, *The Analogy of Love: Divine and Human Love at the Center of Christian Theology* (Charlottesville, Va.: Imprint Academic, 2007); George M. Newlands, *Theology of the Love of God* (Atlanta: John Knox, 1980); Mildred Bangs Wynkoop, *A Theology of Love: The Dynamic of Wesleyanism* (Kansas City: Beacon Hill Press, 1972); Hans Urs von Balthasar, *Love Alone*, trans. Alexander Dru (New York: Herder & Herder, 1969); Daniel Day Williams, *The Spirit and the Forms of Love* (New York: Harper & Row, 1968); John McIntyre, *On the Love of God* (New York: Harper & Brothers, 1962); and Anders Nygren, *Eros and Agape*, trans. Philip S. Watson (1953; repr., New York: Harper & Row, 1969), among many other books.

2   Histories of love include Carter Lindberg, *Love: A Brief History through Western Christianity* (Malden, Mass.: Blackwell, 2008); Liz Carmichael, *Friendship: Interpreting Christian Love* (New York: T&T Clark, 2004); Bernard V. Brady, *Christian Love: How Christians through the Ages Have Understood Love* (Washington, D.C.: Georgetown University Press, 2003); Diane Ackerman, *A Natural History of Love* (New York: Random House, 1994); and Denis de Rougemont, *Love in the Western World*, rev. ed., trans. Montgomery Belgion (Princeton: Princeton University Press, 1983). Philosophical treatments of love include Irving Singer, *Philosophy of Love: A Partial Summing-Up* (Cambridge, Mass.: MIT Press, 2009); John

Cowburn, *Love*, Marquette Studies in Philosophy 36 (Milwaukee: Marquette University Press, 2003); Timothy Jackson, *Love Disconsoled: Meditations on Christian Charity* (New York: Cambridge University Press, 1999); Robert E. Wagoner, *The Meanings of Love: An Introduction to Philosophy of Love* (Westport, Conn.: Praeger, 1997); Vincent Brümmer, *The Model of Love: A Study in Philosophical Theology* (New York: Cambridge University Press, 1993); and Frederick D. Wilhelmsen, *The Metaphysics of Love* (New York: Sheed & Ward, 1962), among others. Bridging history and philosophy is Robert G. Hazo, *The Idea of Love* (New York: Praeger, 1967).

3 Augustine, *The Happy Life*, trans. Roland J. Teske, S.J., in Augustine of Hippo, *Trilogy on Faith and Happiness*, ed. Boniface Ramsey (Hyde Park, N.Y.: New City Press, 2010). *De Beata Vita* is one of the earliest surviving works of Augustine, written probably soon after his conversion sometime in the fall of 386. All references to this work will be made parenthetically in the main text to *HL* followed by paragraph numbers.

4 As Gareth B. Matthews, *Augustine* (Malden, Mass.: Blackwell, 2005), chap. 15, notes, the bishop of Hippo returned time and again to reflect on the nature of happiness over the next forty years.

5 Thus are our temporal loves driven by *cupiditas*, in contrast to our love for eternally abiding realities which is motivated by *caritas*; see William S. Babcock, "*Cupiditas* and *Caritas*: The Early Augustine on Love and Fulfillment," in *Augustine Today*, ed. Richard John Neuhaus (Grand Rapids: Eerdmans, 1993), 1–34.

6 There may be an even deeper relationship between the treatise and the collection of sermons, since in *De Trinitate* Augustine cites from John's Gospel more than from any other source. See Evan F. Kuehn, "The Johannine Logic of Augustine's Trinity: A Dogmatic Sketch," *Theological Studies* 68, no. 3 (2007): 572–94, at 577.

7 Augustine, *The Trinity*, trans. Edmund Hill (Brooklyn, N.Y.: New City Press, 1991). All references to this work will be made parenthetically in the main text to *T* followed by book and section numbers.

8 Augustine, *Ten Homilies on the First Epistle General of St. John*, in Augustine, *Later Works*, ed. John Burnaby (Philadelphia: Westminster, 1955). All references to this work will be made parenthetically in the main text to *TH* followed by homily and paragraph numbers.

9 This "two loves" motif not only becomes central to Augustine's own biography but also structures his magnum opus, *The City of God*. See William Mallard, *Language and Love: Introducing Augustine's Religious Thought through the Confessions Story* (University Park: Pennsylvania State University Press, 1994), esp. chap. 11 regarding Augustine's *Civitas Dei*.

10 Augustine certainly knew what he was saying in making this inversion, as it appears also throughout his corpus (over ten different occasions). For further discussion of this daring inversion in Augustine, see Johannes van Bavel, "The Double Face of Love in Augustine," *Louvain Studies* 12, no. 2 (1987): 116–30. Also, Roland J. Teske, S.J., "Augustine's Inversion of 1 John 4:8," *Augustinian Studies* 39, no. 1 (2008): 49–60, esp. 55, notes that this "love is God" inversion appears

elsewhere in the patristic literature—in Ambrose, Ambrosiaster, Caesarius of Arles, Leo the Great, and others.

11 I am aware that the renaissance of trinitarian theology in the last generation makes it much easier to accept Augustine's reflections on the intra-trinitarian relations. Yet the challenges related to such thinking about the immanent Trinity should not be overlooked. There are two specific challenges for any pentecostal and pneumatological theology. The first concerns the twofold dilemma: on the one hand there is an ambiguous relationship throughout various sites of the scriptural canon between the divine spirit and the human spirit (as most recently laid out by John H. Levison, *Filled with the Spirit* [Grand Rapids: Eerdmans, 2009]), and on the other hand the metaphysics of God as spirit is not easily distinguishable from the deity of the Holy Spirit (this is the post-Nicene problematic). The second, building from this "other hand," has to do with the Oneness Pentecostal insistence that we need to prioritize the scriptural witness over post-Nicene philosophical approaches to the doctrine of God. Given that Oneness Pentecostalism is not a negligible part of the global renewal movement, my own conviction is that any pentecostal theology should engage dialogically with Oneness perspectives rather than dismiss them. For the record, my feelings are that any use of trinitarian language—of Father, Son, and Spirit—ought to remain primarily at the narrative level of the scriptural witness and follow the salvation-historical testimony of the New Testament writers (precisely what I argue in *Spirit Poured Out on All Flesh*, chap. 5). How this works out will be clear in chapters 6–8 of this book when I present my pneumatological theology of love in dialogue with the Lukan, Pauline, and Johannine materials.

12 It is this passage which has suggested that Augustine understood the Spirit as the bond of love between the Father and the Son, although see a recent interpreter who cautions against such a view: Catherine Osborne, "The *nexus amoris* in Augustine's Trinity," in *Studia Patristica*, vol. 22, ed. Elizabeth A. Livingstone (Leuven: Peeters, 1989), 309–14.

13 Earlier in the book, Augustine had already identified the Spirit as "the gift of God," of both the Father and the Son (*T* 5.12, citing there Acts 8:20 and John 4:10).

14 The procession of the Spirit principally from the Father is not understood by Augustine as excluding the Spirit's procession secondarily from the Son as well; this is the basis of Augustine's understanding of the *filioque* (see *T* 15.47–48).

15 This is of course an allusion to Romans 5:5—"hope does not disappoint us, because God's love has been poured into our hearts through the Holy Spirit that has been given to us"—which is quoted explicitly on multiple occasions both in *De Trinitate* and in the homilies on 1 John.

16 Augustine, *The Enchiridion on Faith, Hope, and Charity*, in Augustine, *Late Have I Loved Thee: Selected Writings of Saint Augustine on Love*, ed. John F. Thornton and Susan B. Varenne (New York: Vintage Books, 2006), 91.

17 For a full prosecution of this thesis regarding Augustine's God as incapable of loving, see Thomas Jay Oord, *The Nature of Love: A Theology* (St. Louis: Chalice, 2010), chap. 3.

18 Interestingly, some of Peter Lombard's most controversial doctrines in the *Sentences* were his affirmations "that the Holy Spirit is the Love by which we love God and neighbour" and "that brotherly love, although it is God, is not the Father or the Son, but only the Holy Spirit." Peter Lombard, *The Sentences, Book 1: The Mystery of the Trinity*, trans. Giulio Silano (Toronto: Pontifical Institute of Mediaeval Studies, 2007), 88–89 (Distinction XVII). This was for the Lombard in continuity with Augustine's famous inversion, "love is God," and also enabled the affirmation of the means of the believer's deification in being taken up into the life of the Trinity. Although it is never declared unorthodox, most theologians since have skirted this teaching, with Thomas himself preferring the more modest claims of Augustine on this matter. See Philipp W. Rosemann, "*Fraterna dilectio est Deus*: Peter Lombard's Thesis on Charity as the Holy Spirit," in *Amor Amicitiae—On the Love that Is Friendship: Essays in Medieval Thought and Beyond in Honor of the Rev. Professor James McEvoy*, ed. Thomas A. F. Kelly and Philipp W. Rosemann (Dudley, Mass.: Peeters, 2004), 411–36. I will suggest in a moment, however, that St. Thomas' understanding of the Spirit's gifts of the theological virtues amounts to similar theological results as Peter Lombard's views, albeit without the latter's dogmatic equation of brotherly love and deification.

19 I rely mainly on Thomas Aquinas, *The Summa Theologica*, 2 vols., trans. Laurence Shapcote, rev. Daniel J. Sullivan, Great Books of the Western World 19–20 (Chicago: Encyclopaedia Britannica, 1952). Unless otherwise noted, all references to this work will be made parenthetically in the text and follow standard procedure: identifying, where necessary, (first or second) part, question, article, objection, and/or reply numbers.

20 I am very sympathetic to the substance of Aquinas' handling of the *filioque*, even if it does not resolve all of the ecumenical problems. For the purposes of our discussion, I will follow Aquinas' way of putting it since resolving the question of *filioque* is not essential to the major thesis of this book. For my own treatment of the intra-trinitarian relations, in particular about there being multiple scriptural models for understanding the Spirit's relation to the Son, see *Spirit-Word-Community: Theological Hermeneutics in Trinitarian Perspective* (2002; repr., Eugene, Ore.: Wipf & Stock, 2006), 59–72.

21 Remember, again, that for Aquinas our understanding of divine love is analogical, love being one aspect of the nature of God that is ultimately indivisible and apophatic. As Michael Dodds understands Aquinas' theology of love in relationship to the divine immutability, "Far from being opposed to love, immutability was seen as essential to the absolute gratuity of God's love. Our affirmation of divine immutability did not force us to deny or diminish the compassionate character of God's love, but did induce us to admit the limitations of our knowledge and language, and so kept us from reducing God and his infinite compassionate love to the boundaries of that finite human love and compassion familiar to us." Michael J. Dodds, O.P., *The Unchanging God of Love: Thomas Aquinas and Contemporary Theology on Divine Immutability*, 2nd ed. (Washington, D.C.: Catholic University Press of America, 2008), 242–43. As we shall see, pentecostal approaches to divine

love are less constrained by these apophatic considerations, although I am not unaware of the import of these matters.

22 For more contemporary Catholic theological reflection on the Spirit as gift, see John T. McMahon, *The Gift of God: Come, Holy Spirit* (Westminster, Md.: Newman Press, 1958); Pope Paul VI, *God's Gift—the Holy Spirit!* (Boston: St. Paul Editions, 1978); and Andrew Apostoli, *The Gift of God: The Holy Spirit* (New York: Alba House, 1994). Much more substantive theologically is the work of Australian Catholic systematician David Coffey, *Grace: The Gift of the Holy Spirit* (Manly, Australia: Catholic Institute of Sydney, 1979).

23 Here I follow, in the main, the important work of Paul J. Wadell, *The Primacy of Love: An Introduction to the Ethics of Thomas Aquinas* (New York: Paulist, 1992).

24 Here Thomas cites from Aristotle's *Nicomachean Ethics*, book 8, chap. 5.

25 For an excellent discussion, see Peter King, "Aquinas on the Passions," *Thomas Aquinas: Contemporary Philosophical Perspectives*, ed. Brian Davies (New York: Oxford University Press, 2002), 353–84, esp. 354–58.

26 As Thomas Dixon, *From Passions to Emotions: The Creation of a Secular Psychological Category* (New York: Cambridge University Press, 2003), shows, the richness of the medieval discussion revolving around the passions, appetites, and affectivity has been lost since the Enlightenment, particularly in terms of the emergence of the emotions as the central and all-encompassing category of scientific exploration. I will return to discuss this point in the next chapter.

27 See Michael Dauphinais and Matthew Levering, *Knowing the Love of Christ: An Introduction to the Theology of St. Thomas Aquinas* (Notre Dame, Ind.: University of Notre Dame Press, 2002), 51–52.

28 I fully embrace Aquinas' metaphysics of participation here (II–II.26.4a) but feel he is straining at gnats in trying to prioritize the spiritual love of self over the love of neighbor; in fact, since he ends up granting that corporeally we should be willing to suffer injury on behalf of our neighbor (II–II.26r2 and II–II.26.5), in that sense he arrives at the conclusion that the love of neighbor is privileged over the love of self.

29 I am loath to admit that Aquinas, reflecting the patriarchial and misogynist views of his time, also affirms the love of fathers over mothers because "the father is principle in a more excellent way than the mother, because he is the active principle, while the mother is a passive and material principle. Consequently, strictly speaking, the father is to be loved more" (II–II.26.10a). He might have begun to take steps toward redeeming himself, however, by saying that "a man loves his wife more intensely, but greater reverence should be shown to his parents" (II–II.26.11a).

30 For full discussion, see the classic but still reliable work of Barthélemy Froget, *The Indwelling of the Holy Spirit in the Souls of the Just according to the Teaching of St. Thomas Aquinas*, 2nd ed., trans. Sydney A. Raemers (1921; repr., Westminster, Md.: Newman Press, 1952), esp. part IV.

31 At a third level—and here I mention something I have not yet so far commented on—the Spirit also imparts charismatic graces, which are the extraordinary

charisms of the Spirit, especially those enumerated by St. Paul in 1 Corinthians 12:4-7, directed particularly for the benefit of others (II–II.171–78).

32 This reflects my broad sympathy with the traditional Catholic theological articulation of grace perfecting nature—wonderfully and succinctly overviewed in Neil Ormerod, *Creation, Grace, and Redemption* (Maryknoll, N.Y.: Orbis, 2007), chap. 6 on "Grace and the Supernatural"—even as I remain firmly Protestant in emphasizing the prior initiative of God. My own pentecostal sensibilities, however, lead me to approach these issues pneumatologically from beginning to end, which will take us the rest of this volume to unpack.

33 Paul Tillich, *Systematic Theology*, 3 vols. (Chicago: University of Chicago Press, 1951–1963). All references to this work will be made parenthetically in the text as *ST* followed by volume and page number.

34 Tillich writes that "anxiety is an ontological quality. . . . Anxiety is independent of any special object . . . it is dependent only on the threat of nonbeing—which is identical with finitude. In this sense it has been said rightly that the object of anxiety is 'nothingness'—and nothingness is not an 'object.' Objects are feared. A danger, a pain, an enemy, may be feared, but fear can be conquered by action. Anxiety cannot, for no finite being can conquer its finitude. Anxiety is always present, although often it is latent" (*ST* I.191).

35 Tillich was writing at a time when it was fashionable to distinguish between various types of love, often drawing from ancient Greek and Latin terms. We have now come to see—in, e.g., Gene H. Outka, *Agape: An Ethical Analysis* (New Haven: Yale University Press, 1972), and Alan Soble, ed., *Eros, Agape, and Philia: Readings in the Philosophy of Love* (New York: Paragon House, 1989)—that it is fairly arbitrary to define love variously through this strategy. Jamie Smith suggests in his philosophical anthropology that we are first and foremost desiring and loving creatures and that "*agapē* is rightly ordered *eros*" (James K. A. Smith, *Desiring the Kingdom: Worship, Worldview, and Cultural Formation* [Grand Rapids: Baker Academic, 2009], 79), to which I would also add that *agape* is *philia* that is intentionally shaped by the Spirit's presence and activity. By and large, much of the constructive argument of this volume will proceed with a generic and all-inclusive notion of love as ideally *agape*, qualifying or specifying only as relevant to pentecostal-charismatic spirituality.

36 See my *Discerning the Spirit(s): A Pentecostal-Charismatic Contribution to Christian Theology of Religions*, Journal of Pentecostal Theology Supplemental Series 20 (Sheffield, UK: Sheffield Academic, 2000), 77–85.

37 John Charles Cooper argues—convincingly, in my opinion—that Tillich's Spiritual Presence translates into twentieth-century existential philosophical language the mysticism of St. Paul who repeatedly spoke of being "in Christ" or "in the Spirit." See John Charles Cooper, *The "Spiritual Presence" in the Theology of Paul Tillich: Tillich's Use of St. Paul* (Macon, Ga.: Mercer University Press, 1997).

38 Paul Tillich, "Being and Love," *Pastoral Psychology* 5, no. 43 (1954): 43–46, 48, at 43.

39 Thus while *agape* plays a central role in Tillich's soteriology, it is not only not devoid of erotic elements but is fundamentally constituted by erotic love as well;

this theological thesis is irrefutably demonstrated by Alexander C. Irwin, *Eros toward the World: Paul Tillich and the Theology of the Erotic* (Minneapolis: Fortress, 1991), even as he raises pointed questions about how the deep flaws of Tillich's marital love cast a shadow over his theological legacy.

40   My colleague Nimi Wariboko suggests that here Tillich's famous Protestant Principle should be extended by the Pentecostal Principle; the latter provides an engine with which to begin again what the Protestant Principle resists in terms of the absolutization of law. See Nimi Wariboko, *The Pentecostal Principle: Ethical Methodology in New Spirit* (Grand Rapids: Eerdmans, 2011).

41   Paul Tillich, *The Protestant Era*, abr. ed., trans. James Luther Adams (Chicago: University of Chicago Press, 1957), 155.

42   Tillich's succinct and collected thoughts on this issue can be found in his small book, *Love, Power and Justice: Ontological Analyses and Ethical Applications* (New York: Oxford University Press, 1954).

43   These are matters noted by Tillichian scholars—e.g., Robison B. James, "Dealing with the Personal Encounter Deficit in Tillich, Especially vis-à-vis God," *Bulletin of the North American Paul Tillich Society* 33, no. 4 (2007): 6–20.

44   E.g., any comprehensive historical discussion of theologians who also connected love and the Spirit would necessarily include Maximus the Confessor from the Orthodox tradition, the Victorine and Cistercian theologians (such as Richard of St. Victor in the former case and Bonaventure, Aelred of Rievaulx, and William of St. Thierry in the latter), the anchoress Julian of Norwich, and Jonathan Edwards. None of these, however, made substantive and extensive connections between love and the Spirit; their pneumatological associations were tangential, made in a more explicitly trinitarian framework, or ad hoc or nonsystematic in nature.

Chapter 2

1   As noted by Philipp W. Rosemann in "*Sacra pagina* or *scientia divina*? Peter Lombard, Thomas Aquinas, and the Nature of the Theological Project," *Philotheos* 4 (2004): 284–300, esp. 290–93, Aquinas' *Summa Theologica* can be understood at least in part as representing the emergence of theology as *scientia*, understood as the epistemologically rigorous and philosophically systematic articulation of the poetic language of the scriptural and commentary traditions. See also William J. Abraham, *Canon and Criterion in Christian Theology: From the Fathers to Feminism* (New York: Oxford University Press, 1998), chap. 4; and Alexander W. Hall, *Thomas Aquinas and John Duns Scotus: Natural Theology in the High Middle Ages* (New York: Continuum, 2007), esp. chap. 2.

2   I discuss the convergence of theology and science from an explicitly pentecostal perspective in my "Academic Glossolalia? Pentecostal Scholarship, Multi-disciplinarity, and the Science–Religion Conversation," *Journal of Pentecostal Theology* 14, no. 1 (2005): 61–80.

3   I lay out my theology of nature and my views regarding the relationship between theology and science in my *The Spirit of Creation: Modern Science and Divine*

Action in the Pentecostal-Charismatic Imagination (Grand Rapids: Eerdmans, 2011), esp. chap. 2.

4 E.g., Anthony Walsh, *The Science of Love: Understanding Love and Its Effects on Mind and Body* (Buffalo: Prometheus Books, 1991); and Thomas Jay Oord, *Science of Love: The Wisdom of Well-Being* (Philadelphia: Templeton Foundation, 2004).

5 An excellent overview of Sorokin's life and work, particularly in the context of scientific research on love, is Stephen G. Post's introduction to a new edition of Pitirim A. Sorokin, *The Ways and Power of Love: Types, Factors, and Techniques of Moral Transformation* (1954; repr., Philadelphia: Templeton Foundation, 2002). All references to this book hereafter will be to this reprinted edition of *WPL* and be made parenthetically in the text.

6 This was the title of a book he published in the wake of the Second World War: Pitirim A. Sorokin, *The Reconstruction of Humanity* (Boston: Beacon, 1948). See also Sorokin, *Social Philosophies in an Age of Crisis* (Boston: Beacon, 1950), reprinted as *Modern Historical and Social Philosophies* (New York: Dover, 1963), and *S.O.S.: The Meaning of Our Crisis* (Boston: Beacon, 1951).

7 Sorokin recounts the events leading up the founding of the Center, including Lilly's role, in his autobiography, *A Long Journey: The Autobiography of Pitirim A. Sorokin* (New Haven: College and University Press, 1963), chap. 15. For an overview of the work of the Center, see Pitirim A. Sorokin, *On the Practice of Sociology*, ed. Barry V. Johnston (Chicago: University of Chicago Press, 1998), esp. 305–16.

8 Among the most important of these were two edited Sorokin books: *Explorations in Altruistic Love and Behavior: A Symposium* (Boston: Beacon, 1950), and *Forms and Techniques of Altruistic and Spiritual Growth: A Symposium* (Boston: Beacon, 1954).

9 Pitirim A. Sorokin, *Altruistic Love: A Study of American "Good Neighbors" and Christian Saints* (Boston: Beacon, 1950).

10 This is also because the experience of love is "the *summum bonum* . . . the supreme and highest form of happiness itself" (*WPL* 79).

11 See Pitirim A. Sorokin, "Integralism is My Philosophy," in *This Is My Philosophy: Twenty of the World's Outstanding Thinkers Reveal the Deepest Meanings They Have Found in Life*, ed. Whit Burnett (New York: Harper & Brothers, 1957), 180–89; cf. Vladimir Solovyov, *The Philosophical Principles of Integral Knowledge*, trans. Valeria Z. Nollan (Grand Rapids: Eerdmans, 2008).

12 Sorokin's philosophical integralism functioned for his sociological work somewhat like Tillich's philosophical existentialism did for his theological work; see the discussion of these two contemporaries—for a few years (1955–1962) at Harvard University—by Mary Montgomery Clifford, "Paul Tillich and Pitirim A. Sorokin on Love," *Zygon: The Journal of Religion and Science* 39, no. 1 (2004): 103–10.

13 George Steinmetz, "American Sociology before and after World War II: The (Temporary) Settling of a Disciplinary Field," in *Sociology in America: A History*, ed. Craig Calhoun (Chicago: University of Chicago Press, 2007), 314–66.

14 E.g., F. R. Cowell, *Values in Human Society: The Contributions of Pitirim A. Sorokin to Sociology* (Boston: Sargent, 1970); Joseph Allen Matter, *Love, Altruism, and World Crisis: The Challenge of Pitirim Sorokin* (Chicago: Nelson-Hall, 1974); and, more recent, Elvira del Pozo Aviñó, ed., *Integralism, Altruism and Reconstruction: Essays in Honor of Pitirim A. Sorokin*, Biblioteca Javier Coy d'estudis nord-americans 41 (València, Spain: Universitat de València, 2006).

15 E.g., Stephen G. Post, Byron Johnson, Michael E. McCullough, and Jeffrey P. Schloss, eds., *Research on Altruism and Love: An Annotated Bibliography of Major Studies in Psychology, Sociology, Evolutionary Biology, and Theology* (Philadelphia: Templeton Foundation, 2003).

16 E.g., Samuel Oliner and Pearl M. Oliner, *The Altruistic Personality: Rescuers of Jews in Nazi Europe* (New York: Free Press, 1988).

17 The most important book introducing the work of the IRUL is Stephen G. Post, *Unlimited Love: Altruism, Compassion, and Service* (Philadelphia: Templeton Foundation, 2003). Post has published many other volumes in the last ten years.

18 For an overview of developments since Sorokin, see Keishin Inaba and Kate Loewenthal, "Religion and Altruism," in *The Oxford Handbook of the Sociology of Religion*, ed. Peter B. Clarke (New York: Oxford University Press, 2009), 876–89.

19 An accessible "history" of the major developments in research on altruism in the biological sciences is provided by Lee Alan Dugatkin, *The Altruism Equation: Seven Scientists Search for the Origins of Goodness* (Princeton: Princeton University Press, 2006).

20 Charles Darwin, *The Descent of Man: The Concise Edition*, ed. Carl Zimmer (New York: Plume, 2007), 206–7.

21 Samir Okasha, *Evolution and the Levels of Selection* (New York: Oxford University Press, 2006), chap. 5, entitled "The Gene's-Eye View and Its Discontents."

22 Richard Dawkins, *The Selfish Gene* (New York: Oxford University Press, 1976), with two new editions since.

23 Kin selection was probably named by John Maynard Smith, "Group Selection and Kin Selection," *Nature* 201 (1964): 1145–47, and reciprocal altruism and indirect reciprocity by Robert L. Trivers, "The Evolution of Reciprocal Altruism," *Quarterly Review of Biology* 46, no. 1 (1971): 35–57. In the midst of all of this was William Hamilton, who enabled the extension of the notion of kin selection to that of inclusive fitness; on Hamilton, see Dugatkin, *The Altruism Equation*, chap. 5.

24 See Richard D. Alexander, *The Biology of Moral Systems* (New York: De Gruyter, 1987).

25 Two of the major proponents of what is called multilevel and group selection theory are Elliott Sober and David Sloan Wilson, especially their *Unto Others: The Evolution and Psychology of Unselfish Behavior* (Cambridge, Mass.: Harvard University Press, 1998).

26 Jeffrey Schloss, "Emerging Accounts of Altruism: 'Love Creation's Final Law'?" in *Altruism and Altruistic Love: Science, Philosophy, and Religion in Dialogue*, ed. Stephen G. Post et al. (New York: Oxford University Press, 2002), 212–42, at 214.

27 This would certainly be the case for the work that jump-started the enterprise: Robert M. Axelrod, *The Evolution of Cooperation* (New York: Basic Books, 1984). As a political scientist, Axelrod's application of game theoretical methods to reciprocal altruistic theories has been widely heralded (across disciplines) as providing a plausible explanation for the emergence of cooperation as a strategy for survival in a competitive field. For a state-of-the-question report on the notion of cooperation in the biological sciences, see Peter Hammerstein, ed., *Genetic and Cultural Evolution of Cooperation* (Cambridge, Mass.: MIT Press, 2003).

28 Kenneth M. Weiss and Anne V. Buchanan, *The Mermaid's Tale: Four Billion Years of Cooperation in the Making of Living Things* (Cambridge, Mass.: Harvard University Press, 2009), xi, emphasis in original. See also John L. Casti, "Cooperation: The Ghost in the Machinery of Evolution," in *Cooperation and Conflict in General Evolutionary Processes*, ed. John L. Casti and Anders Karlqvist (New York: John Wiley & Sons, 1995), 63–88.

29 Ernst Fehr and Simon Gächter, "Altruistic Punishment in Humans," *Nature* 415 (2002): 137–40. Researchers have begun, within this framework, to explore the role of religion in fostering expectations of punishment, and how such worldviews thereby also inform cooperative behaviors; see, e.g., Dominic Johnson and Jesse Bering, "Hand of God, Mind of Man: Punishment and Cognition in the Evolution of Cooperation," in *The Believing Primate: Scientific, Philosophical, and Theological Reflections on the Origin of Religion,* ed. Jeffrey Schloss and Michael J. Murray (New York: Oxford University Press, 2009), 26–43.

30 Interestingly, Roughgarden is also an Episcopalian who has urged peace between science and Christian faith in, e.g., *Evolution and Christian Faith: Reflections of an Evolutionary Biologist* (Washington, D.C.: Island Press, 2006).

31 Joan Roughgarden, *The Genial Gene: Deconstructing Darwinian Selfishness* (Berkeley: University of California Press, 2009).

32 See Samir Okasha, Ken Binmore, Jonathan Grose, and Cédric Paternotte, "Cooperation, Conflict, Sex and Bargaining," review of *The Genial Gene*, by Joan Roughgarden, *Biology and Philosophy* 25, no. 2 (2010): 257–67.

33 Matt Ridley, *The Origins of Virtue: Human Instincts and the Evolution of Cooperation* (New York: Viking, 1997), 7.

34 Stephen J. Pope, in *The Evolution of Altruism and the Ordering of Love* (Washington, D.C.: Georgetown University Press, 1994), is one of the first theological ethicists and theologians of love who has attempted to think through the nature of out-group altruism in light of the biological sciences, following (he urges) Aquinas' methodology, not necessarily the Angelic Doctor's formal hierarchy of love.

35 One of the first studies to explore the phenomenon of prosociality vis-à-vis altruism at length was Nancy Eisenberg, *Altruistic Emotion, Cognition, and Behavior* (Hillside, N.J.: Lawrence Erlbaum Associates, 1986).

36 C. Daniel Batson, *The Altruism Question: Towards a Social-Psychological Answer* (Hillsdale, N.J.: Laurence Erlbaum Associates, 1991), 6–7.

37 Batson, *Altruism Question*, 58.

38 Batson, *Altruism Question*, 89.

39 Batson, *Altruism Question*, 174.

40 Batson, *Altruism Question*, 230.

41 Batson's early work on the psychology of altruism paralleled that of Robert H. Frank, *Passions within Reason: The Strategic Role of the Emotions* (New York: Norton, 1988), who argued similarly with regard to the biology of altruism.

42 See Thomas R. Insel, "Implications for the Neurobiology of Love," in *Altruism and Altruistic Love*, ed. Post et al., 254–63, and Mario Beauregard, Jérôme Courtemanche, Vincent Paquette, and Évelyne Landry St-Pierre, "The Neural Basis of Unconditional Love," *Psychiatry Research: Neuroimaging* 172, no. 2 (2009): 93–98.

43 I have written on this in my "The Virtues and Intellectual Disability: Explorations in the (Cognitive) Sciences of Moral Formation," in *Theology and the Science of Morality: Virtue Ethics, Exemplarity, and Cognitive Neuroscience*, ed. James A. Van Slyke et al. (New York: Routledge, forthcoming).

44 Joshua Greene and Jonathan Haidt, "How (and Where) Does Moral Judgment Work?" *Trends in Cognitive Sciences* 6, no. 12 (2002): 517–23, at 517.

45 Lynn G. Underwood, "Compassionate Love: A Framework for Research," in *The Science of Compassionate Love: Theory, Research, and Applications*, ed. Beverley Fehr, Susan Sprecher, and Lynn G. Underwood (Malden, Mass.: Wiley-Blackwell, 2009), 3–25, at 5, emphasis in original.

46 Here I rely especially on Paul Thagard, *The Brain and the Meaning of Life* (Princeton: Princeton University Press, 2010), chap. 9. For a full-length study, see Stein Bråten, ed., *On Being Moved: From Mirror Neurons to Empathy* (Philadelphia: John Benjamins, 2007).

47 William B. Hurlbut, "Empathy, Evolution, and Altruism," in *Altruism and Altruistic Love*, ed. Post et al., 309–30.

48 Andrew Michael Flescher and Daniel L. Worthen, *The Altruistic Species: Scientific, Philosophical, and Religious Perspectives on Human Benevolence* (Philadelphia: Templeton Foundation, 2007), 133–34, emphasis in original.

49 Flescher and Worthen, *Altruistic Species*, 143–44, emphasis in original.

50 Besides empathy, other sociocultural emotions increasingly recognized as playing important roles in the evolutionary psychological origins of altruism among humans are shame, guilt, pride, and honor; see Herbert Gintis, Samuel Bowles, Robert Boyd, and Ernst Fehr, "Explaining Altruistic Behaviour in Humans," in *Oxford Handbook of Evolutionary Psychology*, ed. R. I. M. Dunbar and Louise Barrett (New York: Oxford University Press, 2007), 605–19, esp. 613–17.

51 We are only at the very beginning stages of untangling the complexities involved in understanding human affectivity, which includes not only emotion and passion but feeling and desire, inclination and disposition. But what we do know confirms that the science of the affections will open up windows into human intersubjectivity and interrelationality as well. For preliminary studies, see Colwyn Trevarthen, "The Intersubjective Psychobiology of Human Meaning: Learning of Culture Depends on Interest for Co-operative Practical Work—and Affection for the Joyful Art of Good Company," *Psychoanalytic Dialogues* 19, no. 5 (2009): 507–18, and

Ravi Kumar Kurup and Parameswara Achutha Kurup, "Hypothalamic Digoxin, Hemispheric Dominance, and Neurobiology of Love and Affection," *International Journal of Neuroscience* 113, no. 5 (2003): 721–29. We will return to discuss the affections in greater detail in chap. 5.

52 See A. C. Papanicolaou, *Emotion: A Reconsideration of the Somatic Theory* (New York: Gordon and Breach Science Publishers, 1989).

53 Richard Restak, *The Naked Brain: How the Emerging Neurosociety Is Changing How We Live, Work, and Love* (New York: Harmony Books, 2005).

54 This is exactly what appears to have happened in Walter J. Freeman, *Societies of Brains: A Study in the Neuroscience of Love and Hate* (Hillsdale, N.J.: Lawrence Erlbaum Associates, 1995), which claims as its aim "to give *love* . . . due place and precedence in intentionality" (8, emphasis original) but results in nary a mention of love in the rest of the book, lost as it is in analyses of neuroactivity, sensation/perception, intention/movement, learning processes, and the self-society relationship. To Freeman's credit, the reader comes away with an inkling of how love might be understood as a neurosocial reality, and thus his book can be considered a contribution to the important conversation on the social dimensions of the brain and of human rationality.

55 This is not to deny the contributions of psychology, which I have not focused on. If I were to do so, I would begin with the work of Robert J. Sternberg, including his *The Triangle of Love: Intimacy, Passion, Commitment* (New York: Basic Books, 1988); *Love Is a Story: A New Theory of Relationships* (New York: Oxford University Press, 1998); *Cupid's Arrow: The Course of Love through Time* (New York: Cambridge University Press, 1998); and, edited with Karin Weis, *The New Psychology of Love* (New Haven: Yale University Press, 2006). As we can see, however, even Sternberg's rigorously grounded psychology of love has sprouted wings, transgressing disciplinary boundaries in the process, which is one of the points I take from this exercise.

56 Thomas Lewis, Fari Amini, and Richard Lannon, *A General Theory of Love* (New York: Vintage Books, 2001). All authors are M.D.s in psychiatry, but with distinct emphases in neuroscientific psychodynamics (Lewis), psychoanalysis (Amini), and psychoactive medication (Lannon).

57 Oord, *Science of Love*, 31; see also Thomas Jay Oord, *Defining Love: A Philosophical, Scientific, and Theological Engagement* (Grand Rapids: Brazos, 2010), esp. chaps. 3–5.

58 I want here to emphasize Oord's call for a multilateral and multidisciplinary inquiry into love since it is a danger that the neurocognitive focus on the emotions will overemphasize this approach, thus resulting in a reductionistic view of love as emotionally based; for warnings about what is lost in a research paradigm on the emotions that has by and large been psychologized—i.e., medieval views about the emotions as intertwined with the passions, the appetites, and the affections—see Thomas Dixon, *From Passions to Emotions: The Creation of a Secular Psychological Category* (New York: Cambridge University Press, 2003).

59   On the idea of convergent evolution, the notion that rewinding the evolutionary tape over and over would result in the emergence of pretty much the kind of successful adaptations evident in our own evolutionary history, see Simon Conway Morris, *Life's Solution: Inevitable Humans in a Lonely Universe* (New York: Cambridge University Press, 2003), and Simon Conway Morris, ed., *The Deep Structure of Biology: Is Convergence Sufficiently Ubiquitous to Give a Directional Signal?* (West Conshohocken, Pa.: Templeton Foundation, 2008).

60   This is suggestive of the truth of the theory of reciprocal altruism, which has already received sociological validation—e.g., Samuel P. Oliner, *Do Unto Others: Extraordinary Acts of Ordinary People* (Cambridge, Mass.: Westview, 2003). The truth of a particular biological theory of altruism does not necessarily presume the exclusive truth of the theory's presuppositions (e.g., neo-Darwinian egoism).

61   E.g., Kristen Renwick Monroe, *The Heart of Altruism: Perceptions of a Common Humanity* (Princeton: Princeton University Press, 1996).

62   Eva-Lotta Grantén, *Patterns of Care: Relating Altruism in Sociobiology and the Christian Tradition of Agape*, Lund Studies in Ethics and Theology 12 (Lund, Sweden: Lund University, 2003).

Chapter 3

1   I categorize Pentecostalism here as a "religion" merely descriptively, without any of the pejorative associations that Pentecostals themselves frequently make with regard to that notion (insisting that theirs is a living and vital faith relationship with God, rather than a static or dead form of religiosity). Precedence here involves an important work by pentecostal scholars: Murray W. Dempster, Byron D. Klaus, and Douglas Petersen, eds., *The Globalization of Pentecostalism: A Religion Made to Travel* (Irvine, Calif.: Regnum Books International, 1999).

2   Esp. my *The Spirit Poured Out on All Flesh: Pentecostalism and the Possibility of Global Theology* (Grand Rapids: Baker Academic, 2005), and *In the Days of Caesar: Pentecostalism and Political Theology* (Grand Rapids: Eerdmans, 2010).

3   Notice, e.g., the titles of books on Pentecostalism—Meredith B. McGuire, *Pentecostal Catholics: Power, Charisma, and Order in a Religious Movement* (Philadelphia: Temple University Press, 1981); Ogbu U. Kalu, *Power, Poverty, and Prayer: The Challenges of Poverty and Pluralism in African Christianity, 1960–1996* (New York: Peter Lang, 2000); and Asonzeh F. K. Ukah, *A New Paradigm of Pentecostal Power: A Study of the Redeemed Christian Church of God in Nigeria* (Trenton, N.J.: Africa World Press, 2008).

4   The early Pentecostals did not question the authenticity of the longer ending of Mark; for discussion, see John Christopher Thomas and Kimberly Ervin Alexander, "'And the Signs are Following': Mark 16.9-20—A Journey into Pentecostal Hermeneutics," *Journal of Pentecostal Theology* 11, no. 2 (2003): 147–70.

5   We have no time to comment about this except to say that it is also plausible to comprehend such expressions of Pentecostalism within its power paradigm; for further discussion, see Ralph W. Hood Jr. and W. Paul Williamson, *Them*

That Believe: The Power and Meaning of the Christian Serpent-Handling Tradition (Berkeley: University of California Press, 2008).

6   As discussed by William W. Menzies and Robert P. Menzies, *Spirit and Power: Foundations of Pentecostal Experience* (Grand Rapids: Zondervan, 2000), part II.

7   See John Wimber with Kevin Springer, *Power Evangelism* (San Francisco: Harper & Row, 1986) and *Power Healing* (San Francisco: Harper & Row, 1987); and Kevin Springer, ed., *Power Encounters among Christians in the Western World* (San Francisco: Harper & Row, 1988).

8   The many works of C. Peter Wagner lead the way here—e.g., *Confronting the Powers: How the New Testament Church Experienced the Power of Strategic-Level Spiritual Warfare* (Ventura, Calif.: Regal Books, 1996). See also Rene Holvast, *Spiritual Mapping in the United States and Argentina, 1989–2005: A Geography of Fear* (Boston: Brill, 2008).

9   There has been little confirmation of missionaries communicating to "natives" in their own languages; see D. William Faupel, "Glossolalia as Foreign Language: An Investigation of the Early Twentieth-Century Pentecostal Claim," *Wesleyan Theological Journal* 31, no. 1 (1996): 95–109.

10   E.g., Luke Wesley, *The Church in China: Persecuted, Pentecostal, and Powerful* (Baguio, Philippines: AJPS Books, 2004).

11   E.g., L. Grant McClung Jr., ed., *Azusa Street and Beyond: Pentecostal Missions and Church Growth in the Twentieth Century* (South Plainfield, N.J.: Bridge, 1986); Murray A. Dempster, Byron D. Klaus, and Douglas Petersen, eds., *Called and Empowered: Global Mission in Pentecostal Perspective* (Peabody, Mass.: Hendrickson, 1991); and Gary B. McGee, *Miracles, Missions, and American Pentecostalism* (Maryknoll, N.Y.: Orbis, 2010).

12   Paul Alexander, *Signs and Wonders: Why Pentecostalism Is the World's Fastest Growing Faith* (San Francisco: Jossey-Bass, 2009).

13   E.g., Craig S. Keener, *The Spirit in the Gospels and Acts: Divine Purity and Power* (Peabody, Mass.: Hendrickson, 1997). Note also that the theme of the twenty-seventh annual meeting of the Society for Pentecostal Studies was "Purity and Power: Revisioning the Holiness and Pentecostal/Charismatic Movements for the Twenty-First Century" (held jointly with the Wesleyan Theological Society, March 12–14, 1998, in Cleveland, Tennessee); the session papers have been collected and are available at many university libraries.

14   E.g., Tom Smail, Andrew Walker, and Nigel Wright, *The Love of Power, or, the Power of Love: A Careful Assessment of the Problems within the Charismatic and Word-of-Faith Movements* (Minneapolis: Bethany House, 1994); Roland Howard, *Charismania: When Christian Fundamentalism Goes Wrong* (Herndon, Va.: Mowbray, 1997); and Martyn Percy, *Power and the Church: Ecclesiology in an Age of Transition* (Washington, D.C.: Cassell, 1998).

15   Material from this section has been adapted from parts of my article, "What's Love Got to Do with It? The Sociology of Love and the Renewal of Modern Pentecostalism," *Journal of Pentecostal Theology* 21, no. 1 (2012): forthcoming.

16 By this time Poloma had already published two major studies on the contemporary pentecostal-charismatic renewal—*The Charismatic Movement: Is There a New Pentecost?* (Boston: Twayne Publishers, 1982) and *The Assemblies of God at the Crossroads: Charisma and Institutional Dilemmas* (Knoxville: University of Tennessee Press, 1989)—with a third book in press, to be noted momentarily.

17 See John Arnott, *The Father's Blessing* (Orlando, Fla.: Creation House, 1995), chap. 1, esp. 22–26.

18 Margaret M. Poloma, *Main Street Mystics: The Toronto Blessing and Reviving Pentecostalism* (Walnut Creek, Calif.: AltaMira Press, 2003), 140.

19 Poloma, *Main Street Mystics*, 141.

20 Poloma uses "mysticism" and its cognates as framed by social psychological theories of individual religious experience (see *Main Street Mystics*, 24–31); my usage in the remainder of this chapter is consistent with this, but focuses especially on pentecostal perceptions that the Holy Spirit is directly present to and active through the experiences of believers.

21 Margaret M. Poloma and Ralph W. Hood Jr., *Blood and Fire: Godly Love in a Pentecostal Emerging Church* (New York: New York University Press, 2008).

22 Poloma and Hood, *Blood and Fire*, 145.

23 With regard to these types of love, Poloma and Hood drew on the work of philosopher Rolf M. Johnson, *Three Faces of Love* (DeKalb: Northern Illinois University Press, 2001).

24 Poloma and Hood, *Blood and Fire*, 115–16.

25 As reported, e.g., by Donald E. Miller and Tetsunao Yamamori, *Global Pentecostalism: The New Face of Christian Social Engagement* (Berkeley: University of California Press, 2007).

26 Matthew T. Lee and Margaret M. Poloma, *A Sociological Study of the Great Commandment in Pentecostalism: The Practice of Godly Love as Benevolent Service* (Lewiston, N.Y.: Mellen, 2009), 7.

27 Lee and Poloma, *A Sociological Study of the Great Commandment in Pentecostalism*, 129.

28 Margaret M. Poloma and John C. Green, *The Assemblies of God: Godly Love and the Revitalization of American Pentecostalism* (New York: New York University Press, 2010); all further references to this work will be made parenthetically in the text by *AGGL* followed by page numbers. I should note that as social scientists, both Poloma and Green understand "revitalization" in a descriptive sense; however, as an insider to the Pentecostal movement broadly defined, Poloma herself would probably grant certain latitude to include as part of this understanding an ecclesial notion of renewal.

29 No distinctive correlations were established between either traditionalism or religious experience and volunteering or participation in politics. But all things being equal in these arenas, this does not overthrow my interpretation of the overall thrust of the data nor the thesis of presented here.

30 Poloma has always been sensitive to the methodological complexities involved by her participant-observation as a Christian studying Christian phenomena, and

almost every one of her books includes a chapter or appendix or some other substantial section discussing these issues. I have provided a short overview of how Poloma has negotiated the tensions between (social) scientific reason and faith within a broader discussion of the relationship between science and pentecostal faith in my *The Spirit of Creation: Modern Science and Divine Action in the Pentecostal-Charismatic Imagination* (Grand Rapids: Eerdmans, 2011), chap. 2.

31 For an overview of how the project has continued to develop methodologically in terms of involving theologians, see Matthew T. Lee, Margaret M. Poloma, and Stephen G. Post, "Introduction: The Interdisciplinary Study of Godly Love," in *The Science and Theology of Godly Love*, ed. Matthew T. Lee and Amos Yong (DeKalb: Northern Illinois University Press, forthcoming).

32 The popular literature on, as well as practical guides to, pentecostal and charismatic prayer is extensive. Unfortunately, however, there remains little by way of scholarly analysis of this phenomenon. An informative introductory discussion can be found in chap. 11 of Cephas Narh Omenyo, *Pentecost Outside Pentecostalism: A Study of the Development of Charismatic Renewal in the Mainline Churches in Ghana* (Zoetermeer, Netherlands: Boekencentrum, 2006), especially the section "Prayer, Praise, and Fasting."

33 Myung Soo Park, "Korean Pentecostal Spirituality as Manifested in the Testimonies of Members of Yoido Full Gospel Church," in *David Yonggi Cho: A Close Look at His Theology and Ministry*, ed. Wonsuk Ma, William W. Menzies, and Hyeonsung Bae (Baguio City, Philippines: APTS Press, 2004), 43–67.

34 This reflects the embodied character of pentecostal spirituality, expertly summarized in Russell P. Spittler, "Corinthian Spirituality: How a Flawed Anthropology Imperils Authentic Christian Existence," in *Pentecostal Currents in American Protestantism*, ed. Edith L. Blumhofer, Russell P. Spittler, and Grant A. Wacker (Urbana: University of Illinois Press, 1999), 3–19.

35 Which is not to say that everything that goes on under this label is of the Holy Spirit; for a more cautious interpretation of this phenomenon, see Darren Ayling, "'When Groans and Mumblings are Not Enough': Investigating Being 'Slain in the Spirit' in Acts," in Myk Habets, ed., *The Spirit of Truth: Reading Scripture and Constructing Theology with the Holy Spirit* (Eugene, Ore.: Pickwick, 2010), 168–78.

36 Ronda Chervin, *Why I am a Charismatic, a Catholic Explains: Reflections on Charismatic Prayer and the Longings of the Human Heart* (Liguori, Mo.: Liguori, 1978).

37 A number of essayists highlight this aspect of glossolalia in Mark J. Cartledge, *Speaking in Tongues: Multi-Disciplinary Perspectives* (Waynesboro, Ga.: Paternoster, 2006).

38 An overview is Mark J. Cartledge, *Encountering the Spirit: The Charismatic Tradition* (Maryknoll, N.Y.: Orbis, 2007), chap. 3.

39 "Liminality" refers to the corporate, usually congregational, experience of worship which enables worshipers to transcend their normal daily routines and effectively be transformed to engage their world; for further discussion, see Daniel E. Albrecht, *Rites in the Spirit: A Ritual Approach to Pentecostal/Charismatic*

Spirituality, Journal of Pentecostal Theology Supplemental Series 19 (Sheffield, UK: Sheffield Academic, 1999), esp. chaps. 6–7.

40 This is not to say that everything that happens in "holy laughter" revival circles is of the Spirit; for a sensitive yet critical overview, see B. J. Oropeza, *A Time to Laugh: The Holy Laughter Phenomenon Examined* (Peabody, Mass.: Hendrickson, 1995).

41 Cecil M. Robeck Jr., *The Azusa Street Mission and Revival: The Birth of the Pentecostal Movement* (Nashville: Nelson, 2006), 146.

42 Hillsong Music, "My Greatest Love Is You," lyrics available on numerous Internet sites.

43 For further discussion of Hillsong's pneumatically oriented worship, see Darlene Zschech, "The Role of the Holy Spirit in Worship: An Introduction to the Hillsong Church, Sydney, Australia," in *The Spirit in Worship, Worship in the Spirit*, ed. Teresa Berger and Bryan D. Spinks (Collegeville, Minn.: Liturgical Press, 2009), 285–92, and Mark Evans, *Open Up the Doors: Music in the Modern Church* (Oakville, Conn.: Equinox Publishing, 2006), chap. 5.

44 Julie C. Ma, "Korean Pentecostal Spirituality: A Case Study of Jashil Choi," in *The Spirit and Spirituality: Essays in Honour of Russell P. Spittler*, ed. Wonsuk Ma and Robert P. Menzies (New York: T&T Clark, 2004), 298–313, tells of how Choi, the mother-in-law of Yonggi Cho, the pastor of the largest congregation in the world in Seoul, Korea, is motivated by prayer and fasting to personal evangelism and social ministry.

45 E.g., Heidi Baker with Shara Pradhan, *Compelled by Love: How to Change the World through the Simple Power of Love in Action* (Lake Mary, Fla.: Charisma House, 2008).

46 E.g., Heidi Baker and Rolland Baker, *Expecting Miracles: True Stories of God's Supernatural Power and How You Can Experience It* (Grand Rapids: Chosen, 2007) and *The Hungry Always Get Fed: A Year of Miracles* (Chichester, UK: New Wine Press, 2007). Note that Heidi Baker is not only a pentecostal missionary (to Mozambique) but also a Ph.D., her doctoral dissertation being *Pentecostal Glossolalia: Toward a Reconstructive Theology of Glossolalia* (Ph.D. diss., King's College, London, 1995).

47 As Bruce Stevens—in " 'Why Feel Bad?' A Theory of Affect (Emotions) and the Relationship to Pentecostal Spirituality," *Australasia Pentecostal Studies* 9 (2005–2006): 81–98, at 94—notes, "The experience of 'Baptism in the Spirit' provides an affective flooding in the joy of the Spirit which is experienced as emotionally healing."

Chapter 4

1 The definitive history, so far, is Cecil M. Robeck Jr., *The Azusa Street Mission and Revival: The Birth of the Pentecostal Movement* (Nashville: Nelson, 2006).

2 Some might be concerned that to follow Sorokin's notion of "love energy" would be misleading since it suggests that science might be able to quantitatively

measure the presence and activity of the Holy Spirit as it does electromagnetic energy forces. I think Sorokin's sociology of love admits of scientific measurement, although only in the effects of love rather than in its causal mechanisms. As should become clear in what follows in this chapter and in the remainder of this features of the Spirit's empowering activity but to its transformative effects. See also my concluding chapter in Matthew T. Lee and Amos Yong, eds., *The Science and Theology of Godly Love* (DeKalb: Northern Illinois University Press, forthcoming).

3   A point of entry into the dispute is Michael Bergunder, "Constructing Indian Pentecostalism: On Issues of Methodology and Representation," in *Asian and Pentecostal: The Charismatic Face of Christianity in Asia*, ed. Allan Anderson and Edmond Tang, Regnum Studies in Mission/Asian Journal of Pentecostal Studies Series 3 (Oxford: Regnum, 2005), 177–214, esp. 179–91.

4   The standard accounts of the holiness roots of Pentecostalism are Vinson Synan, *The Holiness-Pentecostal Tradition: Charismatic Movements in the Twentieth Century*, 2nd ed. (Grand Rapids: Eerdmans, 1997), and Donald W. Dayton, *Theological Roots of Pentecostalism* (Metuchen, N.J.: Scarecrow Press, 1987). More important for our purposes because of our focus on black holiness Pentecostalism, which is central to this chapter, are Walter J. Hollenweger, *Pentecostalism: Origins and Developments Worldwide* (Peabody, Mass.: Hendrickson, 1997), part I; Iain MacRobert, *The Black Roots and White Racism of Early Pentecostalism in the USA* (New York: St. Martin's Press, 1988); and Cheryl J. Sanders, *Saints in Exile: The Holiness-Pentecostal Experience in African American Religion and Culture* (New York: Oxford University Press, 1996). For a discussion of the dominant African American character of the Azusa Street mission, see Cecil M. Robeck Jr., "The Azusa Street Mission and Historic Black Churches: Two Worlds in Conflict in Los Angeles' African American Community," in *Afro-Pentecostalism: Black Pentecostal and Charismatic Christianity in History and Culture*, ed. Amos Yong and Estrelda Alexander, Religion, Race, and Ethnicity Series (New York: New York University Press, 2011), 21–41, esp. 29–35.

5   See David Petts, "The Baptism in the Holy Spirit: The Theological Distinctive," in *Pentecostal Perspectives*, ed. Keith Warrington (Carlisle, UK: Paternoster, 1998), 98–119; for more on Parham's role, see the excellent scholarly biography by James R. Goff Jr., *Fields White unto Harvest: Charles F. Parham and the Missionary Origins of Pentecostalism* (Fayetteville: University of Arkansas Press, 1988).

6   See Allan H. Anderson, "The Dubious Legacy of Charles Parham: Racism and Cultural Insensitivities among Pentecostals," *Pneuma: The Journal of the Society for Pentecostal Studies* 27, no. 1 (2005): 51–64, esp. 52–57.

7   I delineate Durham's views over and against other pentecostal interpretations of sanctification and holiness in my *In the Days of Caesar: Pentecostalism and Political Theology* (Grand Rapids: Eerdmans, 2010), chap. 5.1.1.

8   James S. Tinney, "William J. Seymour: Father of Modern-Day Pentecostalism," *Journal of the Interdenominational Theological Center* 4, no. 1 (1976): 34–44, esp. 39. See also William J. Seymour, *The Doctrines and Discipline of the Azusa Street*

Apostolic Faith Mission of Los Angeles, California, ed. Larry Martin (1915; repr., Joplin, Mo.: Christian Life Books, 2000), 42.

9   A fully digitized version of the newsletter is available through the Flower Pentecostal Heritage Center, http://ifphc.org/index.cfm?fuseaction=publications Guide.apostolicfaithazusa (accessed December 21, 2010). In most cases, unnamed articles would have been written or adapted as his own by Seymour, the newsletter editor.

10   Unnamed and untitled, *Apostolic Faith* 1, no. 1 (1906): 1.

11   As represented, e.g., by J. A. B. Wood, *Perfect Love, or, Plain Things for Those Who Need Them: Concerning the Doctrine, Experience, Profession, and Practice of Christian Holiness*, rev. ed. (Chicago: Christian Witness, 1880).

12   Seymour, *Doctrines and Discipline*, 42–43.

13   Unnamed, "United to Jesus," *Apostolic Faith* 1, no. 2 (1906): 3.

14   William J. Seymour, "Questions Answered," *Apostolic Faith* 1, no. 11 (1908): 2; capitalization in original. For further discussion of the theology of love at the Azusa Street Mission, see Charles R. Fox Jr., *William J. Seymour: A Critical Investigation of His Soteriology, Pneumatology, and Ecclesiology* (Ph.D. diss., Regent University School of Divinity, 2009), esp. the section "A Loving Church" (112–16).

15   Unnamed and untitled, from *The Pentecost* 1, no. 1 (1908): 4; also available through the Flower Pentecostal Heritage Center, http://ifphc.org/index.cfm?fusea ction=publicationsGuide.thePentecost (accessed December 21, 2010).

16   See also Kimberly Ervin Alexander, "Boundless Love Divine: A Re-evaluation of Early Understandings of the Experience of Spirit Baptism," in *Passover, Pentecost, and Parousia: Studies in Celebration of the Life and Ministry of R. Hollis Gause*, ed. Steven Jack Land, Rickie D. Moore, and John Christopher Thomas, Journal of Pentecostal Theology Supplemental Series 35 (Blandford Forum, UK: Deo Publications, 2010), 145–70. Cf. Michael Wilkinson, "Charles W. Chawner and the Missionary Impulse of the Hebden Mission," in *Winds from the North: Canadian Contributions to the Pentecostal Movement*, ed. Michael Wilkinson and Peter Althouse, Religion in Americas Series 10 (Boston: Brill, 2010), 39–54, esp. 44.

17   Frank Bartleman, *Azusa Street* (1925; repr., Plainfield, N.J.: Logos International, 1980), 54.

18   See the insightful essay by Renea Brathwaite, "The Azusa Street Revival and Racial Reconciliation: An Afro-Pentecostal Perspective," in *Forgiveness, Reconciliation, and Restoration: Multidisciplinary Studies from a Pentecostal Perspective*, ed. Martin William Mittelstadt and Geoffrey William Sutton (Eugene, Ore.: Pickwick, 2010), 65–87. Brathwaite argues that an idealized view of the Mission overlooks how even within the very early days of the revival its racial harmony was contested and that this gradually unfolded into the segregated pentecostal movement that marked much of its development in the rest of the twentieth century.

19   Unnamed, "The Old Time Pentecost," *Apostolic Faith* 1, no. 1 (1906): 1.

20   Dale T. Irvin, "'Drawing All Together in One Bond of Love': The Ecumenical Vision of William J. Seymour and the Azusa Street Revival," *Journal of Pentecostal Theology* 3, no. 6 (1995): 25–53, at 41.

21   William J. Seymour, "The Same Old Way," *Apostolic Faith* 1, no. 1 (1906): 3.
22   See David D. Daniels III, "The Color of Charismatic Leadership: William Joseph Seymour and Martin Luther King, Jr. as Champions of Interracialism," in *We've Come This Far: Reflections on the Pentecostal Tradition and Racial Reconciliation*, ed. Byron D. Klaus, Encounter: The Pentecostal Ministry Series 2 (Springfield, Mo.: Assemblies of God Theological Seminary, 2006), 66–87, esp. 82.
23   Unnamed, "Beginning of a World Wide Revival," *Apostolic Faith* 1, no. 5 (1907): 1.
24   Steven J. Land, "William J. Seymour: The Father of the Holiness-Pentecostal Movement," in Henry H. Knight III, *From Aldersgate to Azusa Street: Wesleyan, Holiness, and Pentecostal Visions of the New Creation* (Eugene, Ore.: Pickwick, 2010), 218–26, at 225.
25   Frederick L. Ware, "The Church of God in Christ and the Azusa Street Revival," in *The Azusa Street Revival and Its Legacy*, ed. Harold D. Hunter and Cecil M. Robeck Jr. (Cleveland, Tenn.: Pathway Press, 2006), 243–57, esp. 247–49.
26   For details, see David D. Daniels, "Charles Harrison Mason: The Interracial Impulse of Early Pentecostalism," in *Portraits of a Generation: Early Pentecostal Leaders*, ed. James R. Goff Jr. and Grant Wacker (Fayetteville: University of Arkansas Press, 2002), 255–70.
27   Seymour, *Doctrines and Discipline*, 38–39.
28   Ithiel C. Clemmons, *Bishop C. H. Mason and the Roots of the Church of God in Christ* (Bakersfield, Calif.: Pneuma Life, 1996), 57.
29   Clemmons, *Bishop C. H. Mason*, 73.
30   Joe Newman, *Race and the Assemblies of God Church: The Journey from Azusa Street to the "Miracle of Memphis"* (Youngstown, N.Y.: Cambria Press, 2007), argues that the Assemblies leaders were consciously motivated, even if only in part, by white–black issues, while Darrin J. Rodgers, "The Assemblies of God and the Long Journey toward Racial Reconciliation," *Assemblies of God Heritage* 28 (2008): 50–61, 66, suggests that other reasons were more foundational and that race was largely beneath the surface of the denomination's founding. For our purposes, no resolution of this issue is required.
31   For details, see Newman, *Race and the Assemblies of God Church*, chap. 5. Cf. Lois Olena, "I'm Sorry, My Brother," in *We've Come This Far*, ed. Klaus, 130–52, for a detailed examination of the case of Robert Harrison, who was originally refused credentials in 1951 but finally became a "poster child" African American in the Assemblies when he was invited to join the Billy Graham evangelistic team in 1962 (he was also ordained by the Assemblies that year).
32   For more on this observation, see Gastón Espinosa, "Ordinary Prophet: William J. Seymour and the Azusa Street Revival," in *Azusa Street Revival*, ed. Hunter and Robeck, 29–60, esp. 53–54.
33   See, e.g., H. Paul Thompson Jr., "'On Account of Conditions that Seem Unbearable': A Proposal about Race Relations in the Church of God (Cleveland, TN) 1909–1929," *Pneuma: The Journal of the Society for Pentecostal Studies* 25, no. 2 (2003): 240–64; and Harold D. Hunter, "A Journey toward Racial Reconciliation:

Race Mixing in the Church of God of Prophecy," in *Azusa Street Revival*, ed. Hunter and Robeck, 277–96.

34 The laments of Johan Mostert, "Lessons from Our Struggle to Overcome Racial Segregation: A Brief History of the Apostolic Faith Mission of South Africa," in Byron D. Klaus, *We've Come This Far*, ed. Klaus, 153–62, are recognized as applicable also in the U.S.A. See also Cecil M. Robeck Jr., "Historical Roots of Racial Unity and Disunity in American Pentecostalism," *Cyberjournal for Pentecostal-Charismatic Research* 14 (2005), http://www.pctii.org/cyberj/cyberj14.html (accessed June 6, 2011).

35 See Frank D. Macchia, "From Azusa to Memphis: Evaluating the Racial Reconciliation Dialogue among Pentecostals," *Pneuma: The Journal of the Society for Pentecostal Studies* 17, no. 2 (1995): 203–18, along with the set of "Roundtable: Racial Reconciliation" articles in *Pneuma: The Journal of the Society for Pentecostal Studies* 18, no. 1 (1996): 113–40.

36 In short, mere rhetoric needs to be translated into concrete action that dismantles racism; see Derrick R. Rosenior, "The Rhetoric of Pentecostal Racial Reconciliation: Looking Back to Move Forward," in *A Liberating Spirit: Pentecostals and Social Action in North America*, ed. Michael Wilkinson and Steven M. Studebaker, Pentecostals, Peacemaking, and Social Justice Series 2 (Eugene, Ore.: Pickwick, 2010), 53–84, which is a distillation of Rosenior's dissertation, *Toward Racial Reconciliation: Collective Memory, Myth, and Nostalgia in American* (Ph.D. diss., Howard University, 2005).

37 The definitive work on this topic so far is Paul Alexander, *Peace to War: Shifting Allegiances in the Assemblies of God*, C. Henry Smith Series 9 (Telford, Pa.: Cascadia Publishing House, 2009); my focus in what follows, though, is on the pacifist commitments of COGIC.

38 See Jay Beaman, *Pentecostal Pacifism: The Origin, Development, and Rejection of Pacific Belief among the Pentecostals* (Hillsboro, Kan.: Center for Mennonite Brethren Studies, 1989), chap. 1.

39 Theodore Kornweibel Jr., "Race and Conscientious Objection in World War I: The Story of the Church of God in Christ," in *Proclaim Peace: Christian Pacifism from Unexpected Quarters*, ed. Theron F. Schlabach and Richard T. Hughes (Urbana: University of Illinois Press, 1997), 58–81, esp. 61–62, 71, 75.

40 Theodore Kornweibel Jr., "Bishop C. H. Mason and the Church of God in Christ during World War I: The Perils of Conscientious Objection," *Southern Studies* 26, no. 4 (1987): 261–81, at 272.

41 Charles Harrison Mason, "The Kaiser in the Light of the Scriptures," in *Preaching with Sacred Fire: An Anthology of African American Sermons, 1750 to the Present*, ed. Martha Simmons and Frank A. Thomas (New York: Norton, 2010), 436–39, at 439.

42 See J. O. Patterson, German R. Ross, and Julia Mason Atkins, eds., *History and Formative Years of the Church of God in Christ* (Memphis: Church of God in Christ, 1969), 23–24, and Lucille J. Cornelius, *The Pioneer: History of the Church of God in Christ* (Memphis: Church of God in Christ, 1975), 68.

43 See Alexander, *Peace to War*, 154, for the full AG Constitutional Resolution, adopted April 1–10, 1914, from which I quote in the remainder of this paragraph.

44 For an overview of some of the issues, see Murray W. Dempster, "'Crossing Borders': Arguments Used by Early American Pentecostals in Support of the Global Character of Pacifism," *European Pentecostal Theological Association Bulletin* 10, no. 2 (1991): 63–88.

45 Peter Althouse, "Canadian Pentecostal Pacifism," *Eastern Journal of Practical Theology* 4, no. 2 (1990): 32–43, at 39.

46 Much of this paragraph comes from the COGIC's Amendments to the Constitution, article 17 (1926), available at http://www.harvestcelebration.org/ReadingRoom/COGIC%20History/COGIC%20Amendments%201926.htm (accessed December 21, 2010).

47 See the COGIC's "Military/Institutional Chaplains Directive" (1974), available at http://cogic.net/cogiccms/military-institutional-chaplaincy/history-motto-and-mission/ (accessed December 21, 2010); see also the *Official Manual with the Doctrines and Discipline of the Church of God in Christ 1973* (Memphis: Church of God in Christ, 1973), 130–31.

48 Unnamed, "To the Baptised Saints," *Apostolic Faith* 1, no. 9 (1907): 2.

49 Church of God in Christ, "What We Believe," available at http://cogic.net/cogic-cms/default/cogic-history/what-we-believe/ (accessed December 20, 2010).

50 Craig Scandrett-Leatherman argues a variant of this thesis, suggesting that for Mason and the COGIC, the baptism of the Spirit was not merely a baptism into holy love and power but a baptism into the nonviolent love of Jesus and the power of bold resistance, even amidst persecution and harassment, as conscientious objectors to war. See his "Rites of Lynching and Rights of Dance: Historic, Anthropological, and Afro-Pentecostal Perspectives on Black Manhood after 1865," in *Afro-Pentecostalism*, ed. Yong and Alexander, 95–118, esp. 103–8.

51 AG Resolution passed August 28, 1967, as cited in Alexander, *Peace to War*, 237.

52 One who has blazed a path for such a pacifist reading of Luke-Acts is Martin William Mittelstadt, "Spirit and Peace in Luke-Acts: Possibilities for Pentecostal/Anabaptist Dialogue," *Didaskalia* 20 (2009): 17–40, although he is careful to acknowledge that we cannot formulate a full apology for pacifism from these two books alone (37).

53 See also Joel Shuman, "Pentecost and the End of Patriotism: A Call for the Restoration of Pacifism among Pentecostal Christians," *Journal of Pentecostal Theology* 4, no. 9 (1996): 70–96, esp. 94–96.

54 As noted also by Paul N. Alexander, "Spirit-Empowered Peacemaking: Toward a Pentecostal Peace Fellowship," *Journal of the European Pentecostal Theological Association* 22 (2002): 78–102, at 96.

55 Here I borrow from Murray W. Dempster, "Pacifism in Pentecostalism: The Case of the Assemblies of God," in *Proclaim Peace*, ed. Schlabach and Hughes, 31–57, who has repeatedly pointed out that the early Pentecostals understood pacifism as "the moral sign of a restored New Testament apostolic church" (35).

56　The nonviolent witness of South African pentecostal Frank Chikane is a case in point; see my "Justice Deprived, Justice Demanded: Afropentecostalisms and the Task of World Pentecostal Theology Today," *Journal of Pentecostal Theology* 15, no. 1 (2006): 127–47, esp. 130–34, and *The Spirit Poured Out on All Flesh: Pentecostalism and the Possibility of Global Theology* (Grand Rapids: Baker Academic, 2005), 66–68.

57　E.g., Glen Stassen, ed., *Just Peacemaking: Ten Practices for Abolishing War,* 2nd ed. (Cleveland: Pilgrim Press, 2004).

58　A forthcoming book-length monograph will make this argument at length: Paul Alexander, *Jesus Shaped and Spirit Empowered: Peace with Justice from a Pentecostal Perspective*, Pentecostal Manifestos Series 7 (Grand Rapids: Eerdmans, 2013). Having said this, however, I am not sure about defending an absolutist form of pacifism. Timothy Jackson, e.g., argues that Christian love and political violence (just wars defending the innocent) are not mutually exclusive; rather the latter may be a limited but viable instrument of love of God and neighbor, and authentic love may sometimes cause such violence (i.e., love includes traditional contrasts like judgment/mercy, rather than only one pole of such contrasts). In the end, though, Jackson argues for an expansive theology of agape that can appeal to both pacifists and just war theorists alike; see Timothy P. Jackson, "Christian Love and Political Violence," in *The Love Commandments: Essays in Christian Ethics and Moral Philosophy*, ed. Edmund N. Santurri and William Werpehowski (Washington, D.C.: Georgetown University Press, 1992), 182–220, and *The Priority of Love: Christian Charity and Social Justice* (Princeton: Princeton University Press, 2003), chap. 3.

Chapter 5

1　Steven J. Land, *Pentecostal Spirituality: A Passion for the Kingdom*, Journal of Pentecostal Theology Supplemental Series 1 (Sheffield, UK: Sheffield Academic, 1993); all further references to this work will be made parenthetically in the text by *PS* followed by page numbers.

2　In effect, prayer at the center of pentecostal spirituality (*PS* 165–73) both shapes and expresses the pentecostal affections and by doing so moves pentecostal practice and informs pentecostal worship and confession. See also Steven J. Land, "Praying in the Spirit: A Pentecostal Perspective," in *Pentecostal Movements as an Ecumenical Challenge*, ed. Jürgen Moltmann and Karl-Josef Kuschel (Maryknoll, N.Y.: Orbis, 1996), 85–93. Land's theology of prayer is deeply informed by that of one of his teachers, Don E. Saliers, *The Soul in Paraphrase: Prayer and the Religious Affections* (New York: Seabury Press, 1980).

3　At one level, pentecostal theology has by and large accepted these fairly traditional Reformation categories. But a closer reading of Land will show that he is struggling to articulate the pentecostal difference that might be registered if pentecostal experience were allowed to revision this classical ordo salutis. My own work has been devoted, at least in part, to show that, as Land himself has argued, a pentecostal soteriology and theology of grace would resonate with Wesleyan sensibilities regarding a more dynamic via salutis with wider theological implications. For more on the pentecostal via salutis, see my *The Spirit Poured Out on All Flesh: Pentecostalism and the Possibility of Global Theology* (Grand Rapids: Baker Academic, 2005), chap. 2, and *Theology and Down Syndrome: Reimagining Disability in Late Modernity* (Waco, Tex.: Baylor University Press, 2007), chap. 8; cf. also Kenneth J. Archer, *The Gospel Revisited: Towards a Pentecostal Theology of Worship and Witness* (Eugene, Ore.: Pickwick, 2011), chap. 4.

4 Land's theology of the affections is informed by the thought of Wesley; see, e.g., Gregory S. Clapper, *John Wesley on Religious Affections: His Views on Experience and Emotion and Their Role in the Christian Life and Theology*, Pietist and Wesleyan Studies 1 (Metuchen, N.J.: Scarecrow Press, 1989), and Henry H. Knight III, "True Affections: Biblical Narrative and Evangelical Spirituality," in *The Nature of Confession: Evangelicals and Postliberals in Conversation*, ed. Timothy R. Phillips and Dennis L. Ockholm (Downers Grove, Ill.: InterVarsity, 1996), 193–200.

5 Although Land makes passing references to the work of the great Puritan theologian Jonathan Edwards, in particular Edwards' classic *Religious Affections*, he does not at this point refer explicitly to Edwards' insight that the dispositional character of the Christian affections are interwoven with the inclinations of the heart. For a brief discussion of this important point, see John E. Smith, "Religious Affections and the 'Sense of the Heart,'" in *The Princeton Companion to Jonathan Edwards*, ed. Sang Hyun Lee (Princeton: Princeton University Press, 2005), 103–14, esp. 104. See also Brad Walton, *Jonathan Edwards,* Religious Affections, *and the Puritan Analysis of True Piety, Spiritual Sensation, and Heart Religion*, Studies in American Religion 74 (Lewiston, N.Y.: Mellen, 2002).

6 I say "intimates" because Land never puts it quite this way in his book, but this in effect is what his apocalyptic affections suggest. For further explication of how pentecostal spirituality is caught up in such a now-but-not-yet stance, based fundamentally on the fact that the outpouring of the Spirit on the Day of Pentecost inaugurates the kingdom (see Acts 2:17, which, curiously, Land only alludes to but does not refer to directly, so far as I can tell), see my *In the Days of Caesar: Pentecostalism and Political Theology* (Grand Rapids: Eerdmans, 2010), chap. 8.

7 The dispensationalist framing of pentecostal eschatology, especially at the popular level, may pose some challenges for academic pentecostal theology since the general trend of pentecostal scholarship—e.g., Peter Althouse and Robby Waddell, eds., *Perspectives in Pentecostal Eschatologies: World without End* (Eugene, Ore.: Pickwick, 2010)—has been to jettison dispensationalism given its incompatibility with pentecostal spirituality. But can pentecostal spirituality be so easily extricated from the dispensationalist presuppositions so crucial to the missionary urgency of pentecostal praxis? I will return to this important question below.

8 This reflects also the influence of Jürgen Moltmann's eschatological theology. See, e.g., Frederic B. Burnham, Charles S. McCoy, and M. Douglas Meeks, eds., *Love: The Foundation of Hope: The Theology of Jürgen Moltmann and Elisabeth Moltmann-Wendel* (San Francisco: Harper & Row, 1988).

9   See Gregory S. Clapper, *The Renewal of the Heart Is the Mission of the Church: Wesley's Heart Religion in the Twenty-First Century* (Eugene, Ore.: Cascade, 2010), and Kenneth J. Collins, *The Theology of John Wesley: Holy Love and the Shape of Grace* (Nashville: Abingdon, 2007).

10 Steven J. Land, "Be Filled with the Spirit: The Nature and Evidence of Spiritual Fullness," *Ex Auditu* 12 (1996): 108–20, esp. 117–18.

11 Thus Land's pentecostal holiness theology resonates with contemporary Wesleyan theologies that emphasize love as being at the core of holiness and vice versa; see, e.g., Thomas Jay Oord and Michael Lodahl, *Relational Holiness: Responding to the Call of Love* (Kansas City: Beacon Hill, 2005).

12 Cf. Henry H. Knight, "From Aldersgate to Azusa: Wesley and the Renewal of Pentecostal Spirituality," *Journal of Pentecostal Theology* 4, no. 8 (1996): 82–98.

13 This is the epistemological aspect of Land's theology of affectivity, which has been more recently made explicit in James K. A. Smith, *Thinking in Tongues: Pentecostal Contributions to Christian Philosophy* (Grand Rapids: Eerdmans, 2010), chap. 3, esp. 71–80.

14 As argued by Stephen Post, one of the foremost of contemporary theologians of love, "*Agape* is an affection of the heart, an attunement of the person's deepest center that issues in a faithful will to exist for God and others as well as for one's own true fulfillment. . . . But foremost, *agape* invites the neighbor to change and to be changed into a new being with a new heart centered on God." Stephen G. Post, *A Theory of Agape: On the Meaning of Christian Love* (Lewisburg, Pa.: Bucknell University Press), 116.

15 Samuel Solivan, *The Spirit, Pathos, and Liberation: Toward an Hispanic Pentecostal Theology*, Journal of Pentecostal Theology Supplemental Series 14 (Sheffield, UK: Sheffield Academic, 1998), 12; all further references to this work will be made parenthetically in the text by *SPL* followed by page numbers.

16 E.g., Allan Figueroa Deck, ed., *Frontiers of Hispanic Theology in the United States* (Maryknoll, N.Y.: Orbis, 1992), and Ada María Isasi-Díaz, *En La Lucha = In the Struggle: A Hispanic Women's Liberation Theology* (Minneapolis: Fortress, 1993).

17 Abraham J. Heschel, *The Prophets* (New York: Harper & Row, 1962).

18 Daniel Castelo, *The Apathetic God: Exploring the Contemporary Relevance of Divine Impassibility* (Eugene, Ore.: Wipf & Stock, 2009), 34–35, reminds us that Heschel as a Jewish theologian presumes a robust theology of divine transcendence and thus does not collapse the differences between divine pathos and human pathos; hence, the scriptural witness to God's suffering should be understood amidst the larger picture of divine covenant-keeping rather than as a static attribute.

19 Eldin Villafañe, *The Liberating Spirit: Toward an Hispanic American Pentecostal Social Ethic* (Grand Rapids: Eerdmans, 1993), being the initial salvo of a corpus of work that has grown increasingly less parochially focused on pentecostal issues. Villafañe has long taught at Gordon Conwell Theological Seminary in the Boston area.

20 Villafañe, *Liberating Spirit*, 212–13, makes three points about love: (1) that it moved Jesus to action; (2) that the scope and depth of Christian love is to match

that of Jesus'; and (3) that there is a social dimension to love, which is linked to justice. We will return in the next section to love's manifestation in the social domain.

21 Elsewhere I have engaged in a much more extensive exegesis of the Day of Pentecost narrative in dialogue with Solivan and others; see my *The Spirit Poured Out on All Flesh*, chap. 4.

22 See Jung Young Lee, *God Suffers for Us: A Systematic Inquiry into a Concept of Divine Passibility* (The Hague: Martinus Nijhoff, 1974), esp. his account of the empathetic role of the Spirit in God's interactions with creaturely suffering (67–70). See also Choan-Seng Song's "love as the possibility of theology," the notion that the divine love is grounded, at least in part, in the divine pain that is felt on behalf of and in solidarity with creatures, in *Third-Eye Theology: Theology in Formation in Asian Settings*, rev. ed. (Maryknoll, N.Y.: Orbis, 1991), chap. 3.

23 Here I rely on Reinhard Hütter, *Suffering Divine Things: Theology as Church Practice*, trans. Doug Stott (Grand Rapids: Eerdmans, 2000), whose work I have appropriated elsewhere, but toward similar ends—see Yong, *Hospitality and the Other: Pentecost, Christian Practices, and the Neighbor* (Maryknoll, N.Y.: Orbis, 2008), 59–61. See also Steven M. Studebaker, "The Pathos of Theology as a Pneumatological Derivative or a Poiemata of the Spirit? A Review Essay of Reinhard Hütter's Pneumatological and Ecclesiological Vision of Theology," *Pneuma: The Journal of the Society for Pentecostal Studies* 32, no. 2 (2010): 269–82.

24 Thus orthopathos is powerfully redemptive, rather than leaving God impotently subjected to suffering the effects of creaturely disobedience; on this point, see Andrew K. Gabriel, *The Lord Is the Spirit: The Holy Spirit and the Divine Attributes* (Eugene, Ore.: Pickwick, 2011), 150–51.

25 Classically, the passions have been understood along with the appetites and reason as part of a tripartite anthropology, at least among the medieval scholastics. The emotions, on the other hand, have been consistently contrasted with reason in a long tradition reaching back to the Stoics. The affections, more recently, have been viewed as dispositional or inclinational feelings that move the will to action.

26 Solivan's theological intuitions are given anthropological substance in the work of André Corten, *Pentecostalism in Brazil: Emotion of the Poor and Theological Romanticism*, trans. Arianne Dorval (New York: St. Martin's, 1999), who observes how the emotions function in pentecostal worship and piety to enable engagement with poverty. However, Corten suggests, Pentecostalism is more likely to produce an antipolitical posture that neglects engaging with structural injustice, in contrast to the focus of liberation theological methodologies.

27 Frank D. Macchia, *Baptized in the Spirit: A Global Pentecostal Theology* (Grand Rapids: Zondervan, 2006); all further references to this work will be made parenthetically in the text by *BS* followed by page numbers.

28 Leading the way here has been Roger Stronstad, *The Charismatic Theology of St. Luke* (Peabody, Mass.: Hendrickson, 1984). See also James B. Shelton, *Mighty in Word and Deed: The Role of the Holy Spirit in Luke–Acts* (Peabody, Mass.: Hendrickson, 1991), and Robert P. Menzies, *Empowered for Witness: The Spirit in*

Luke–Acts, Journal of Pentecostal Theology Supplemental Series 6 (Sheffield, UK: Sheffield Academic, 1994).

29   Even renowned pentecostal scholars like Gordon D. Fee have weighed in on the evangelical side of this debate; see particularly "Hermeneutics and Historical Precedent: A Major Problem in Pentecostal Hermeneutics," in his important book, *Gospel and Spirit: Issues in New Testament Hermeneutics* (Peabody, Mass.: Hendrickson, 1991), chap. 6.

30   E.g., Max Turner, *Power from on High: The Spirit in Israel's Restoration and Witness in Luke–Acts*, Journal of Pentecostal Theology Supplemental Series 9 (Sheffield, UK: Sheffield Academic, 1996), and Youngmo Cho, *Spirit and Kingdom in the Writings of Luke and Paul: An Attempt to Reconcile These Concepts* (Waynesboro, Ga.: Paternoster, 2005).

31   I discuss some of the major concerns about dispensationalism in my *In the Days of Caesar*, chap. 8.1.2; see also Peter Althouse, *Spirit of the Last Days: Pentecostal Eschatology in Conversation with Jürgen Moltmann*, Journal of Pentecostal Theology Supplement Series 25 (New York: T&T Clark, 2003), and Matthew K. Thompson, *Kingdom Come: Revisioning Pentecostal Eschatology*, Journal of Pentecostal Theology Supplement Series 37 (Blandford Forum, UK: Deo Publishing, 2010).

32   Frank D. Macchia, *Spirituality and Social Liberation: The Message of the Blumhardts in the Light of Wuerttemberg Pietism*, Pietist and Wesleyan Studies 4 (Metuchen, N.J.: Scarecrow Press, 1993).

33   Macchia, *Spirituality and Social Liberation*, 167.

34   More recent scholarship, see e.g., Simeon Zahl, *Pneumatology and Theology of the Cross in the Preaching of Christoph Friedrich Blumhardt: The Holy Spirit between Wittenberg and Azusa Street* (New York: T&T Clark, 2010), esp. 64n8—has suggested that the younger Blumhardt had a much more pessimistic anthropology throughout much of his later life and thus was more cautious about the realizable potentiality of the kingdom than Macchia presumes, but my argument does not rely on having to adjudicate these issues in Blumhardtian historiography.

35   This is the thesis of Macchia's most recent book, *Justified in the Spirit: Creation, Redemption, and the Triune God* (Grand Rapids: Eerdmans, 2010).

36   Macchia's thesis is an elaboration of Stephen's understanding that the dwelling place of God was no longer limited to the temple but encompassed the heavens and the earth (Acts 7:48-49). I discuss Stephen's cosmic vision in my *Who Is the Holy Spirit? A Walk with the Apostles* (Brewster, Mass.: Paraclete Press, 2011), chap. 16. See also Thompson, *Kingdom Come*, part III, where he discusses, in dialogue with and through extension of Macchia's work, "the entire sanctification of the universe" and "the final healing and justification of the cosmos" (the subtitles of chaps. 8 and 9, respectively).

37   The implication of this quotation is that Macchia defends a variant of the *filioque*, regarding the spiration of the Spirit from the Son as well, to use classical pneumatological notions. He bases this claim, however, on the Lukan identification of the Son's role in sending the Spirit at Pentecost (see Acts 2:33) rather than on the Johannine texts traditionally referenced. This is consistent with Thomas Aquinas'

view regarding the procession of the Spirit *through* the Son (see the discussion in chap. 2 above).

38 This is how Macchia finally bridges the soteriological and the charismatic dimensions of the Spirit's work, by distinguishing between the dual conversions of the Spirit's baptism into divine love. This is consistent with my own dynamic soteriology that includes various crisis experiences subsequent to conversion; see my *The Spirit Poured Out on All Flesh*, chap. 2.

39 Macchia seems to acknowledge just as much in his "Afterword" to Matthew T. Lee and Margaret M. Poloma, *A Sociological Study of the Great Commandment in Pentecostalism: The Practice of Godly Love as Benevolent Service* (Lewiston, N.Y.: Mellen, 2009), 149–52.

40 A pentecostal theologian who has called attention to the "analogy of love" in another context, one dominated by Barth's analogy of faith, which was itself a reaction to the analogy-of-being tradition, is David R. Nichols, "The Search for a Pentecostal Structure in Systematic Theology," *Pneuma: The Journal of the Society for Pentecostal Studies* 6, no. 2 (1984): 57–76, at 72. Nichols' point, also reiterated by Steven Land (*PS* 38), is that pentecostal spirituality invites an alternative modality of operation, one informed by pentecostal sensibilities rather than those of either liberal or mainline theological traditions. I would affirm this move, although I would be less inclined to set any pentecostal analogy of faith off from, or as being over and against, other analogical approaches, instead seeing inclusive and dialogical possibilities in the pentecostal option.

41 Not surprisingly, then, we observe the confluence of theology of the Spirit and theology of love in the work of charismatic evangelical theologian Clark H. Pinnock, *Flame of Love: A Theology of the Holy Spirit* (Downers Grove, Ill.: InterVarsity, 1996). See also Reformed theologian Gary D. Badcock, *Light of Truth and Fire of Love: A Theology of the Holy Spirit* (Grand Rapids: Eerdmans, 1997), as well as Catholic theologians Brian P. Gaybba, *The Spirit of Love: Theology of the Holy Spirit* (London: Geoffrey Chapman, 1987), and Donald J. Goergen, *Fire of Love: Encountering the Holy Spirit* (New York: Paulist, 2006).

Chapter 6

1 I discuss the important role of Luke-Acts for pentecostal theology in my *The Spirit Poured Out on All Flesh: Pentecostalism and the Possibility of Global Theology* (Grand Rapids: Baker Academic, 2005), chap. 2.1, and *In the Days of Caesar: Pentecostalism and Political Theology* (Grand Rapids: Eerdmans, 2010), chap. 3. See also Martin William Mittelstadt, *Reading Luke-Acts in the Pentecostal Tradition* (Cleveland, Tenn.: CPT Press, 2010).

2 While we will stay close to the New Testament text for most of the remainder of this book, our focus is not on the grammatical level. Instead, we will be working theologically in general and from out of our pentecostal resources in particular. For this reason, while there are various words for love in the Greek New Testament—e.g., *philia*, *storge*, *epithymia*, *agape*—we will, unless otherwise indicated,

not rely on these distinctions, staying with the general word *love,* since these meanings are more intertwined than not. For excellent discussions of how vast and overlapping the semantic range of these New Testament terms for love was in the first century, see Leon Morris, *Testaments of Love: A Study of Love in the Bible* (Grand Rapids: Eerdmans, 1981), esp. chap. 6; Victor Paul Furnish, *The Love Command in the New Testament* (Nashville: Abingdon, 1972), the appendix; and James Barr, "Words for Love in Biblical Greek," in L. D. Hurst and N. T. Wright, *The Glory of Christ in the New Testament: Studies in Christology in Memory of George Bradford Caird* (New York: Oxford University Press, 1987), 3–18. A more comprehensive discussion focused on *agape* but noting appearances and synonymous uses of the other terms is Ceslaus Spicq, *Agape in the New Testament,* 3 vols., trans. Marie Aquinas McNamara and Mary Honoria Richter (St. Louis: Herder, 1963–1966).

3   See Richard B. Hays, *The Moral Vision of the New Testament: A Contemporary Introduction to New Testament Ethics* (San Francisco: HarperSanFrancisco, 1996), 201–2.

4   One of the more important books written by a pentecostal biblical scholar on this theme is Craig S. Keener, *Gift and Giver: The Holy Spirit for Today* (Grand Rapids: Baker Academic, 2001). See also Risto Saarinen, *God and the Gift: An Ecumenical Theology of Giving* (Collegeville, Minn.: Liturgical Press, 2005), 36–45, for a discussion of the pervasiveness of the notion of giving and the gift in the New Testament.

5   Unless otherwise noted, all scriptural references in this section will be to the book of Acts.

6   Demetrius K. Williams, "'Upon All Flesh': Acts 2, African Americans, and Intersectional Realities," in *They Were All Together in One Place? Toward Minority Biblical Criticism,* ed. Randall C. Bailey, Tat-siong Benny Liew, and Fernando F. Segovia, SBL Semeia Studies 57 (Boston: Brill, 2009), 289–310, deploys ideological criticism to alert us to how a merely universalistic reading of Acts 2 without the appreciation of the many particular ways in which humans are constituted— ethnically, racially, socially, economically, in terms of class and gender, etc.—ends up being exclusive of such particularities. My own work has been sensitive to these readings of Acts specifically from an Asian American perspective—e.g., "The Future of Asian Pentecostal Theology: An Asian American Assessment," *Asian Journal of Pentecostal Studies* 10, no. 1 (2007): 22–41, among a number of other articles and book chapters on pentecostal and evangelical readings of Acts. The following presumes the importance of particularity amidst the universalizing thrust of the Acts narrative.

7   For more on how the Third Gospel foreshadows the universal scope of the apostolic mission in Acts, see Thomas J. Lane, *Luke and the Gentile Mission: Gospel Anticipates Acts,* European University Studies Series 23 (New York: Peter Lang, 1996), and Stephen G. Wilson, *The Gentiles and the Gentile Mission in Luke-Acts,* Society for New Testament Studies Monograph Series 23 (New York: Cambridge University Press, 1973).

8   In fact, the "ends of the earth" (ἐσχάτου τῆς γῆς) of Acts 1:8 literally means the "ends of time"; see also Vítor Westhelle, "Liberation Theology: A Latitudinal Perspective," in *The Oxford Handbook of Eschatology*, ed. Jerry L. Walls (New York: Oxford University Press, 2008), 311–27, esp. 320–23.

9   Note that my references to God's "universal redemption" even in light of this Lukan "universal restoration" do not presume the heterodox doctrine of universalism—that all will actually be saved—since I am agnostic about what will happen in this regard. My claim is only that God "desires everyone to be saved and to come to the knowledge of the truth" (1 Tim 2:4), and in that sense the gospel has universal reach and range. Elsewhere (see *In the Days of Caesar*, 351–52) I have suggested that the possibility of the salvation of any, much less of all, is dependent in part on if, how, and to what extent those who have received the Holy Spirit bear witness to the gospel.

10   I have expanded on this thesis in my *Who Is the Holy Spirit? A Walk with the Apostles* (Brewster, Mass.: Paraclete Press, 2011), which provides a pentecostal reading of the book of Acts as well as of the Third Gospel.

11   I suggest, following Earl Richard, "Pentecost as a Recurrent Theme in Luke–Acts," in *New Views on Luke and Acts*, ed. Earl Richard (Collegeville, Minn.: Liturgical Press, 1990), 133–49, that there is literary justification for rereading Luke in light of the Day of Pentecost motif. This is not to say that the Day of Pentecost is either the only or the dominant interpretive theme of the Lukan corpus; it is to say that an argument can be made for the coherence of both Lukan volumes in light of the outpouring of the Spirit. This section thus asks how the gift of the Spirit on that Jewish feast day might now be understood in the life and ministry of Jesus.

12   In this section, by contrast to the preceding one, all scriptural references will be to the Gospel of Luke unless otherwise noted. By the way, if Mary is recognized as the "mother of God" (*theotokos*) in Christ, then might she also be understood as the mother of love or of charity? For hints in this direction, see Benedict XVI, encyclical letter *Deus Caritas Est* (December 25, 2005), §41, available at http://www.vatican.va/holy_father/benedict_xvi/encyclicals/documents/hf_ben-xvi_enc_20051225_deus-caritas-est_en.html.

13   See Michael Prior, *Jesus the Liberator: Nazareth Liberation Theology (Luke 4:16-30)*, Biblical Seminar 26 (Sheffield, UK: Sheffield Academic, 1995); cf. Beth Grant, "Implications of Luke 4:18 and the Mission of the 21st Century Pentecostal Church," in *Luke–Acts*, vol. 4 of *A Biblical Theology of the Holy Spirit: Contemporary Issues in Pneumatology*, ed. James E. Richardson (Springfield, Mo.: Global University, 2009), 155–78.

14   See Sharon H. Ringe, *Jesus, Liberation, and the Biblical Jubilee: Images for Ethics and Christology* (Philadelphia: Fortress, 1985); cf. James A. Sanders, "Sins, Debts, and Jubilee Release," in *Luke and Scripture: The Function of Sacred Tradition in Luke–Acts*, ed. Craig A. Evans and James A. Sanders (Minneapolis: Fortress, 1993), 84–92.

15 It is this pneumatological dimension that I would foreground in Susan R. Garrett's insightful discussion, *The Demise of the Devil: Magic and the Demonic in Luke's Writings* (Minneapolis: Fortress, 1989).

16 As noted by Peter Rhea Jones, "The Love Command in Parable: Luke 10:25-37," *Perspectives in Religious Studies* 6, no. 3 (1979): 223–42, esp. 226, this question assumes that according to some readings of the Torah in the time of Jesus, even if Jews were to love their countrymen and women as well as sojourners (as delineated, e.g., in Lev 19), there were others who were beyond the pale of neighborliness. The disputed issues here anticipate Thomas Aquinas' construction of a hierarchy of love. Jesus, as we shall see here, overturns the presuppositions of this question by linking benevolent love to one's enemies.

17 Norman H. Young, "The Commandment to Love Your Neighbor as Yourself and the Parable of the Good Samaritan (Luke 10:25-37)," *Andrews University Seminary Studies* 21, no. 3 (1983): 265–72, is a good place to start, but he is not motivated by explicitly pentecostal concerns, so the pneumatological connection I wish to make is absent.

18 Luke Timothy Johnson, *The Gospel of Luke*, Sacra Pagina 3 (Collegeville, Minn.: Liturgical Press, 1991), 174.

19 See John R. Donahue, "Who Is My Enemy? The Parable of the Good Samaritan and the Love of Enemies," in Willard M. Swartley, ed., *The Love of Enemy and Nonretaliation in the New Testament* (Louisville, Ky.: Westminster John Knox, 1992), 137–56.

20 While there is strong evidence, gathered by John Meier, that this injunction to love enemies goes back to the historical Jesus, Meier also cautions against "blithe homiletic generalizations proclaiming love to be the center of Jesus' message." Not only are the love commands minimal across the broad scope of Jesus' teachings, there are also counter-indicators, such as when, at the conclusion of the parable of the ten pounds, it is said, "But as for these enemies of mine who did not want me to be king over them—bring them here and slaughter them in my presence" (Luke 19:27). I recognize the force of Meier's admonishments but remind my readers that I seek only to explicate a pneumatological theology of love, not argue the historical claim about love being the be-all and end-all of Jesus' life, teachings, and ministry. See John P. Meier, *Law and Love*, vol. 4 of *A Marginal Jew: Rethinking the Historical Jesus* (New Haven: Yale University Press, 2009), chap. 36, on "Widening the Focus: The Love Commandments of Jesus," at 481.

21 See further my *Spirit Poured Out on All Flesh*, 240–44, as well as my discussion of the parable of the sheep and the goats in Matthew 25 in chap. 5 of my *The Bible, Disability, and the Church: A New Vision of the People of God* (Grand Rapids: Eerdmans, 2011).

22 As we shall see, I effect a slight realignment of Land's categories in what follows.

23 For the central role of testimony in pentecostal spirituality, see Mark J. Cartledge, *Testimony in the Spirit: Rescripting Ordinary Pentecostal Theology* (Burlington, Vt.: Ashgate, 2010), esp. 15–17.

24 In this section, I will alternate between Luke and Acts, and references will follow the lead citation in each paragraph unless noted otherwise.

25 I put it this way because the man healed at the Beautiful Gate is now also able to enter into the temple courts; see my discussion in *Who Is the Holy Spirit*, chap. 8.

26 See Kindalee Pfremmer De Long, *Surprised by God: Praise Responses in the Narrative of Luke–Acts*, Beihefte zur Zeitschrift für die neutestamentliche Wissenschaft und die Kunde der älteren Kirche 166 (New York: De Gruyter, 2009).

27 Verse 47 could also read, "The reason that I [am able to] tell you that her many sins are forgiven is the fact that she is showing so much love"; see L. Gregory Jones, *Embodying Forgiveness: A Theological Analysis* (Grand Rapids: Eerdmans, 1995), 161, brackets in original.

28 See Joel B. Green, *The Gospel of Luke* (Grand Rapids: Eerdmans, 1997), 313–14.

29 See Martin William Mittelstadt, "Pentecostals and the Gospel of Peace: Spirit and Reconciliation in Luke-Acts," in *Forgiveness, Reconciliation, and Restoration: Multidisciplinary Studies from a Pentecostal Perspective*, ed. Martin William Mittelstadt and Geoffrey W. Sutton (Eugene, Ore.: Pickwick, 2010), 3–22.

30 See Joseph Grassi, *Peace on Earth: Roots and Practices from Luke's Gospel* (Collegeville, Minn.: Liturgical Press, 2004).

31 This is my meager contribution to a pentecostal theology of peace more rigorously articulated by Paul Alexander, "Nonviolent Direct Action in Acts 2: The Holy Spirit, the Early Church, and Martin Luther King, Jr.," in *Trajectories in the Book of Acts: Essays in Honor of John Wesley Wyckoff*, ed. Paul Alexander, Jordan Daniel May, and Robert G. Reid (Eugene, Ore.: Wipf & Stock, 2010), 114–24.

32 No doubt the apostolic life of prayer was modeled after that of their Spirit-anointed prophet from Nazareth—e.g., Luke 3:21; 5:16; 6:12; 9:18; 11:1; 18:1; 22:39-46; see also David Crump, *Jesus the Intercessor: Prayer and Christology in Luke–Acts*, Wissenschaftliche Untersuchungen zum Neuen Testament 2.49 (1992; repr., Grand Rapids: Baker, 1999).

33 This eschatological dimension to the prayer of the apostolic community is emphasized in Steven F. Plymale, *The Prayer Texts of Luke-Acts*, American University Studies 118 (New York: Peter Lang, 1991), esp. chap. 4.

34 The result is a slight revision of Land's triadic correlations, particularly where Land links prayer with compassion and witness with courage; see Steven J. Land, *Pentecostal Spirituality: A Passion for the Kingdom*, Journal of Pentecostal Theology Supplemental Series 1 (Sheffield, UK: Sheffield Academic, 1993), 139.

35 My hermeneutical position briefly summarized here has been defended at—some would say exhaustive—length in my *Spirit-Word-Community: Theological Hermeneutics in Trinitarian Perspective* (2002; repr., Eugene, Ore.: Wipf & Stock, 2006).

Chapter 7

1 Of course, this does not mean we will avoid the secondary literature altogether. But again, we bring very focused perspectives—ones informed by pentecostal

experience, spirituality, and hermeneutics—to our endeavor, and this also will be registered in conversation with our dialogue partners.

2   Some of the more prominent are D. A. Carson, *Showing the Spirit: A Theological Exposition of 1 Corinthians 12–14* (Grand Rapids: Baker, 1987); Robert L. Thomas, *Understanding Spiritual Gifts: A Verse-by-Verse Study of 1 Corinthians 12–14*, rev. ed. (Grand Rapids: Kregel Publications, 1999); and Ralph P. Martin, *The Spirit and the Congregation: Studies in 1 Corinthians 12–15* (Grand Rapids: Eerdmans, 1984).

3   Some have noted that "love itself is not named among the gifts of the Spirit"—e.g., Allan Barr, "Love in the Church: A Study of First Corinthians, Chapter 13," *Scottish Journal of Theology* 3, no. 4 (1950): 416–25, at 418; cf. Arnold Bittlinger, *Gifts and Graces: A Commentary on I Corinthians 12–14*, trans. Herbert Klassen and Michael Harper (1967; repr., Grand Rapids: Eerdmans, 1972), 74–75—and that it would be more accurate instead to say that love is a fruit of the Spirit, following Galatians 5:22. Yes, love is not one of the *spiritual gifts* enumerated in 1 Corinthians 12, but I will argue in this chapter the theological thesis that love is given through the Spirit and in that sense is a gift of the Spirit, even perhaps the most excellent and most desirable one.

4   David Lim, *Charismata, a Fresh Look: A Pentecostal Perspective and Commentary on 1 Corinthians 12–14* (Clayburn, B.C.: Western Pentecostal Bible College, 1979); French L. Arrington, *Divine Order in the Church: A Study of 1 Corinthians* (Grand Rapids: Baker, 1978), chap. 8; and Siegfried S. Schatzmann, *A Pauline Theology of Charismata* (Peabody, Mass.: Hendrickson, 1987), 29–47, among other pentecostal scholars.

5   In this section, all scriptural references will be to 1 Corinthians, unless otherwise noted.

6   I argue in another place that such considerations in Paul provide us with important clues for thinking afresh about theology of disability; see my *The Bible, Disability, and the Church: A New Vision of the People of God* (Grand Rapids: Eerdmans, 2011), chap. 4.

7   Bert Dominy, "Paul and Spiritual Gifts: Reflections on I Corinthians 12–14," *Southwestern Journal of Theology* 26, no. 1 (1983): 49–68, at 50.

8   See the excellent discussion of "The Spirit, Power, and Weakness," in Gordon D. Fee, *God's Empowering Presence: The Holy Spirit in the Letters of Paul* (Peabody, Mass.: Hendrickson, 1994), 822–26, who suggests that what we find in Paul is a veritable pneumatological *via media* between pentecostal triumphalism (with its focus on power) and evangelical humility (with its emphasis on weakness).

9   Robert Thomas notes that "Fifteen characteristics of love appear, fifteen that are most appropriate to affairs in Corinth" (*Understanding Spiritual Gifts*, 13); see also José Enrique Aguilar Chiu, *1 Cor 12–14: Literary Structure and Theology*, Analecta Biblica 166 (Rome: Editrice Pontificio Istituto Biblico, 2007), esp. 281–95.

10   Charles Talbert, "Paul's Understanding of the Holy Spirit: The Evidence of 1 Corinthians 12–14," *Perspectives in Religious Studies* 11, no. 4 (1984): 95–108, at 100–101.

11 Dominy, "Paul and Spiritual Gifts," 57.

12 As suggested by James Patrick, "Insights from Cicero on Paul's Reasoning in 1 Corinthians 12–14: Love Sandwich or Five Course Meal?" *Tyndale Bulletin* 55, no. 1 (2004): 43–64, esp. 52–53. Patrick suggests that the "love sandwich" (of chap. 13 surrounded by chaps. 12 and 14) reflects the Ciceronian structure designed to amplify the rhetorical persuasiveness of the argument and that within this framework love defines the identity of the charismatic life.

13 Emphasized by Hans Conzelmann, *1 Corinthians: A Commentary on the First Epistle to the Corinthians*, Hermeneia Series, trans. James W. Leitch (Philadelphia: Fortress, 1975), 224.

14 Raymond F. Collins, *First Corinthians*, Sacra Pagina 7 (Collegeville, Minn.: Liturgical Press, 1999), 485.

15 Emphasizing the pneumatological dynamic of this "way of love" illuminates Kierkegaard's intuition that these "works of love," as he calls them, are actually love itself achieving what imperfect humans are incapable of accomplishing on their own. How, we might ask? Through the Spirit, I would answer. See Søren Kierkegaard, *Works of Love: Some Christian Reflections in the Form of Discourses*, trans. Howard and Edna Hong (New York: Harper & Row, 1962).

16 I thank Thomas Jay Oord for helping me to clarify this insight.

17 David A. Ackerman, "Fighting Fire with Fire: Community Formation in 1 Corinthians 12–14," *Evangelical Review of Theology* 29, no. 4 (2005): 347–62, esp. 357–60.

18 Russell Morton, "Gifts in the Context of Love: Reflections on 1 Corinthians 13," *Ashland Theological Journal* 31 (1999): 11–23, at 20.

19 In the remainder of this chapter, all scriptural references will be to the book of Romans unless otherwise indicated. Note though about the context of Romans 8 that "The setting for the passage is that of a lawcourt, as in Job 1–2 and Zechariah 3, in which a prosecutor accuses a justified Christian. But the Christian does not have to fear a prosecutor" (Joseph A. Fitzmyer, *Romans: A New Translation with Introduction and Commentary*, Anchor Bible 33 [New York: Doubleday, 1992], 529)—because of the legal work of Christ. I will return to discuss this aspect of the argument in Romans in the next section of this chapter.

20 Paul's language here leads scholars to suggest that the *sitz im leben* of the letter involved persecution of "the 'weak' who consisted predominantly of Jewish Christians whose leaders had been expelled from Rome by the Edict of Claudius [CE 54]." Robert Jewett, *Romans: A Commentary*, Hermeneia Series (Minneapolis: Fortress, 2007), 546.

21 We do not need here to resolve the conundrums attending to the mystery of how divine sovereignty preserves rather than cancels out creaturely freedom. A whole host of issues are pertinent, some of which I discuss elsewhere—e.g., "Divine Omniscience and Future Contingents: Weighing the Presuppositional Issues in the Contemporary Debate," *Evangelical Review of Theology* 26, no. 3 (2002): 240–64, and "Divine Knowledge and Relation to Time," in *Philosophy of Religion: Introductory Essays*, ed. Thomas Jay Oord (Kansas City: Beacon Hill, 2003),

136–52. My own preference, consistent with the Wesleyan-Holiness theology of prevenient grace that is also present in the holiness-pentecostal tradition, is to talk about *divine initiative* rather than sovereignty precisely in order not to undermine human responsibility.

22 Adrienne von Speyr appropriately titles her reflections on this Pauline chapter *The Victory of Love: A Meditation on Romans 8*, trans. Lucia Wiedenhöver (San Francisco: Ignatius, 1990).

23 John A. Bertone, "The Function of the Spirit in the Dialectic between God's Soteriological Plan Enacted but Not Yet Culminated: Romans 8.1-27," *Journal of Pentecostal Theology* 7, no. 15 (1999): 75–97, at 76n4. The extensivity of references to the Spirit in this chapter is also what led Wesleyan scholar A. Skevington Wood to write a book entitled *Paul's Pentecost: Studies in the Life of the Spirit from Romans 8* (Exeter, UK: Paternoster, 1963). Wood's last chapter, on vv. 31-39, is entitled "The Sustenance of the Spirit."

24 See Robert Jewett, "The Corruption and Redemption of Creation: Reading Rom. 8:18-23 within the Imperial Context," in *Paul and the Roman Imperial Order*, ed. Richard A. Horsley (Harrisburg, Pa.: Trinity Press International, 2004), 25–46, esp. 43–44.

25 John Bertone, "The Experience of Glossolalia and the Spirit's Empathy: Romans 8:26 Revisited," *Pneuma: The Journal of the Society for Pentecostal Studies* 25, no. 1 (2003): 54–65, at 57. See also the groundbreaking article by Frank D. Macchia, "Sighs Too Deep for Words: Towards a Theology of Glossolalia," *Journal of Pentecostal Theology* 1, no. 1 (1992): 47–73.

26 The emotional character of human prayers "too deep for words" is highlighted by Bertone, "Experience of Glossolalia," 57–58.

27 The Spirit who stirs up our passions, prayers, and hopes for the redemption of the cosmos here is the same Spirit who enables our passionate prayer for the arrival of kingdom amid the *polis* of this world in Luke, as I show in my *Who Is the Holy Spirit? A Walk with the Apostles* (Brewster, Mass.: Paraclete Press, 2011), chap. 32.

28 My pneumatological reading of Romans, as concerning the gift of the Spirit to the world that recapitulates the salvation of the world and its restoration to God, is not new, having roots among patristic theologians like Origen—e.g., Maureen Beyer Moser, *Teacher of Holiness: The Holy Spirit in Origen's Commentary on the Epistle to the Romans*, Early Christian Studies 4 (Piscataway, N.J.: Gorgias Press, 2005).

29 See Jewett, *Romans*, 532.

30 Elsewhere Paul also writes of the Christian hope as assured in pneumatological terms: "He who has prepared us for this very thing is God, who has given us the Spirit as a guarantee" (2 Cor 5:5). And even if the letter to the Ephesians is not authentic to Paul, it says of those in Christ that they are "marked with the seal of the promised Holy Spirit; this is the pledge of our inheritance towards redemption as God's own people, to the praise of his glory" (Eph 1:13b-14).

31 I am aware that there is a long debate about whether or not Romans 7:7-25 refers to the pre- or post-conversion life. I lean toward the latter for the reasons given,

although I do not think my argument cannot be adjusted if a consensus emerges about the former.

32 James D. G. Dunn calls this section "Love as the Norm for Social Relationships"; see Dunn, *Romans 9–16*, Word Biblical Commentary 38b (Waco, Tex.: Word Books, 1988), 736.

33 As Walter Wilson notes, this passage in Romans "represents the nearest thing we have to a general statement of Paul's program for Christian ethical thought and behavior . . . [with] ἀγάπη ('love') as the basic perspective and motivation of Christian ethical conduct. . . . For Paul ἀγάπη governs all ethical relations and attitudes, both inside and outside the body of believers." Walter T. Wilson, *Love without Pretense: Romans 12.9-21 and Hellenistic-Jewish Wisdom Literature*, Wissenschaftliche Untersuchungen zum Neuen Testament 2.46 (Tübingen: J. C. B. Mohr, 1991), 5, 212.

34 The issues are complex, as there may have also been some Gentile Christians who were convinced of Jewish practices or some Jewish Christians who felt themselves free of the law; issues of social status and superstitions are intertwined. A book-length discussion is Mark Reasoner, *The Strong and the Weak: Romans 14.1–15.13 in Context* (New York: Cambridge University Press, 1999).

35 Interestingly, this is one of the few references in Paul to the kingdom of God. Scholars have long debated why the kingdom discourse that dominates the Gospel accounts is practically absent in Paul. It is possible that for Paul, life in the Spirit denotes the already-but-not-yet appearance of the kingdom of God. Romans 14:17, along with the main thrust of Romans 8, provides further confirmation for the thesis argued by Youngmo Cho that Paul innovated and transformed "the kingdom" prevalent in the evangelists into his notion of "life in the Spirit." See Cho, *Spirit and Kingdom in the Writings of Luke and Paul: An Attempt to Reconcile These Concepts* (Waynesboro, Ga.: Paternoster, 2005).

36 The connection between Romans 14 and 12:3 is highlighted in J. Paul Sampley, "The Weak and the Strong: Paul's Careful and Crafty Rhetorical Strategy in Romans 14:1–15:13," in *The Social World of the First Christians: Essays in Honor of Wayne A. Meeks*, ed. L. Michael White and O. Larry Yarbrough (Minneapolis: Fortress, 1995), 40–52, esp. 47–48.

37 Again, this is the central thesis of Macchia's most recent book, which we mentioned in passing in chap. 5: Frank D. Macchia, *Justified in the Spirit: Creation, Redemption, and the Triune God* (Grand Rapids: Eerdmans, 2010).

Chapter 8

1 Judith M. Lieu, *I, II, and III John: A Commentary* (Louisville: Westminster John Knox, 2008), e.g., recognizes the complexity of the critical issues and so suggests that it is best to approach the Johannine epistles on their own terms, without any a priori assumptions about their relationship to the Gospel (6–9, 17–18). For some purposes, this may well be the safest course of interpretive action; for others, such as our canonical-theological approach, this is unduly constricting, even

if we will not run roughshod over the text and its original context (to the degree that historical criticism gives us access to the historicity "behind" the text).

2   In fact, unlike 2 and 3 John, the author is not named in the First Letter. All extant manuscripts of the Johannine epistles, however, identify John as their author, and this, along with other reasons internal and external to the letter, encourages us to assume Johannine authorship. So in the following pages I will periodically refer to the author of these Johannine materials by name, but I mean nothing more than that "John" serves as a convenient shorthand for the processes through which the final form of these documents have come down to us. For a brief discussion of the role of letter titles in antiquity in general and vis-à-vis 1 John in particular, see John Christopher Thomas, *The Pentecostal Commentary on 1 John, 2 John, 3 John* (New York: T&T Clark, 2004), 5–6.

3   See Stephen S. Smalley, *1, 2, 3 John*, rev. ed., Word Biblical Commentary 51 (Nashville: Nelson, 2007), xx–xxi.

4   André Feuillet, *Le Mystère de l'amour divin dans la théologie johannique* (Paris: J. Gabalda, 1972), 180, quoted in Judith M. Lieu, *The Theology of the Johannine Epistles* (New York: Cambridge University Press, 1991), 66n73. On the chiastic structuring of 1 John around the theme of love, see John Christopher Thomas, *The Spirit of the New Testament* (Leiden, UK: Deo Publishing, 2005), chap. 17.

5   Smalley, *1, 2, 3 John*, 201.

6   All scriptural references in this section will be to 1 John unless otherwise noted.

7   There has been much scholarly ink spilled over what exactly was the historical issue "behind" the letter. I do not think we can say much more than that it was related to an early form of Gnosticism, especially a set of docetic beliefs that minimized the incarnational (enfleshed) character of God's salvation offered in Christ. For more discussion, see Rudolf Schnackenburg, *The Johannine Epistles: Introduction and Commentary*, trans. Reginald and Ilse Fuller (New York: Crossroad, 1992), 17–24.

8   This warning of Raymond E. Brown, *The Epistles of John: Translated with Introduction, Notes, and Commentary* (Garden City, N.Y.: Doubleday, 1982), 556, made with regard to the reference to the Spirit in 1 John 3:24, applies also to the reference in 4:13.

9   This is why 1 John has been read as a "critical theological epistemology"; see R. W. L. Moberly, "'Test the Spirits': God, Love, and Critical Discernment in 1 John 4," in *The Holy Spirit and Christian Origins: Essays in Honor of James D. G. Dunn*, ed. Graham N. Stanton, Bruce W. Longenecker, and Stephen C. Barton (Grand Rapids: Eerdmans, 2004), 296–307, at 297.

10   Thus, as Judith Lieu notes, love of God and love of community are inextricable (*Theology of the Johannine Epistles*, 65). Similarly, James Moffatt, *Love in the New Testament* (London: Hodder & Stoughton, 1929), argues that the close links between God's love and brotherly love constitute the distinctiveness of the Christian religion. See also Karl Rahner, *The Love of Jesus and the Love of Neighbor*, trans. Robert Barr (New York: Crossroad, 1983).

11   Even if "our joy" should be retained rather than the "your joy" that is found in

some manuscripts, the "our" is inclusive of the readership in light of the solidarity between the Johannine author(s) and the wider community, a solidarity
either already existing or hoped for following reception of the Epistle; see Brown,
Epistles of John, 173.

12 As explicated in Mary Ann Fatula, *The Holy Spirit: Unbounded Gift of Joy* (Collegeville, Minn.: Liturgical Press, 1998).

13 The definitive study so far is Gary M. Burge, *The Anointed Community: The Holy
Spirit in the Johannine Tradition* (Grand Rapids: Eerdmans, 1987).

14 Unless otherwise noted, all scriptural references in the rest of this chapter will be
to the Gospel of John.

15 Robert E. Tourville, *The Gospel of John: A Verse-by-Verse Commentary from the
Classical Pentecostal Perspective* (New Wilmington, Pa.: House of Bon Giovanni,
1986), 413.

16 E.g., George R. Beasley-Murray, *John*, 2nd ed., Word Biblical Commentary 36
(Nashville: Nelson, 1999), 381.

17 See also Craig S. Keener, "Sent Like Jesus: Johannine Missiology (John 20:21-22),"
Asian Journal of Pentecostal Studies 12, no. 1 (2009): 21–45.

18 Historically, there has been a great deal of commentary on the forgiveness of sins
authorized in this text and its relationship to the baptismal rite and the sacra-
ment of confession. From a pentecostal and generally free church perspective, I
would agree with Craig Keener that "It is anachronistic to read into this passage
the later Catholic doctrine of penance or others' views about admission to baptism"; however, I will not belabor this point because it does not touch on our task
of exploring John's pneumatology of love. See Craig S. Keener, *The Gospel of John:
A Commentary* (Peabody, Mass.: Hendrickson, 2003), 2:1206.

19 See Marianne Meye Thompson, "The Breath of Life: John 20:22-23 Once More,"
in *Holy Spirit and Christian Origins*, ed. Stanton, Longenecker, and Barton, 69–78,
esp. 76.

20 Tricia Gates Brown, *Spirit in the Writings of John: Johannine Pneumatology in
Social-Scientific Perspective* (New York: T&T Clark, 2003), thus suggests viewing
the Spirit as a representative broker in place of the absent Jesus, the ultimate broker between God and the world.

21 For efforts to trace the derivation of the Paraclete idea from Greco-Roman and
Second Temple Jewish sources, see Hans Windisch, *The Spirit-Paraclete in the
Fourth Gospel*, trans. James W. Cox (Philadelphia: Fortress, 1968). One scholar,
Eskil Franck, *Revelation Taught: The Paraclete in the Gospel of John*, Coniectanea
Biblical New Testament Series 14 (Lund, Sweden: CWK Gleerup, 1985), argues
that the Paraclete is embodied in the Beloved Disciple of the Fourth Gospel (13:23,
20:2, 21:20). For thorough discussion of the historical-critical issues, not many of
which have seen resolution in the last generation, see George Johnston, *The Spirit-
Paraclete in the Gospel of John*, Society for New Testament Studies Monograph
Series 12 (Cambridge: Cambridge University Press, 1970).

22 Tourville, *Gospel of John*, 301–2, is one of the few commentators who have noted
the "and" conjunction between verses 15 and 16; all I am doing is make explicit

that the "helping" aspect of the Paraclete's work (which Tourville emphasizes) relates to the keeping of the commandments as a response to Jesus' love (which Tourville does not quite pinpoint).

23 Thus love "means for John the very life of God determining the relation between the Father and the Son"; see Matthew Vellanickal, *The Divine Sonship of Christians in the Johannine Writings*, Analecta Biblica 72 (Rome: Biblical Institute Press, 1977), 315.

24 I get the language of "indwelling" in this paragraph from Raymond E. Brown, *The Gospel according to John: Introduction, Translation, and Notes*, The Anchor Bible 29, 2 vols. (Garden City, N.Y.: Doubleday, 1970), 2:648.

25 The world's lack of love for God and hatred of Jesus have been percolating throughout the Gospel narrative (see 5:42, 7:7, 8:42, 16:2, 17:14). But note that "the Gospel of John defines love and hate entirely with respect to a person's stance toward Jesus," so that from the community's point of view, the world's hatred is not personal to them (only to Jesus); see Adele Reinhartz, "Love, Hate, and Violence in the Gospel of John," in *Violence in the New Testament*, ed. Shelly Matthews and E. Leigh Gibson (New York: T&T Clark, 2005), 109–23, at 110.

26 For a succinct discussion of the connection between the Paraclete passages and the disciples' need for help to survive in a hostile world, see Charles H. Talbert, *Reading John: A Literary and Theological Commentary on the Fourth Gospel and the Johannine Epistles* (New York: Crossroad, 1992), 215–16.

27 As John Christopher Thomas summarizes, "The primary purpose of the Farewell Materials in the Fourth Gospel is to prepare the disciples for Jesus' departure by providing for their time without him through a variety of means," and "The promise of continual cleansing, provision despite denials, the coming of the Paraclete, and solidarity with Jesus all serve to encourage and enable the believer as he/she walks the path of discipleship with the master." John Christopher Thomas, *He Loved Them until the End: Farewell Materials in the Gospel According to John* (Pune, India: Fountain Press, 2003), 27, 83.

28 As I argue in my "'The Light Shines in the Darkness': Johannine Dualism and the Challenge of Christian Theology of Religions Today," *Journal of Religion* 89, no. 1 (2009): 31–56.

29 Cornelis Bennema, *Encountering Jesus: Character Studies in the Gospel of John* (Colorado Springs: Paternoster, 2009), chap. 3.

30 Bennema, *Encountering Jesus*, 207.

31 E.g., "he is the atoning sacrifice for our sins, and not for ours only but also for the sins of the whole world," and "we have seen and do testify that the Father has sent his Son as the Saviour of the world" (1 John 2:2, 4:14).

32 With regard to "for he gives the Spirit without measure" (3:34b), Craig Keener (*Gospel of John*, 1:583) comments, "the lack of specified object for 'gives' (and perhaps its present tense) might support the idea of giving to the world, so in the end it is difficult to settle on the preferred interpretation; but 'receives' the Spirit without measure might fit Jesus as the recipient better. The Father's enormous love for the Son (3:35) becomes the Johannine measure of God's love for the disciples

(17:23), as Christ's sacrifice attests (3:16)." I would simply add that what the grammar does not prohibit, the theological thrust of the Johannine tradition encourages: that we understand God's measureless gift of the Spirit through Christ as intended for the world.

33 Sandra M. Schneiders, "The Raising of the New Temple: John 20.19-23 and Johannine Ecclesiology," *New Testament Studies* 52, no. 3 (2006): 337–55, at 353.

34 Schneiders, "Raising of the New Temple," 354, brackets in original.

35 As Timothy Jackson observes, forgiveness enables the liberation of the forgiver from personal torment, touches the consciences of others, fosters the solidarity that hastens the incoming kingdom, imitates Christ and enacts his direct commandment, and is not irresponsible, since not holding grudges is not the same as not holding actions culpable and following up on consequences of actions is not to be paralyzed by the past. Timothy P. Jackson, *The Priority of Love: Christian Charity and Social Justice* (Princeton: Princeton University Press, 2003), chap. 4, esp. 147–55.

36 To be sure, as John Meier forcefully reminds us, for the Johannine community "love of enemies does not exist on the radar screen." But it should also be noted that nowhere in the Johannine tradition are the disciples told to hate the world in return, which contrasts with that of the Qumran community, which asserted, "He shall admit into the Covenant of Grace all those who have freely devoted themselves to the observance of God's precepts, that they may be joined to the counsel of God and may live perfectly before Him in accordance with all that has been revealed concerning their appointed times, and that they may love all the sons of light, each according to his lot in God's design, and *hate all the sons of darkness*, each according to his guilt in God's vengeance" (1QS 1:9-11, emphasis added). Thus while we might wish John could have said more positive things about the enemies who hated them because of Christ, we can also be thankful that not more was said vis-à-vis those enemies. John P. Meier, *Law and Love*, vol. 4 of *A Marginal Jew: Rethinking the Historical Jesus* (New Haven: Yale University Press, 2009), 567, and Geza Vermes, ed., *The Complete Dead Sea Scrolls in English*, trans. Vermes (New York: Penguin, 1997), 98–99.

37 Thus 20:23 is what speech-act theorists call a perlocutionary statement, one that not only tells us about something but brings about a new state of affairs. In the words of biblical scholar Raymond Brown, "It is an effective, not merely a declaratory, power against sin, a power that touches new and old followers of Christ, a power that challenges those who refuse to believe" (Brown, *Gospel according to John*, 2:1044).

Chapter 9

1 This was, of course, John Wesley's testimony; see, e.g., chap. 2 of Francis J. McConnell, *John Wesley* (New York: Abingdon, 1939).

2 As beautifully portrayed in James D. Whitehead and Evelyn Eaton Whitehead, *Holy Eros: Pathways to a Passionate God* (Maryknoll, N.Y.: Orbis, 2009).

3   See Dennis Ngien, *Gifted Response: The Triune God as the Causative Agency of Our Responsive Worship* (Milton Keynes, UK: Paternoster, 2008).

4   This theological anthropology presumes that our psyches and our spiritual lives are emergent levels of complexity from our brains and bodies, a thesis explicated in more detail in my *Theology and Down Syndrome: Reimagining Disability in Late Modernity* (Waco, Tex.: Baylor University Press, 2007), chap. 6, and *The Spirit of Creation: Modern Science and Divine Action in the Pentecostal-Charismatic Imagination* (Grand Rapids: Eerdmans, 2011), esp. chap. 2.

5   The result is a shift from *creatio ex nihilo* to *creatio ex amore*, so that the creation and its creatures participate with God "in the ongoing adventure of creation until love is all in all." James H. Olthuis, "A Radical Ontology of Love: Thinking 'with' Radical Orthodoxy," in *Radical Orthodoxy and the Reformed Tradition: Creation, Covenant, and Participation*, ed. James K. A. Smith and James H. Olthuis (Grand Rapids: Baker Academic, 2005), 277–93, esp. 292, at 293.

6   Not to mention that, as the Psalmist said, "By the word of the Lord the heavens were made, and all their host by the breath of his mouth. . . . When you hide your face, they [the animals] are dismayed; when you take away their breath, they die and return to their dust. When you send forth your spirit, they are created; and you renew the face of the ground" (Ps 33:6; 104:29-30).

7   This highlights the dynamic nature of the creation so that, as James Olthuis (again and elsewhere) notes, "love replaces being-as-power as the highest category. For in the degree that one is not in love, one is deficient in being. . . . 'I am loved, therefore I am'. . . . The passive 'am loved' also suggests that whether or not we are existentially able to love is inextricably related to whether we were first loved," as indeed we were, insists the Christian doctrine of creation. Olthuis, "Crossing the Threshold: Sojourning Together in the Wild Spaces of Love," in *The Hermeneutics of Charity: Interpretation, Selfhood, and Postmodern Faith*, ed. James K. A. Smith and Henry Isaac Venema (Grand Rapids: Brazos, 2004), 23–40, at 34.

8   I expand on this in my "*Ruach*, the Primordial Waters, and the Breath of Life: Emergence Theory and the Creation Narratives in Pneumatological Perspective," in *The Work of the Spirit: Pneumatology and Pentecostalism*, ed. Michael Welker (Grand Rapids: Eerdmans, 2006), 183–204, esp. 190-200.

9   See, e.g., John Templeton, *Agape Love: A Tradition Found in Eight World Religions* (Philadelphia: Templeton Foundation, 1999), and Jacob Neusner and Bruce Chilton, eds., *Altruism in World Religions* (Washington, D.C.: Georgetown University Press, 2005); cf. Xinzhong Yao, *Confucianism and Christianity: A Comparative Study of Jen and Agape* (Brighton, UK: Sussex Academic Press, 1997), and Rusmir Mahmutćehajić, *On Love: In the Muslim Tradition*, trans. Celia Hawkesworth, Abrahamic Dialogues Series 7 (New York: Fordham University Press, 2007).

10 As unpacked in my trilogy on this topic: *Discerning the Spirit(s): A Pentecostal-Charismatic Contribution to Christian Theology of Religions*, Journal of Pentecostal Theology Supplement Series 20 (Sheffield, UK: Sheffield Academic, 2000); *Beyond the Impasse: Toward a Pneumatological Theology of Religions* (Grand Rapids:

Baker Academic, 2003); and *Hospitality and the Other: Pentecost, Christian Practices, and the Neighbor* (Maryknoll, N.Y.: Orbis, 2008).

11 This kenotic power of the Spirit is discussed by Andrew K. Gabriel, *The Lord Is the Spirit: The Holy Spirit and the Divine Attributes* (Eugene, Ore.: Pickwick, 2011), chap. 7, and Bradford McCall, "Kenosis and Emergence: A Theological Synthesis," *Zygon: The Journal of Religion and Science* 45, no. 1 (2010): 149–64. See also John C. Polkinghorne, ed., *The Work of Love: Creation as Kenosis* (Grand Rapids: Eerdmans, 2001).

12 This aspect of the divine vulnerability vis-à-vis a freely evolving creation is registered by W. H. Vanstone, *The Risk of Love* (New York: Oxford University Press, 1978); see also Mark Manolopoulos, *If Creation Is a Gift* (Albany: State University of New York Press, 2009), esp. chap. 5, on the ambiguity of creation's responses to the divine gift of creative freedom.

13 See also Eugene F. Rogers Jr., *After the Spirit: A Constructive Pneumatology from Resources outside the Modern West* (Grand Rapids: Eerdmans, 2005), for more on the materiality and physicality of the Spirit who is always distinct from but with (interacting with, to be more precise) the Son.

14 So that, as Thomas A. Smail, *The Giving Gift: The Holy Spirit in Person* (1988; repr., Lima, Ohio: Academic Renewal Press, 2002), 140–43, says, there is both the Father and the Son's giving of the Spirit on the one hand, and the Father and Spirit's mutual giving of Son on the other hand.

15 This is where I would affirm, with Stephen K. Moroney, *God of Love and God of Judgment* (Eugene, Ore.: Wipf & Stock, 2009), that the divine judgment on sin is also an expression of the divine love; see also D. A. Carson, *The Difficult Doctrine of the Love of God* (Leicester, UK: InterVarsity, 2000), chap. 4.

16 This point draws on the work of D. Lyle Dabney, "*Pneumatologia Crucis*: Reclaiming *Theologia Crucis* for a Theology of the Spirit Today," *Scottish Journal of Theology* 53, no. 4 (2000): 511–24, and "Naming the Spirit: Towards a Pneumatology of the Cross," in *Starting with the Spirit*, vol. 2 of *Task of Theology Today*, ed. Gordon Preece and Stephen Pickard (Adelaide: Australia Theological Forum, 2001), 28–58; see also Yong, "A Theology of the Third Article? Hegel and the Contemporary Enterprise in First Philosophy and First Theology," in *Semper Reformandum: Studies in Honour of Clark H. Pinnock*, ed. Stanley E. Porter and Anthony R. Cross (Carlisle, UK: Paternoster, 2003), 208–31, esp. 226–30.

17 With roots actually in Augustine, see Arie Baars, " 'Opera Trinitatis Ad Extra Sunt Indivisa' in the Theology of John Calvin," in *Calvinus sacrarum literarum interpres: Papers of the International Congress on Calvin Research*, ed. Herman J. Selderhuis, Reformed Historical Theology 5 (Göttingen: Vandenhoeck & Ruprecht, 2008), 131–41, esp. 132–33.

18 This is my pneumatological contribution to ongoing formulations of a trinitarian theology of love. Anthony Kelly puts it this way: "God is confessed as Trinity because God has been revealed as Love, and that the more we allow the notion of love to interpret the Trinity and the Trinity to interpret the meaning of love, the more radically healthy Christian theology will be"; Michael Downey argues that

"First, the love of God and the life flowing from it is altogether, that is, completely, gift. Second, this gift is the mystery of all three together in one love. Third, by this gift we are invited, all of us together, into communion with the God whose name above all naming is Love." Kelly, *The Trinity of Love: A Theology of the Christian God* (Wilmington, Del.: Glazier, 1989), xiii; Downey, *Altogether Gift: A Trinitarian Spirituality* (Maryknoll, N.Y.: Orbis, 2000), 14–15.

19 See Scott J. Jones, *The Evangelistic Love of God and Neighbor: A Theology of Witness and Discipleship* (Nashville: Abingdon, 2003), and John Piper, *God Is the Gospel: Meditations on God's Love as the Gift of Himself* (Wheaton: Crossway Books, 2005).

20 Robbie B. H. Goh, "Hillsong and 'Megachurch' Practice: Semiotics, Spatial Logic, and the Embodiment of Contemporary Evangelical Protestantism," *Material Religion: The Journal of Objects, Art, and Belief* 4, no. 3 (2008): 284–304, at 293.

21 See Heidi Baker with Shara Pradhan, *Compelled by Love: How to Change the World through the Simple Power of Love in Action* (Lake Mary, Fla.: Charisma House, 2008).

22 Jules Toner does not quite link radical love with the love of enemies to the point of death, but he does emphasize how affective affirmation is central to the deep mutuality that characterizes the loving and self-sacrificial commitments between lovers and their beloveds; see Jules Toner, *Love and Friendship*, Marquette Studies in Philosophy 26 (Milwaukee: Marquette University Press, 2003), esp. 145–48.

23 As Miroslav Volf puts it, the world is sinful, so God judges it, but God loves the world, so God is in a dilemma. What then is God's response? "God forgives," even indiscriminately! Forgiveness involves condemnation but also the generous release of debt (which overcomes guilt) that transforms the memory of the forgiver. On the one hand, forgiveness does not require repentance (it is unconditional), but on the other hand, as a social reality repentance and even restitution and reconciliation should be the *consequence* of forgiveness. In the end, our forgiveness is not our own but is God's forgiveness in Christ working through us (and, I would add: forgiveness is the Spirit's, in empowering our voices, actions, behaviors, and hearts!). See Miroslav Volf, *Free of Charge: Giving and Forgiving in a Culture Stripped of Grace* (Grand Rapids: Zondervan, 2006), 140, 177–83.

24 See William Klassen, *Love of Enemies: The Way to Peace* (Philadelphia: Fortress, 1984).

25 Amid the reigning paradigm of greed and competitiveness in the evolutionary sciences, Philip Hefner, *The Human Factor: Evolution, Culture, and Religion* (Minneapolis: Fortress, 1993), 207, underscores that this Christian commandment focused on loving our enemies is the ultimate *skandolon*. But the good news is that beneath this struggle lies a more primordial peace, one made possible again by the gift of God in Christ and the Spirit.

26 The Spanish philosopher-mystic Miguel de Unamuno wrote, "The end of charity, the end of love for God, is to cause God to be all in all, and all of us all in God. It is the perfect consciousness-raising of the universe, that is, its socialization, its divinization, that nature be society and society perfect, kinship, family. And

then it will be possible to call Him Father openly"; de Unamuno, *Treatise on Love of God*, ed. and trans. Nelson R. Orringer (Urbana: University of Illinois Press, 2007), 55.

27 The letter to the Ephesians also notes not the destruction of the opposition but their redemption: "God put this power to work in Christ when he raised him from the dead and seated him at his right hand in the heavenly places, far above all rule and authority and power and dominion, and above every name that is named, not only in this age but also in the age to come. And he has put all things under his feet and has made him the head over all things for the church, which is his body, the fullness of him who fills all in all" (1:20-23).

28 I provide a more extensive argument for this thesis in my *In the Days of Caesar: Pentecostalism and Political Theology* (Grand Rapids: Eerdmans, 2010), chap. 4.3.

29 See also Robert W. Caldwell, *Communion in the Spirit: The Holy Spirit as the Bond of Union in the Theology of Jonathan Edwards* (Milton Keynes, UK: Paternoster, 2006), parts I and II of which unpack these themes as displayed in the trinitarian theology of Edwards.

Select Bibliography

Ackerman, David A. "Fighting Fire with Fire: Community Formation in 1 Corinthians 12–14." *Evangelical Review of Theology* 29, no. 4 (2005): 347–62.

Alexander, Paul. *Peace to War: Shifting Allegiances in the Assemblies of God.* Henry Smith Series 9. Telford, Pa.: Cascadia Publishing House, 2009.

———. *Signs and Wonders: Why Pentecostalism Is the World's Fastest-Growing Faith.* San Francisco: Jossey-Bass, 2009.

Alexander, Richard. *The Biology of Moral Systems.* New York: De Gruyter, 1987.

Anonymous. *Apostolic Faith* 1, no. 1 (1906).

———. *The Pentecost* 1, no. 1 (1908): 4.

Arnott, John. *The Father's Blessing.* Orlando: Creation House, 1995.

Baker, Heidi, with Shara Pradhan. *Compelled by Love: How to Change the World through the Simple Power of Love in Action.* Lake Mary, Fla.: Charisma House, 2008.

Bartleman, Frank. *Azusa Street.* Plainfield, N.J.: Logos International, 1980.

Batson, C. Daniel. *The Altruism Question: Toward A Social-Psychological Answer.* Hillsdale, N.J.: Laurence Erlbaum, 1991.

"Beginning of a World Wide Revival," *Apostolic Faith* 1, no. 5 (2007): 1.

Bennema, Cornelis. *Encountering Jesus: Character Studies in the Gospel of John.* Colorado Springs: Paternoster, 2009.

Bertone, John A. "The Function of the Spirit in the Dialectic between God's Soteriological Plan Enacted But Not Yet Culminated: Romans 8.1-27." *Journal of Pentecostal Theology* 7, no. 15 (1999): 75–97.

Brown, Raymond. *The Epistles of John*. Garden City, N.Y.: Doubleday, 1982.

———. *The Gospel According to John: Introduction, Translation, and Notes*. Garden City, N.Y.: Doubleday, 1970.

Chervin, Ronda. *Why I Am a Charismatic, a Catholic Explains: Reflections on Charismatic Prayer and the Longings of the Human Heart*. Liguori, Mo.: Liguori, 1978.

Clemmons, Ithiel. *Bishop C. H. Mason and the Roots of the Church of God in Christ*. Bakersfield, Calif.: Pneuma Life Publishers, 1996.

Collins, Raymond F. *First Corinthians*. Sacra Pagina 7. Collegeville, Minn.: Liturgical Press, 1999.

Dabney, D. Lyle. "Naming the Spirit: Towards a Pneumatology of the Cross." In *Starting with the Spirit*, Vol. 2 of *Task of Theology Today*, edited by Gordon Preece and Stephen Pickard, 28–58. Australia Theological Forum, 2001.

———. "*Pneumatologia Crucis*: Reclaiming *Theologia Crucis* for a Theology of the Spirit Today." *Scottish Journal of Theology* 53, no. 4 (2000): 511–24.

Daniels, David D., III. "The Color of Charismatic Leadership: William Joseph Seymour and Martin Luther King, Jr. as Champions of Interracialism." In *We've Come This Far: Reflections on the Pentecostal Tradition and Racial Reconciliation*, edited by Byron D. Klaus. Springfield, Mo.: Assemblies of God Theological Seminary, 2006.

Darwin, Charles. *The Descent of Man: The Concise Edition*. Edited by Carl Zimmer. New York: Plume, 2007.

Dauphinais, Michael and Michael Levering. *Knowing the Love of Christ: An Introduction to the Theology of St. Thomas Aquinas*. Notre Dame, Ind.: University of Notre Dame Press, 2002.

Dawkins, Richard. *The Selfish Gene*. New York: Oxford University Press, 1976.

Dempster, Murray W. "Pacifism in Pentecostalism: The Case of the Assemblies of God." In *Proclaim Peace: Christian Pacifism from Unexpected Quarters*, edited by Theron Schlabach and Richard Hughes, 31–57. Champaign: University of Illinois Press, 1997.

Dixon, Thomas. *From Passions to Emotions: The Creation of a Secular Psychological Category*. New York: Cambridge University Press, 2003.

Dominy, Bert. "Paul and Spiritual Gifts: Reflections on I Corinthians 12–14." *Southwestern Journal of Theology* 26, no. 1 (1983): 49–68.

Fatula, Mary Ann. *The Holy Spirit: Unbounded Gift of Joy*. Collegeville, Minn.: Liturgical Press, 1998.

Fehr, Ernst and Simon Gächter, "Altruistic Punishment in Humans." *Nature* 415 (2002): 137–40.

Feuillet, André. *Le Mystère de l'amour divin dans la théologie johannique*. Paris: J. Gabalda, 1972.

Flescher, Andrew Michael, and Daniel L. Worthen. *The Altruistic Species: Scientific, Philosophical, and Religious Perspectives of Human Benevolence.* Philadelphia: Templeton Foundation, 2007.

Goh, Robbie B. H. "Hillsong and 'Megachurch' Practice: Semiotics, Spatial Logic, and the Embodiment of Contemporary Evangelical Protestantism." *Material Religion: The Journal of Objects, Art, and Belief* 4, no. 3 (2008): 284–304.

Heschel, Abraham. *The Prophets.* New York: Harper & Row, 1962.

Hurlbut, William B. "Empathy, Evolution, and Altruism." In *Altruism & Altruistic Love: Science, Philosophy, & Religion in Dialogue,* edited by Stephen G. Post, Lynn G. Underwood, Jeffrey Schloss, and William B. Hurlbut, 309–30. New York: Oxford University Press, 2002.

Hütter, Reinhard. *Suffering Divine Things: Theology as Church Practice.* Translated by Doug Stott. Grand Rapids: Eerdmans, 2000.

Irvin, Dale T. "'Drawing All Together in One Bond of Love': The Ecumenical Vision of William J. Seymour and the Azusa Street Revival." *Journal of Pentecostal Theology* 3, no. 6 (1995): 25–53.

Johnson, Luke. *The Gospel of Luke.* Sacra Pagina 3. Collegeville, Minn.: Liturgical Press, 1991.

Jones, Scott J. *The Evangelistic Love of God and Neighbor: A Theology of Witness and Discipleship.* Nashville: Abingdon, 2003.

Kornweibel, Theodore, Jr. "Bishop C. H. Mason and the Church of God in Christ during World War I: The Perils of Conscientious Objection." *Southern Studies* 26, no. 4 (1987): 261–81.

———. "Race and Conscientious Objection in World War I: The Story of the Church of God in Christ." In *Proclaim Peace: Christian Pacifism from Unexpected Quarters,* edited by Theron F. Schlabach and Richard T. Hughes, 58–81. Urbana: University of Illinois Press, 1997.

Land, Steven. "Be Filled with the Spirit: The Nature and Evidence of Spiritual Fullness." *Ex Auditu* 12 (1996): 108–20.

———. *Pentecostal Spirituality: A Passion for the Kingdom.* Journal of Pentecostal Theology Supplemental Series 1. Sheffield, UK: Sheffield Academic, 1993.

———. "William J. Seymour: The Father of the Holiness-Pentecostal Movement." In *From Aldersgate to Azusa Street: Wesleyan, Holiness, and Pentecostal Visions of the New Creation,* edited by Henry H. Knight III, 218–26. Eugene, Ore.: Pickwick, 2010.

Lee, Jung. *God Suffers for Us: A Systematic Inquiry into a Concept of Divine Passibility.* The Hague: Martinus Nijhoff, 1974.

Lee, Matthew. *A Sociological Study of the Great Commandment in Pentecostalism: The Practice of Godly Love as Benevolent Service.* Lewiston, N.Y.: Mellen, 2009.

Lewis, Thomas, Fari Amini, and Richard Lannon. *A General Theory of Love.* New York: Vintage Books, 2001.

Macchia, Frank. *Baptized in the Spirit: A Global Pentecostal Theology*. Grand Rapids: Zondervan, 2006.

———. *Justified in the Spirit: Creation, Redemption, and the Triune God*. Grand Rapids: Eerdmans, 2010.

———. *Spirituality and Social Liberation: The Message of the Blumhardts in the Light of Wuerttemberg Pietism*. Pietist and Wesleyan Studies 4. Metuchen, N.J.: Scarecrow Press, 1993.

Mason, Charles. "The Kaiser in the Light of the Scriptures." In *Preaching with Sacred Fire: An Anthology of African American Sermons, 1750 to the Present*, edited by Martha Simmons, 436–39. New York: Norton, 2010.

Miller, Donald, and Tetsunao Yamamori. *Global Pentecostalism: The New Face of Christian Social Engagement*. Berkeley: University of California Press, 2007.

Mostert, Johan. "Lessons from Our Struggle to Overcome Racial Segregation: A Brief History of the Apostolic Faith Mission of South Africa." In *We've Come This Far*, edited by Byron D. Klaus, 153–62. Springfield, Mo.: Assemblies of God Theological Seminary, 2007.

Newman, Joe. *Race and the Assemblies of God Church: The Journey from Azusa Street to the "Miracle of Memphis."* Youngstown, N.Y.: Cambria Press, 2007.

Ngien, Dennis. *Gifted Response: The Triune God as the Causative Agency of Our Responsive Worship*. Milton Keynes, UK: Paternoster, 2008.

Okasha, Samir. *Evolution of the Levels of Selection*. New York: Oxford University Press, 2006.

"The Old Time Pentecost." *Apostolic Faith* 1, no. 1 (1906): 1.

Oord, Thomas Jay. *Science of Love: The Wisdom of Well-Being*. Philadelphia: Templeton Foundation, 2004.

———. *The Nature of Love: A Theology*. St. Louis: Chalice Press, 2010.

Park, Myung Soo. "Korean Pentecostal Spirituality as Manifested in the Testimonies of Members of Yoido Full Gospel Church." In *David Yonggi Cho: A Close Look at His Theology and Ministry*, edited by Wonsuk Ma, 43–67. Baguio City, Philippines: APTS Press, 2004.

Piper, John. *God Is the Gospel: Meditations on God's Love as the Gift of Himself*. Wheaton, Ill.: Crossway Books, 2005.

Poloma, Margaret M. *Main Street Mystics: The Toronto Blessing and Reviving Pentecostalism*. Walnut Creek, Calif.: AltaMira Press, 2003.

Poloma, Margaret M., and John Green. *The Assemblies of God: Godly Love and the Revitalization of American Pentecostalism*. New York: New York University Press, 2010.

Poloma, Margaret, and Ralph Hood. *Blood and Fire: Godly Love in a Pentecostal Emerging Church*. New York: New York University Press, 2008.

Pope, Stephen J. *The Evolution of Altruism and the Ordering of Love*. Washington, D.C.: Georgetown University Press, 1995.

Renwick-Monroe, Kristen. *The Heart of Altruism: Perceptions of a Common Humanity*. Princeton: Princeton University Press, 1996.

Restak, Richard. *The Naked Brain: How the Emerging Neurosociety Is Changing How We Live, Work, and Love*. New York: Harmony Books, 2005.

Ridley, Matt. *The Origins of Virtue: Human Instincts and the Evolution of Cooperation*. New York: Viking, 1997.

Robeck, Cecil, Jr. *The Azusa Street Mission and Revival: The Birth of the Global Pentecostal Movement*. Nashville: Nelson, 2006.

Roughgarden, Joan. *The Genial Gene: Deconstructing Darwinian Selfishness*. Berkeley: University of California Press, 2009.

Schloss, Jeffrey. "Emerging Accounts of Altruism: 'Love Creation's Final Law'." In *Altruism and Altruistic Love: Science, Philosophy, and Religion and Dialogue*, edited by Stephen G. Post, Lynn G. Underwood, Jeffrey Schloss, and William B. Hurlburt, 212–42. New York: Oxford University Press, 2002.

Schneiders, Sandra M. "The Raising of the New Temple: John 20.19-23 and Johannine Ecclesiology." *New Testament Studies* 52, no. 3 (2006): 337–55.

Seymour, William J. "Questions Answered." *Apostolic Faith* 1, no. 11 (1908): 2.

———. "The Same Old Way." *Apostolic Faith* 1, no. 1 (1906): 3.

Smalley, Stephen S. *1, 2, 3 John*. Rev. ed. Word Biblical Commentary 51. Nashville: Thomas Nelson, 2007.

Solivan, Samuel. *Spirit, Pathos and Liberation: Toward a Hispanic Pentecostal Theology*. Journal of Pentecostal Theology Supplemental Series 14. Sheffield, UK: Sheffield Academic, 1998.

Sorokin, Pitirim. *A Long Journey: The Autobiography of Pitirim A. Sorokin*. New Haven: College and University Press, 1963.

———. *Altruistic Love: A Study of American "Good Neighbors" and Christian Saints*. Boston: Beacon, 1950.

———. *The Reconstruction of Humanity*. Boston: Beacon, 1948.

Steinmetz, George. "American Sociology before and after World War II: The (Temporary) Settling of a Disciplinary Field." In *Sociology in America: A History*, edited by Craig Calhoun, 314–66. Chicago: University of Chicago Press, 2007.

Talbert, Charles. "Paul's Understanding of the Holy Spirit: The Evidence of 1 Corinthians 12–14." *Perspectives in Religious Studies* 11, no. 4 (1984): 95–108.

Thagard, Paul. *The Brain and the Meaning of Life*. Princeton: Princeton University Press, 2010.

Thompson, Marianne Meye. "The Breath of Life: John 20:22-23 Once More." In *Holy Spirit and Christian Origins*, edited by Graham Stanton, Bruce Longenecker, and Stephen Barton, 69–78. Grand Rapids: Eerdmans, 2005.

Tillich, Paul. "Being and Love," *Pastoral Psychology* 5, no. 43 (1954): 43–46, 48.

———. *Love, Power, and Justice: Ontological Analyses and Ethical Applications*. New York: Oxford University Press, 1954.

———. *Protestant Era*. Abridged. Translated by James Luther Adams. Chicago: University of Chicago Press, 1957.

———. *Systematic Theology*. 3 vols. Chicago: University of Chicago Press, 1951–1953.

Tinney, James S. "William J. Seymour: Father of Modern-Day Pentecostalism." *Journal of the Interdenominational Theological Center* 4, no. 1 (1976): 34–44.

"To the Baptised Saints." *Apostolic Faith* 1, no. 9 (1907): 2.

Tourville, Robert E. *The Gospel of John: A Verse-by-Verse Commentary from the Classical Pentecostal Perspective*. New Wilmington, Pa.: House of Bon Giovanni, 1986.

Underwood, Lynn G. "Compassionate Love: A Framework for Research." In *The Science of Compassionate Love: Theory, Research, and Applications*, edited by Beverley Fehr, Susan Sprecher, and Lynn G. Underwood, 3–25. Malden, Mass.: Wiley-Blackwell, 2009.

"United to Jesus." *Apostolic Faith* 1, no. 2 (1906): 3.

Villafañe, Eldin. *The Liberating Spirit: Toward a Hispanic American Pentecostal Social Ethic*. Grand Rapids: Eerdmans, 1993.

Wadell, Paul. *The Primacy of Love: An Introduction to the Ethics of Thomas Aquinas*. New York: Paulist Press, 1992.

Walsh, Anthony. *The Science of Love: Understanding Love and Its Effects on Mind and Body*. Buffalo: Prometheus Books, 1991.

Ware, Frederick L. "The Church of God in Christ and the Azusa Street Revival." In *The Azusa Street Revival and Its Legacy*, edited by Harold D. Hunter and Cecil M. Robeck Jr., 243–57. Cleveland, Tenn.: Pathway Press, 2006.

Weiss, Kenneth M., and Anne V. Buchanan. *The Mermaid's Tale: Four Billion Years of Cooperation in the Making of Living Things*. Cambridge, Mass.: Harvard University Press, 2009.

Williams, Demetrius K. "'Upon All Flesh': Acts 2, African Americans, and Intersectional Realities." In *They Were All Together in One Place: Toward Minority Biblical Criticism*, SBL Semeia Studies 57, edited by Randall C. Bailey, Tatsiong Benny Liew, and Fernando F. Segovia, 288–310. Atlanta: Society of Biblical Literature, 2009.

Yong, Amos. *Discerning the Spirit(s): A Pentecostal-Charismatic Contribution to Christian Theology of Religions*. Sheffield, UK: Sheffield Academic, 2000.

———. "What's Love Got to Do with It? The Sociology of Love and the Renewal of Modern Pentecostalism." *Journal of Pentecostal Theology* 21, no. 1 (2012): forthcoming.

Scripture Index

Subject Index